FISHERIES AND TOXICOLOGY

FISHERIES AND TOXICOLOGY

Edited by

Prof. (Dr.) Mona S.A. Zaki
Department of Hydrobiology
National Research Center, Cairo, Egypt

Dr. Pawan Kumar 'Bharti'
Centre for Agro-Rural Technologies (CART-India)
20, Jamaalpur Man, Raja Ka Tajpur
Bijnore (UP) - 246 735 (India)
E-mail: gurupawanbharti@rediffmail.com

&

Dr. Avnish Chauhan
Dept. of Applied Science
Phonics Group of Institutions
Roorkee, Haridwar (Uttarakhand) (India)

DISCOVERY PUBLISHING HOUSE PVT. LTD.
NEW DELHI-110 002

Published by:
Namit Wasan
DISCOVERY PUBLISHING HOUSE PVT. LTD.
4383/4B, Ansari Road, Darya Ganj
New Delhi-110 002 (India)
Phone : +91-11-23279245, 43596065, 23253475
E-mail : discoverybooksindia@gmail.com
discoverypublishinghouse@gmail.com
namitwasan9@gmail.com
web : www.discoverypublishinggroup.com

First Edition: 2018

ISBN: 978-93-5056-452-3

Fisheries and Toxicology

Printed at:
Infinity Imaging Systems
Delhi

Preface

Aquatic systems reflect perturbations in the environment. So, fish and invertebrates can often be used to indicate the health of an aquatic system because chemicals can accumulate in invertebrates from the water and sediment and in fish from water, sediment, and the food chain. The monitoring of these effects is extremely important to regulate and remediate pollution. To test the toxicity, they can apply biomarkers to detect low-level pollution in aquatic systems.

Toxicology is the study of the effects of manufactured chemicals and other anthropogenic and natural materials and activities on aquatic organisms at various levels of organization, from sub-cellular through individual organisms to communities and ecosystems.

The effects of pollutants on the whole organism can be considered as neuro-physiological, reproductive and behavioural effects. These effects can often be inter-related: neurological changes can affect behaviour; changes in behaviour can affect reproduction and so on. A compound doesn't always put forth an effect on a target organism or a community. It always depends on the concentration of that compound and the time of exposure to it. These effects eventually can be either acute or chronic. Acute toxicity occurs rapidly, are clearly defined, often fatal and rarely reversible. Chronic effects develop after long exposure to low doses or long after exposure and may ultimately cause death.

The effects of pollution on freshwater species are registered in the loss of some species, with maybe some profits for some of them. There normally is a reduction in diversity but not necessarily numbers of individual species, and a change in the balance of such processes as predation, competition and materials cycling. Because of the complexity of pollution, the effects of take-up in the aquatic life are also depended on the pollutants characteristic feature. If two or more poisons are present together in an effluent they may exert a combined effect to an organism, which can be additive, antagonistic or synergistic.

This book provides comprehensive coverage of the fundamental principles and current practices and trends in the field of fisheries and aquatic toxicology.

This book updates the subject matter, illustrations and problems to incorporate new concepts and issues related to fisheries and toxicology.

Particularly thanks are due to all contributors from Egypt, and publisher also for their contribution and assistance.

I hope this book will be of benefit to both present and future colleagues, who teach, study and working in the field of environment, ecology, biotechnology, freshwater ecology, aquatic ecosystem, environmental pollution and fisheries.

Dr. Pawan Kumar 'Bharti'
(*gurupawanbharti@rediffmail.com*)

Contents

1

Biochemical, Clinicophathlogical and Microbial Changes in Clarias Gariepinus Exposed to Pesticide Malathion and Climate Changes

Mona S. Zaki*[1]; Susan O. Mostafa[2]; Soad Nasr[3]
Noor El Deen A I[1]; Nagwa S. Ata[4]; Isis M Awad[2]

ABSTRACT

The effect of Malathion on Biochemical changes in catfish (Clarias gariepinus) after exposure to Malathion 4.5 mg/l for 98 hours and high temperature 30°. The obtained results showed significant increase in cooper, sodium, cortisol, urea as well as ALT and AST. It was concluded that Malathion produces metabolic stress, cell damage with malfunction of haemopoeitic system. The microbiological examination revealed presence of E-coli, Acromonas Sp, Vibrio. We can conclude that in fish reared on low CHO diet there was hyperglycemia due to increase in insulin and cortisol hormone. (Macrocytic hypochromic anemia was observed in fish in 38H and 98H treatment of Malathion. The hemogram shows increase in MCV and decrease of HB%, PCV and RBC's count. There is decrease in IgM. There was petichial haemorage in some part of

1. Dept. of Hydrobiology, National Research centre, Giza, Egypt.
2. Dept. of Biochemistry, National Research centre, Giza, Egypt.
3. Dept. of Parasitology, National Research centre, Giza, Egypt.
4. Dept. of Microbiology, National Research centre, Giza, Egypt.

skin, ascites and erosion due to complications of bacterial infections and there is vertebral column curvature syndrome. [Report and Opinion, 2009;1(6):6-11]. (ISSN 1545-4570).

Key words: Malathion Biochemical changes, Haematological changes, Microbial changes, IgM.

INTRODUCTION

The organophosphorous insecticide malathion (Fig. 1.1) is used to control pests, which attack many economic crops, (Anderson,1990). In Egypt, the Ministry of Agriculture recommended the use of malathion against pests which attack vegetable crops, ornamental plants, medicinal and aromatic plants and for protection of stored grains. Malathion is also used to control different mosquito and fly species, household insects, animal ectoparasites and human head and body lice (Roberts, 1989). The wide use of malathion is attributed to its relatively low mammalian toxicity. But like DDT and other pesticides that have been found to cause irreparable damage to human and environmental health, malathion may pose a greater risk than the product label would lead one to believe.

$$\begin{array}{ll} CH_3 & O\,P - S - CH - CO_2 - C_2\,H_5 \\ CH_3 & O\,CH_2 - CO_2 - C_2\,H_5 \end{array}$$

Fig. 1.11: **"Malathion"**

Shown to be mutagenic, a possible carcinogen, implicated in vision loss, causing myriad negative health effects in human and animal studies, damaging to nontarget organisms, and containing highly toxic impurities, malathion has a legacy of serious problems (Cabello *et, al.* 2001).

According to a report by the Washington, D.C. based group, *World Resources Institute* (WRI), many pesticides appear to be increasing the incidence of infections, pneumonia, ear infections, and tuberculosis. The three pesticides listed as causing this problem were DDT, malathion, and the pesticide aldicarb (Breener, 1992).

The environmental protection agency (EPA) has been stating for years that they would require more detailed tests for chemical effects upon the immune and nervous system. However, to date, these requirements have not been implemented. Perhaps the biggest unknown risk from malathion is its potential to increase risk of contracting bacteria or viral infections such as encephalitis, this paradoxical situation arises since exposure to malathion can weaken a person's immune system (Giri *et, ul.* 2001).

Other effects of malathion for which there is no research, but seriously needed include its ability to cause: Learning disabilities, short term memory damage, increase risk of allergies (Cabello *et, al.* 2001).

Research has accumulated which indicates that nutritional factors can significantly modify the host response to environmental toxicants. Correction of malnutrition can clearly mitigate the effects of many toxicants; however, evidence is mounting that supraphysiologic doses of nutrients (nutritional supplements) can further lessen toxicity. The possibility that nutrition could be implemented as a secondary prevention strategy on a public health scale raises important ethical and policy issues. Nutritional strategies can lessen, but not abolish, toxic effects; moreover, they require dissemination and compliance, which are unlikely to be fully effective (Hu *et, al.*1995).

Malathion accumulate in fish mainly in the visceral fat, where as the gills and muscles retain a lower amount subsequently, with an increase in fat consumption. For example, at the time of migration and hibernation, pesticides may enter the more sensitive organs and induce poisoning (Bruno and Stamps, 1987), (Barton and Iwama, 1991), (Bennett and Wolke, 1987) (Pickering and Duston, 1983). It has been presumed for decades that environmental pollutants especially pesticides can affect one or more of the immunological functions in the fish. It is almost common knowledge cat fish frequently then become more susceptible to various diseases given the extreme variety of pesticides used (Vergut and Studnicka, 1994), (Areechon and Plumb, 2000). Andreson, 1990 suggested a decreased disease resistance in fish exposed to various pesticides. There is so little is known about how pesticides affect the immune systems of fishes (Cabello *et, al.* 2001).

The chemical name is: S-1 2 bis (ethoxycaronyl) ethyl 0,0-dimethyl-phoshordithioate (IUPAC).

Trade names: Malathion, Cythion, Fyfanon and Calmathion (Royal Society of Chemistry, 1993).

The present study discusses the effect of low CHO diet on cat fish, which also exposed to Malathion (4.5 mg/l) as pesticide for 98H. Some microbiological and clincopathological parameters were interproted.

MATERIAL AND METHODS

Experimental Condition

Catfish (50-60 gram/each) were obtained from River Nile Rashid branch, El-Kanater El-Khyria. Fish were acclimatized to laboratory conditions one week before infection in 115 L. glass aquaria with a flow system and dechlorinated tap water. Two groups of fishes were used.

The 1st group (15 fishes) was maintained kept on low carbohydrate diet but free from any toxicants, and kept on a balanced diet that meets its requirements from nutrients as described by (Robberts, 1989).

The 2nd group (15 fishes) were kept under the low CHO diet but were exposed to Malathion (4.5 mg/l) during 98 H hours (Areechon and plumb 1990). The diet ingredient is shown in (Table 1.1).

Table 1.1: Ingredients and Proximate Chemical Composition of Diets Used in Experiments

Ingredients	Diets I (Control)	Diets 2
Fish meal	30	30
Meat meal	8	10
Bone meal	1	3
Skimmed milk	3	4
Soybean	5	7
Wheat bran	20	20
Wheat flour	20	5
Yeast	10	15
God liver oil	1	4
Minenral & Vitamin* premix	2	2
Proximate Chemical Composition:		
Crude protein (CP) %	35.87	38.89
Metabolizable energy/kg	2297.21	2415.4
Ether extract (EE) %	2.78	2.86
Grude fiber (CF) %	3.91	4.27
Ash %	8.735	10.25
Calcium (Ca) %	3.094	3.99
Phosphorous (Ph) %	2.069	2.53
Lysine %	2.105	2.29
Methionine %	0.562	0.613

Copper, dissolved oxygen, temperature, pH, ammonia and nitrites were analyzed daily, while water alkalinity, hardness carbon dioxide, sodium, potassium and chlorides were analyzed before and after each water renewal using commercial kits of Bohringer, France, as shown in (Table 1.2). Malathion was obtained from National Institute of Pesticide, Dokki, Cairo. The 98h LC50 of Malathion for channel cat fish determined in separate study was 9.65 mg (Areechon and Plumb, 1990).

*** Mineral and vitamin premix per/kg of pelleted food :**

Vit.A, 8000 U; Vit. D, 9001, Vit. E 21 U, vit. K, 4 mg; Vit. B2 3.6 mg; niacin 20 mg choline chloride, 160 mg; pantothenic acid, 7 mg; pyridoxine, 0.2 mg; Vit. B 12, 5 ug; Mn, 70 mg, Zn 60 mg, Fe 20 mg, Cu 2 mg, I 1 mg, Co 0.2 mg.

Table 1.2: Water Quality Characteristics in Tanks. Initial Conditions Values are Mean ± SE

pH	5.40 ± 0.1
Temperature °C	18°C ± 0.904
Nitrates mg/l	0.020 ± 0.04
Un ionized ammonia (mg/l)	0.0014 ±0.004
Carbonic dioxide (mg/l)	4.1 ± 0.5
Alkalinity (mg/l)	31.8 ± 2.8
Permanganate oxidabole matter (mg/l)	3.54 ± 0.53
Hardness (mg/l)	34.6 ± 0.1
Chlorides (mg)	8.4 ± 0.6
Potassium (mg/l)	0.12 ± 0.007
Sodium (mg/l)	5.68 ± 0.01

Blood Sampling

Blood samples were taken after 24h, 38h, 98h. The fish were anaesthetized by 1/1000 aqueous solution of Ms 222 and bled from the caudal vein. Blood samples were taken with heparinized microhaematocrit tube. The tubes were centrifuged at 3000 r.p.m. for 10 min. Serum was separated and stored at 20°C until used.

Tested kits supplied form biomerieux (France) were used for determination of the activity of serum glutamic pyruvic transaminase (ALT) and glutamic oxaloacetic transaminase (AST) as described by (Reitman and Frankel, 1957).Serum glucose was assessed according to (Trinder, 1969). Haematocrit value was carried out by using micro-haematocrite capillary tubes centrifuged at 1200 r.p.m. for 5 min. mean corpuscular volume (MCV). Reticulocytis count according to (Drabkin, 1946). Serum cortisol level was determined using radioimmunoassay technique according to the method of (Pickering and Pottinger, 1983). Serum iron were determined using atomic absorption according to (Barham *et al.*, 1972). Values of sodium and potassium in serum were determined by flame photometer according to method described by (Silversmit, 1965). Serum creatinine was measured according to (Bartels *et al.*, 1972). Enzymatic determination of urea was done according to (Patton and Crouch, 1988). Insulin was estimated by radioimmunoassay method using oat. A Cout insulin Kits obtained from Diagnostic Corporation (DPC) west 96th street, Los Ageles U.S.A. (Pickering and Duston, 1983).

Bacterial Isolation

Aseptic swabs from the skingills, base of fins and blood of tested fish were cultivated on blood agar, MacConky agar, Nutrient agar, TSA, Nutrient broth, and peptone water (Oxoid and Difco).

Inoculated media were incubated at 37ºC for 48 hours. Bacterial isolates were identified by examination of the colony morphology and biochemical characteristic described by (Nagae *et al.*, 1993). Bacteria were detected by accounting colonies using surface spread plate technique according to quantitative method described by (Bruno & Stamps 1987).

Measurement of Serum Immunoglobulin M (IgM)

IgM Determination

The serum IgM was measured according to (Fuda *et al.* 1991).

Preparation of Antisera

Antisera of cat fish was prepared by immunizing rabbits as described by (Hara, 1976).

(Cat fish) IgM Antibody

The procedure for labeling antibody of fragment with enzyme was performed according to the method of (Nagae *et al.*, 1993).

Elisa Assay Procedure

Assays were carried out in 96 well polystyrene ELISA microtiter plates (Titertex, Horsham, PA).

Antibody Coating

The micortiter plates were coated with rabbit Anticat fish IgM which was fractionated by DE-52 at a concentration of 40 ug/ml in 0.01 M PBS. A volume of 150 µl was dispensed into each well and incubated for 4 hr at 4º.

Blocking

After one washing with 200 µl of 0.01 M PBS + 0.1% Tween 20 per well and two washings with 200 µl of PBS + 1% thimerosol was added to each well and included for 2hr at room temperature.

Incubation of Samples and Standards

After washing as described above 100 µl of sample and standard were placed into the appropriate wells in the microtiterplates and incubated at room temperature.

Incubation with Peroxidase Labeled Antibody

After washings as described above, each well received 150 µl of peroxidase labeled antibody 1:1600 in PBS-BSA, followed by incubation 12 hr at room temperature.

Enzymatic Color Reaction

The plates were washed as described above and 150 µl 0-phenylenediamine (3 mg/ml 0.1 M citric acid-phosphate buffer (pH 5.0) containing 0.02% H2O2 were added to each well for enzymatic color reaction.

The reaction was stopped after 30 min at room temperature by adding 100 µl of 4NHCI. The absorbance at 492 nm was 2250 (Richmond, CA).

Double antibody sandwish Elisa according to the method of (Matsubara *et al.* 1985) for determination of IgM described. After one washing with 200 µl of 0.01 M PBS + 0.1% Tween 20 per well.

STATISTICAL ANALYSIS

The obtained data were statistically subjected to the students't-test (Gad and Weil, 1983).

RESULTS

Experimental exposure to Malathion (4.5 mg/l) revealed that there was a significant increase in the level of serum creatinine ALT, AST, urea, potassium and insulin, were increased in the 24 hours and 38 h and 98 h non-significantly. There was a significantly increase of cortisol, glucose, copper during all times of experiments. Concerning iron there was a significant decrease of iron level (Table 1.3).

Table 1.3: Effect of Low CHO Diet on Some Biochemical and Hormonal Parameters in Cat Fish Exposed to Malathion (4.5 mg/l)

Parameters	Control	24 Hours	38 Hours	98 Hours
AST (U/l)	77.0 ± 0.53	80.7 ± 0.60	83 ± 0.51	100 ± 0.85**
ALT (U/l)	15.3 ± 0.33	17.4 ± 0.24	18.9 ± 0.83	23.0 ± 0.83*
Urea (mg/dl)	4.3 ± 0.51	4.9 ± 0.76	4.9 ± 0.83	5.1 ± 0.83*
Creatinine (mg/dl)	0.67 ± 0.62	0.69 ± 0.72	0.90 ± 0.51*	1.3 ± 0.53*
Na (Meq/L)	117 ± 1.3	127 ± 2.3*	128 ± 4.5*	142 ± 5.4*
K (Meq/L)	2.58 ± 0.12	3.65 ± 0.13	1.3 ± 0.8	5.00 ± 0.80*
Cortisol (ng/dl)	0.85 ± 0.23	0.88 ± 0.54	0.91 ± 0.39	1.5 ± 0.45**
Glucose (mg/dl)	52 ± 0.59	54.1 ± 0.50	68 ± 0.59	85 ± 0.23**
Insulin (ng)	7.6 ± 0.3	8.5 ± 0.4	11.7 ± 2.4	12.8 ± 0.63**
Copper (mg %)	181 ± 4.0	187 ± 2.3	168 ± 1.3	148 ± 0.45**
Iron (mg %)	190 ± 1.26	176 ± 5.2	168 ± 3.3	151 ± 4.3*
IgM Ng/Ml	0.85 ± 1.32	0.78 ± 1.20	0.63 ± 0.60	0.65 ± 0.44*

*P < 0.01 **P < 0.05

Hematological results in the present work revealed anemia indicated by a significant reduction in RBCs count, HB concentration PCV%, MCV and increase in reticulocyte count especially in 38 h, (Table 1.4).

Concerning microbiological examination, the results showed that the isolated microorganisms from internal organs (liver and kidneys), gills, and fins were Aeromonas Vibrio Sp and E. coli. (Table 1.5). With regard to IgM, a significant decrease was observed by exposing cat fish to the pesticide. (Table 1.3).

Table 1.4: Effect of Low CHO Diet on Hematological Parameters in Fish Exposed to Malathion (4.5 mg/l) for 98 H

Time Groups	Parameters				
	RBCs (106/mm³)	HB gm/dl	P.V.C.(%)	MCV Fl.	Reticulocyte %
Control	3.2 ± 0.34	7.7 ± 0.33	8.7 ± 0.33	31 ± 0.51	1.21 ± 0.2
24 hours	3.3 ± 0.34	8.6 ± 0.10	8.6 ± 0.11	37 ± 0.41	1.92 ± 0.3
38 hours	3.9 ± 0.63	8.7 ± 0.17*	7.87 ± 0.11	38 ± 0.73	2.3 ± 0.4
98 hours	3.7 ± 0.62	8.3 ± 0.28*	6.3 ± 0.37*	39 ± 0.83*	2.4 ± 0.4*

*P < 0.01

Table 1.5): Bacterial Isolates Recovered from Fish Exposed to Malathion (4.5 mg/l)

Bacterial Strain	External Surface	Kidneys	Liver	Gills
E. Coli	2 x 10	3 x 10	2 x 10	1 x 10
Aeromons Sp.	3 x 10	6 x 10	3 x 10	2 x 10
Vibrio/Sp.	2 x 10	1 x 10	2 x 10	2 x 10

There was petichial haemorhage in some part of skin and erosion due to complications of bacterial infection and vertebral column curvature syndrome.

DISCUSSION

It was evident that decrease in the level of CHO with Malathion 4.5 mg/l in fish diet caused a significant increase in glucose level during the experimental period, also insulin level was slightly increased. It is well known that any stress factor such as handling, incubation, anaestesia etc. has been shown to cause hyperglycemia followed by hyperinsulinemia (Yallow and Bawman, 1983).

Low CHO diet with Malathion causes a significant increase of cortisol level which may be due to the activation of hypothalamus, pituitary internal axis. Induced a significant increase in cortisol level, these results coincide with those observed by (Barton and Iwama, 1991), who observed that serum cortisol increased linearly in salminid fish fed on 5% CHO diet.

One consistent effect of cortisol was the reduction in the hemoglobin, PCV% and iron levels, as a result of decrease in appetite in the rainbow trout, or more likely to be the direct result of a catabolic effect, or cortisol of the fish tissues.

This present study revealed that, sodium and potassium concentrations were significantly increased. This retention may be attributable to kidney impairment where the kidney is the normal pass way for Na and K this may explain the main cause for elevation of the serum creatinine and urea in the treated groups.

Marked elevation was noticed in the activity of Asparate Amino Transferase (AST) and Alanine Amino Transferase (ALT). The liver is the primary organ of detoxification as well as a major site for detoxification reaction. Therefore, significant increase in the liver enzymes suggests explanation Malathion affected the liver cells or may be attributed to secondary bacterial infection.

The present results agree with (Bruno & Stamps 1987) they observed that aquatic pollution with heavy metals cause immunosuppression and contribute to outbreaks of infections, and bacterial diseases in fish. We can say that Malathion can affect fish after 24h and there are some complications with this pesticide.

IgM level was determined to find out information about fish immune system, which was previously investigated in different species by many authors as (Matsubara *et al.*, 1985) and (Fuda *et al.*, 1991).

There is a significant decrease in IgM level in fish with Malathion, if compared with control groups. Anderson *et al.*, 1982 found a relation between corisol and IgM as when cortisol increased IgM decrease.

IgM is one of the most important factors in the immune factor to neutralize bacteria and render them more susceptible to phagocytosis (Mona S. Zaki *et al.*, 2003). It is well known that in mammals immunoglobulin production is closely related to endocrine status for example thyroid hormone enhances the production of immunoglobulin (Chen, 1980) cortisol intensity suppress immunoglobulins production (Pickering & Pottinger, 1983).

In conclusions Malathion will reduce humoral immune response as detected by decrease of IgM level and cortisol elevation.

REFERENCES

1. Areechon and Plumb (2000). Sublethal Effects of Malathion on Channel Catfish, Ictalurus Punctatus. Bull. Environ. Contain. Toxicol. 44: 435-442.
2. Areechon, N. and Plumb, J.A. (1990) Sublethal Effects of Malathion on Channel Catfish, Ictalurus Punctatus, Department of Fisheries and Allied Aquacultures and Alabama Agriculture Experiment Station, Auburn University, Alabama 36849, USA.
3. Anderson, D.P. (1990). Immunological Indicators Effects of Environmental Stress on Immune Protection and Decrease Outbreaks. Am. Fish Soc. Symp.8, 38-43.
4. Anderson, D.P.; Roberson, B.S. and Dixon, O.W. (1982). Immunosuppression Induced by Corticosteroid or an Alkylating Agent in Rainbow Trout. Dev. Comp. Immol. Suppl. 2, 197-200.
5. Barham, W.T.; Smit, G.J. and Schoobee, H.J.J. (1972). Determination of Iron in Serum Fish Boil. 17, 275.
6. Bartels, H.; Bohmer, M.and Heierli, C.(1972). Clinical Chemistry Acta, 37, 139.
7. Barton, B.A. and Iwama, G.K. (1991). Physiological Changes in Fish from Stress in Aquaculture with Emphasis on the Response and Effects of Corticosteroids. Annual Review of Fish Disease, 1, 43-49.

8. Bennett, R.O. and Wolke, R.F. (1987a). The Effect of Sublethal Endrin Exposure on Rainbow Trout, Salmo Garidneri Richardson, I. Evaluation of Serum Cortisol Concentrations and Immune Responsiveness. J. Fish Biol. 31: 375-379.
9. Brenner, L. (1992) Journal of Pesticide Reform, Volume 12, Number 4, Winter 1992. Northwest Coalition for Alternatives to Pesticides, Eugene, OR
10. Bruno, D. and Stamps, D.J. (1987). Fry Journal of Fish Diseases, 10, 513. Bull. NRC, Egypt. Vol. 28, No. 2, pp. 245-257.
11. Cabello, G. et,al. (2001).A Rat Mammary Tumor Model Induced by the Organophosphorus Pesticides Parathion and Malathion Possibly Through Acetylcholinesterase Inhibition. Environ. Health Perespect, 101: 471-479.
12. Chen, Y. (1980). Effect of Thyroxine on the Immune Response of Mice in vivo and vitro. Immunol. Org. 9, 269.
13. Drabkin, D.J. (1946). Biol. Chem. 164, 703.
14. Fuda, H.; Sayano, K. Yamaji, F. and Haraj (1991). Serum Immunoglobulin N. (IgM) during Early Development of masu salmon on corhyrchus masu. Comp. Biochem. Physiol. 99A, 637.
15. Gad, S.C. and Weil, C.S. (1983). Statistics for Toxicologists. In Hayes, A.W. 2nd Ed. Principles and Methods of Toxicology. Raven Press, New York, pp. 273-320.
16. Giri, Set, al. (2002). Genotoxic Effects of Malathion: An organophosphorus Insecticide, Using Three Mammalian Bioassays in vivo, 514: 223-231. Journal of Pesticide Reform, 23 (4)
17. Hara, A. (1976). Iron Binding Activity of Female Specific Serum Proteins Rainbow Trout salmo and chum salman Ocorchynchus. J. of Biochem. And hysiology, 427, 549.
18. Hermre, Torrissen, O. and Waagba, R. (1999). Comparative Biochemistry and Physiology, (In press).
19. Hu, H., Kotha,S. and Brennan, T (1995) The Role of Nutrition in Mitigating Environmental Insults: Policy and Ethical Issues Environmental Health Perspectives Volume 103, Supplement 6, September 1995.
20. Joseph, A. and Roger, W.G. (1979). Clinical Chemistry Principles and Procedures 4th Boston, pp. 168-197.
21. Matsubara, A.; Mihara, S. and Kusuda, R. (1985). Quantitation of Yellow Tail Immunoglobulin by Enzyme-linked Immunosorbent Assay (Elisa). Bull. Japan Sac. Sci. fish, 51, 921-927.
22. Mona, S. Zaki, Osfor, M.H. Bayomi, F.S. and Abouel-Gheit, E.N. (2003). Impact of Low Dietary Carbohydrate Diets on some Nutritional and Clinicopathological Parameters of Tiliptia Nilotica Infected with Saprolegnia Parastitia and Exposed to Copper Sulphate Applied Bull. NRC, Egypt, 28.No. (2); 245-257.
23. Nagae, M.; Fuda, H.; Hara, A.; Hamuchi, A. (1993). Changes in serum immunoglobulin M. (IgM) Concentrations during Early Development of Churm Salmon as Determined by Sensitive ELISA. Comp. Biochem. Physiology, 602-613.
24. Patton, C.J. and Crouch, S.R. (1988). Analytical chemistry, 49, 64. c.f. Bio-Merieus Laboratory Reagents and products France Kit.
25. Pickering, A.D. and Duston, J. (1983). Analysis of Cortisol Hormone J. Fish Biol. 23, 163-172.
26. Ckering A.D. and Puttinger, P. (1983).Analysis of Hormone Gen. Com. Endocrinal, 49, 232-239.

27. Reitman, S. and Frankel, S. (1957). Analysis of Liver Function Am. J. Clin. Pathol. 28, 56-64.
28. Roberts, R.J. (1989). Nutritional Pathology of Teleosts. In Fish Pathology. (Ed. By R.J. Roberts) pp. 337-362 Bailiere Tindall London.
29. Silversmit, A.B. (1965). For Determination of Serum Sodium and Potassium Med. 45, 175-177.
30. Trinder, P. (1969). For Determination of serum glucose Ann. Clin. Biochem. 6, 24-26.
31. Vergut, C. and Studnicka, M. (1994). Effects of Lindane Exposure on Rainbow Trout Immunity III. Effect on Non-specific Immunity and B lymphocyte Functions Ecotoxicol. Environ. Safty 27: 324-328.
32. Yalow, R. and Bawman, W.A. (1983). Plalsma insulin in Health and Disease. In "Diabetes Mellius. Theory and Practicle pp. 119-150 (Eds.) Ellelnberg M. and H. Riking Exerpta Medica, New York.

2

Field Studies Encysted Metacercariae Infested Natural Male Tilapias and Monosex Tilapias in Kafr El-Sheikh Governorate Fish Farms

Eissa, I.A.M.[1]; Gado, M.S.[2]; Laila, A.M.[3]
Mona S. Zaki*[3]; Noor El-Deen, A.E[3]

ABSTRACT

The present study was carried out on 1800 specimens of Tilapia fishes *Oreochromis niloticus (O.niloticus)* (*phenotypic, hybrids and monosex O.niloticus* of different size and body weight. They were randomly collected at different seasons from Kafr El- Sheikh Governorate cultured fish farms. The clinical signs of most examined fishes revealed no pathognomonic abnormalities on the external body surface except black spots were detected on skin and fins. Tilapia fishes were shown emaciation. The postmortem findings the black spots were detected on skin and fins. Encysted metacercariae including *Euclinostomum heterostomum, Posthodiplostomum cuticola, Heterophidae* and *Haplorochoidae* were investigated and recorded. The highest prevalence possessed in hybrids while monosex *O.niloticus* occupied the last position. The histopathological examination in different organs of infested fish revealed pathological changes in gills and musculatures.

1. Dept. of Fish Diseases and Management, Fac. of Vet. Med. Suez Canal University, Egypt.
2. Dept. of Fish Diseases and Management, Fac. of Vet. Med., kafr El -Sheikh University, Egypt.
3. Dept.of Hydrobiology, Vet. Division, National Research Centre, Giza, Egypt.

Key word: Encysted metacercariae, *O.niloticus, Hybrids, monosex*

INTRODUCTION

Encysted metacercariae parasitic diseases have the upper hand in fish parasitic diseases regarding the low body gain, high mortality. In addition, such diseases lead to gastrointestinal abrasions which facilitate the invasion of the opportunistic microorganisms. Where unfavourable environmental conditions contribute to stress, which weakens immunity and opens the pathway to pathogens Kabata, (1985), Eissa, (2002). The prevalence rate of encysted metacercariae in *Oreochromis sp* collected from the River Nile at Al-Monib area was considered the highest in egypt and the prevalence of encysted metacercariae was higher in females than that of males Taghreed B.El-Deen (2005). In addation, the prevalence of digenea in summer and spring followed by winter while the lowest one was in autumn Osman (2001), while, Tawfik (2005) recorded a prevalence of digenia was in winter. Histopathological alterations of infested male phenotypic, hybrids and monosex *O. niloticus*. It was concluded that monosex *O. cniloticus* are less exposed to parasitic diseases than hybrid and phenotypic *O. niloticus*.

MATERIALS AND METHODS

Fish

A total number of 1800 cultured *Oreochromis niloticus (O.niloticus)* of various life stages; fry, fingerling and adult Tilapia of different Male fish types (phenotypic *O. niloticus*, hybrids and monosex (hormone treated) were 100, 200 and 300 for each type fish, respectively. The length of fry, fingerlings and adult specimens were ranged from 1-1.5, 2-8 and 20-30 cm. Body weights ranged from 0.9-15.0, 17-28.7 and 105-220 g respectively.

Clinical Examination

The collected fishes were examined clinically according to the methods described by Noga (1996).

Experimental Infection

Experimental Puppies

Six puppies, 4-6 weeks old, weighing 1.750-2.050g; were hygienically caged in suitable steel cages with wire – mesh floor. The puppies were fed on bread soaked in pasteurized milk and supplied with clean water according to Farris (1967). The dogs were proved to be free from any parasitic infestations by three successive fecal examinations with one-week interval. Moreover, they were given orally dose of broad-spectrum anthelmintic; Yomesan® (*Niclosamide*) *"Bayer"* at a rate of 0.25 g./Kg body weight. A frequent removal of the feces and washing the floor of the cages with hot water and soap was adopted.

Experimental Ducklings

Eighteen ducklings, 3-weeks old, weighing 120-130 g; were reared conventionally in separate special cages. They were fed on a ration of 25% protein content and provided with clean water. Their feces were examined daily for three successive days to ensure their clearance of parasitic infestations. In deed, they were provided with a dose of broad-spectrum anthelmintic drug, Ban-minth (*Pyrantel Tartrate, 12.5%*) *"Pfizer"* at a rate of 0.15 g./Kg body weight. A frequent removal of the faeces and washing the floor of the cages with hot water and soap was adopted.

Preparing Fish Musculature for Experimental Infection

From heavily infected regions of the examined fish; the musculature and gills containing viable unidentified metacercariae cysts were collected and weighed and given orally to the parasites-free experimentally infected puppies and ducklings.

Experimental Infection of Puppies

The puppies were divided into three groups; two puppies for each. The puppies from each group were fed on 50 grams of infested musculatures and gills for three successive days according to (Shaapan, 1997).

Experimental Infection of Ducklings

The ducks were divided into three groups; six ducklings for each. The ducklings from each group were fed on two grams infested musculatures and gills for three successive days according to (Amany Abbass, 1997).

Detection of the Eggs After Experimental Infection

The stools of the infected puppies and ducklings were daily examined for detection of trematodes eggs using the flotation sedimentation technique described by Soulsby (1978) in order to determine the prepatent period, which is the first day of egg appearance after the last day of infection was calculated.

Collection of the Adult Flukes

When the number of eggs in the stools of infected puppies and ducklings began to decrease; all puppies and ducklings were killed. The small intestine was subdivided into 3 parts (duodenum. jejunum, and ileum), where each part was separately opened and the contents and the scraped mucosa were collected in suitable jars containing normal saline. Several washings with normal saline were carried out to remove the coarse particles of intestinal contents and mucous that may be attached to the parasites. The sediments were examined with binocular microscope, then the flattened trematodes were picked up in a small bottles containing 10% formalin using Pasteur pipette. Permanent mounting of the collected trematodes and metacercariae; were carried out using

Drury and Wallington (1980), to prepare permanent stained mounts of metacercariae and adults.

Relaxation of Trematodes

The trematodes were mounted on a glass slide and covered with a thin glass slide. Care was necessary to avoid the use of strong pressure on delicate helminthes parasites.

Fixation of Obtained Trematodes

It was carried out using formalin saline 5% as a fixative and left overnight.

Washing

The specimens were then washed with tap water for 15 min; to get rid of any traces of formalin solution.

Staining

The specimens were stained with acetic acid alum carmine (Kruse and Pritchard, 1982).The carmine powder, acetic acid and 100 ml of distilled water were put in a mortar to be soaked for 20 minutes. Then they were boiled gently for 1 hour, at the same time the alum was dissolved in the distilled water (900 ml), and then added to the cooled carmine solution. The solution composite was heated again for 1 hour, and cooled filtered. After filtration, 1 g of salicylic acid was added to the filtered solution to inhibit the growth of molds.

Differentiation

It was done as slowly as possible using a dilute solution of acid- alcohol. It is much better to carry out this process under the dissecting microscope; in order to determine accurately the out most differentiation of internal structures of the trematodes.

Dehydration

It was carried out in ascending grades of ethyl alcohol (30%, 50%, 70%, 90% and absolute alcohol).The time of dehydration depending on the size of the specimen.

Clearing

This process was carried out with clove oil as long as, to complete the clearing of the adult trematodes.

Mounting

It was proceeded with Canda balsam and then the specimens were covered with cover slide and left to dry at 35-38 ºC in an incubator.

Identification of Parasites

The identification of the encysted metacercariae was undertaken according to Kabata (1985).

Histopathological Examination

It was carried out for the naturally infested fish. Specimens from skin, gills and musculatures were taken in different grades of alcohol, cleared in xylol then embedded in paraffin wax. Sections of 4-5 microns were obtained and mounted on glass slide and stained with Haematoxyline and Eosin (H & E), according to Drury and wallington (1980).

RESULTS

Clinical Examination

The infested fishes showed no pathognominic lesion except black spots were detected on skin and fins (Fig. 2.1).

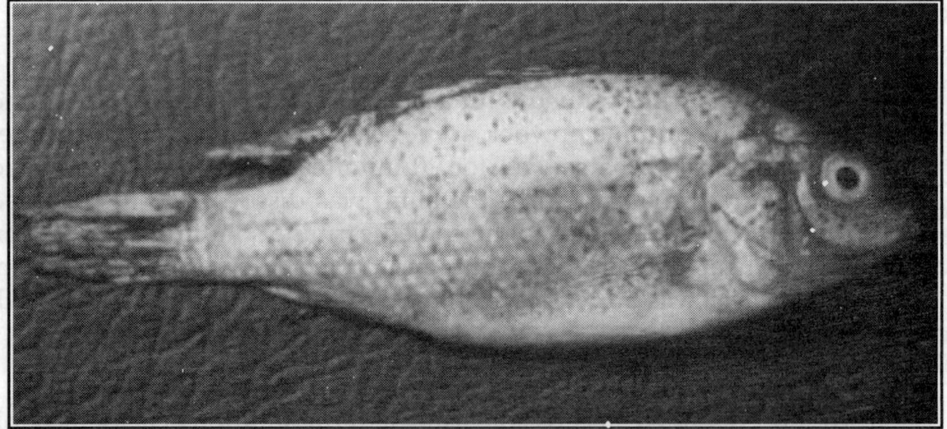

Fig. 2.1: **Phenotypic *Oreochromis niloticus* with Black Spots on the Skin and Fins**

Fig. 2.2: **Phenotypic *Oreochromis niloticus* Showing Encysted Metacercariae in the Posterior Kidney**

Parasitological Examination

Microscopic smears were taken from skin of examined fish, showed identified as the examined black cyst in stained smears taken from skin and orbital cysts were identified as *Myxobolus dermatobia*, cysts were found inside the skin and fins were identified as *Posthodiplostomum cuticola* metacercariae, Cysts were embedded in gill lamellae and musculature were related to *Heterophid* metacercariae and *Haplorchoid* metacercariae.

Experimental infestation of puppies and ducklings with unidentified encysted metacercariae form different types of Tilapia fishes *O.niloticus* (phenotypic (group 1), hybrid (group 2) and monosex (group 3): (Tables 2.1 and 2.2). The obtained adult flukes from the upper part (duodenum) of the small intestine of experimentally infested puppies with unidentified metacercariae encysted in phenotypic *O. niloticus* musculatures was identified as *Prohemostomum vivid, Mesostephanus appendiculatus,Paracoenogonimus ovatus* and *Euclinostomum heteroatom from* midgut of the small intestine of experimentally infested puppies. Gills infested with encysted metacercariaes revealed multiple parasitic cysts in primary and secondary lamellae the parasitic cysts appear surrounded with connective tissue proliferation. Oedematus musculature and infested with encysted metacercariaes were appear surrounded with serous fluid which contains a network of fibrin (Plate 2.2).

DISCUSSION

The present study deals with most of different encysted metacercariae parasitic diseases among naturally infested the cultured Tilapia sp *O. niloticus* (phenotypic, hybrid and monosex) in Kafr El- Sheikh fish farms. The internal organs of naturally infested fish appeared pale, anemic with enlargement and congestion of spleen, liver with distended gallbladder. Signs of emaciation with petechial haemorrhage on the surface of abdomen and slight bulging of stomach was observed.

Concerning the identified encysted metacercariae, they were (*Euclinostomum heterostomum, Posthodiplostomum cuticola, Heterophidae* and *Haplorchoidae*). Such results are nearly similar to those of the original descriptions of Yamaguti (1985), Eissa *et al.*, (1996), Shaapan (1997), Gado and El-Bahy (1999), Ibrahim, (2000), Mousa *et al.*, (2000) and Eman Bazha (2003). The identification of *Prohemostomum vivax, Mesostephanus appendiculatus* and *Paracoenogonimous ovatus* was dependent on the morphological characters of the obtained adult trematodes recovered from the experimental infestation in puppies and ducklings, these results nearly similar to that recorded with Olfat Mahdy and Shaheed,. (2000): (1991) who recovered them from ducks fed on *Tilapia sp* and Shaapan (1997) who recovered them from dogs.

Table 2.1: Unidentified Encysted Metacercariae (EMC) in Experimentally Infested Puppies

Puppies Group	Type of Tilapia	No. of Inf. Puppies	Source of EMC	No. of EMC per/g	No. of + vepuppies	No. of Recovered Trematodes	Percent of Recovered EMC%	Isolated Trematodes	Prepatent Period (days)
Group 1	Male phenotypic *O. niloticus.*	1	Musculatures	25/10 g	1	153	61.2	*Prohemostomum vivax.*	7-10 days
		1	Gills	4 gill filament contain 5 EMC	1	5	25	*Mesostephanus appendiculatus*	7-10 days
Group 2	Male hybrids *O. niloticus.*	1	Musculatures	33/10 g	1	215	65.2	*Prohemostomum vivax* and *Mesostephanus appendiculatus*	7-10 days
		1	Gills	4 gill filament contain 7 EMC	1	10	35.4	*Mesostephanus appendiculatus*	7-10 days
Group 3	Male monosex *O. niloticus.*	1	Musculatures	6/10 g	1	17	28.3	*Prohemostomum vivax*	7-10 days
		1	Gills	4 gill filament containing 2 EMC	1	2	25	*Mesostephanus appendiculatus.*	7-10 days

Table 2.2: Unidentified Encysted Metacercariae (EMC) in Experimentally Infested Ducklings

Ducks Group	Type of Tilapia	No. of Infected Ducks	Source of EMC	No. of EMC per/g	No. of + ve. Ducks	No. of Recovered Trematodes	Percent of Recovered EMC %	Isolated Trematodes	Prepatent Period (days)
Group 1	Male phenotypic *O. niloticus.*	2	Musculatures	25/10 g	1	5	2	*Paracoenogonimus ovatus.*	7-10 days
		2	Gills	4 gill filament containing 5 EMC	0	0	0		7-10 days
Group 2	Male hybrids *O. niloticus.*	2	Musculatures	23/g	2	9	2.7	*Paracoenogonimus ovatus.*	7-10 days
		2	Gills	4 gill filament containing 7 EMC	0	0	0	0	7-10 days
Group 3	Male monosex *O. niloticus.*	2	Musculatures	5/10 g	0	0	0	0	7-10 days
		2	Gills	4 gill filament containing 2 EMC	0	0	0	0	7-10 days

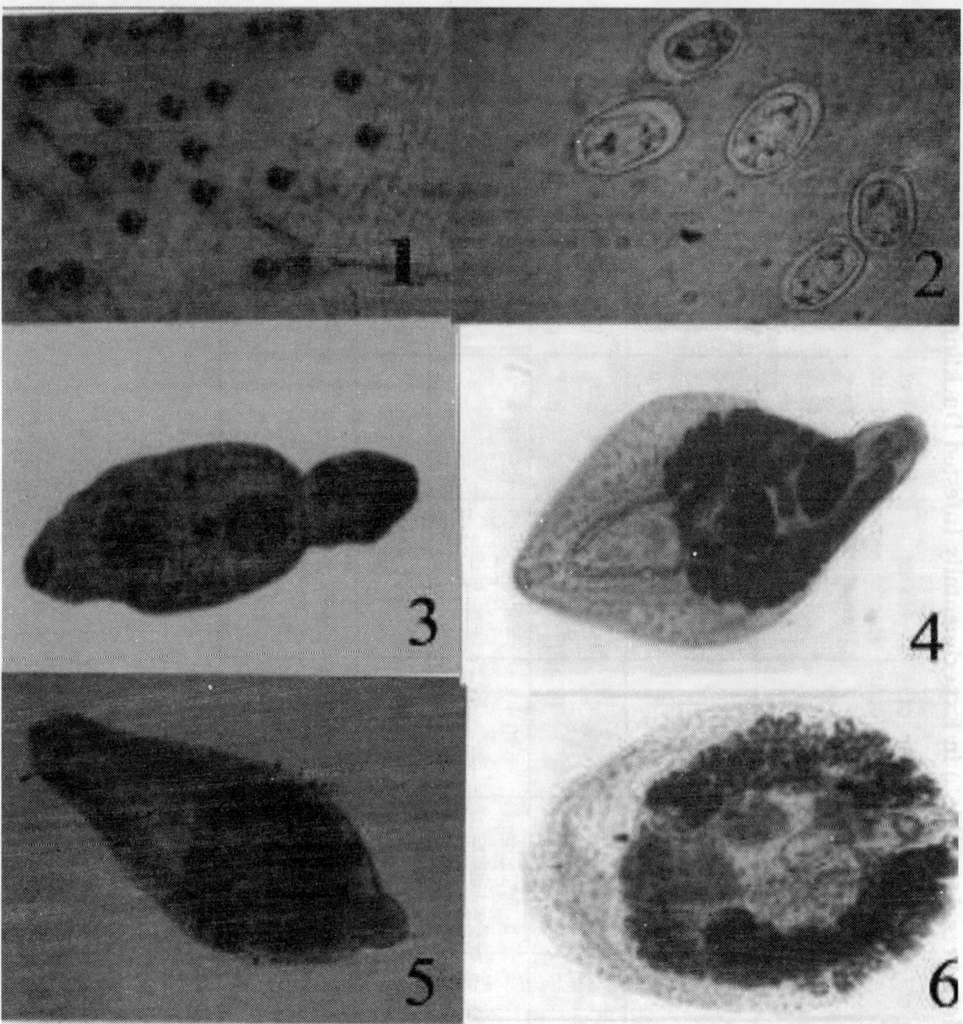

Plate 2.1: (1) Heavy Infestation of *Haplorchoidae* Encysted Metacercariae in Musculature.Wet mount X150. (2) Heavy Infestation of Heterophidae Encysted Metacercariae in Musculature. Stain: Acetic Acid Alum Carmine X40. (3) Larva of *Posthodiplostomum cuticola*. Wet Mount X 40. (4) *Mesostephanus appendiculatis*. Stain: Acetic Acid Alum Carmine X 40. (5) *Prohemostomum vivax*. Stain: Acetic Acid Alum Carmine X 40. (6) *Paracoenogonimous ovatus*. Stain: Acetic acid alum Carmine X 40.

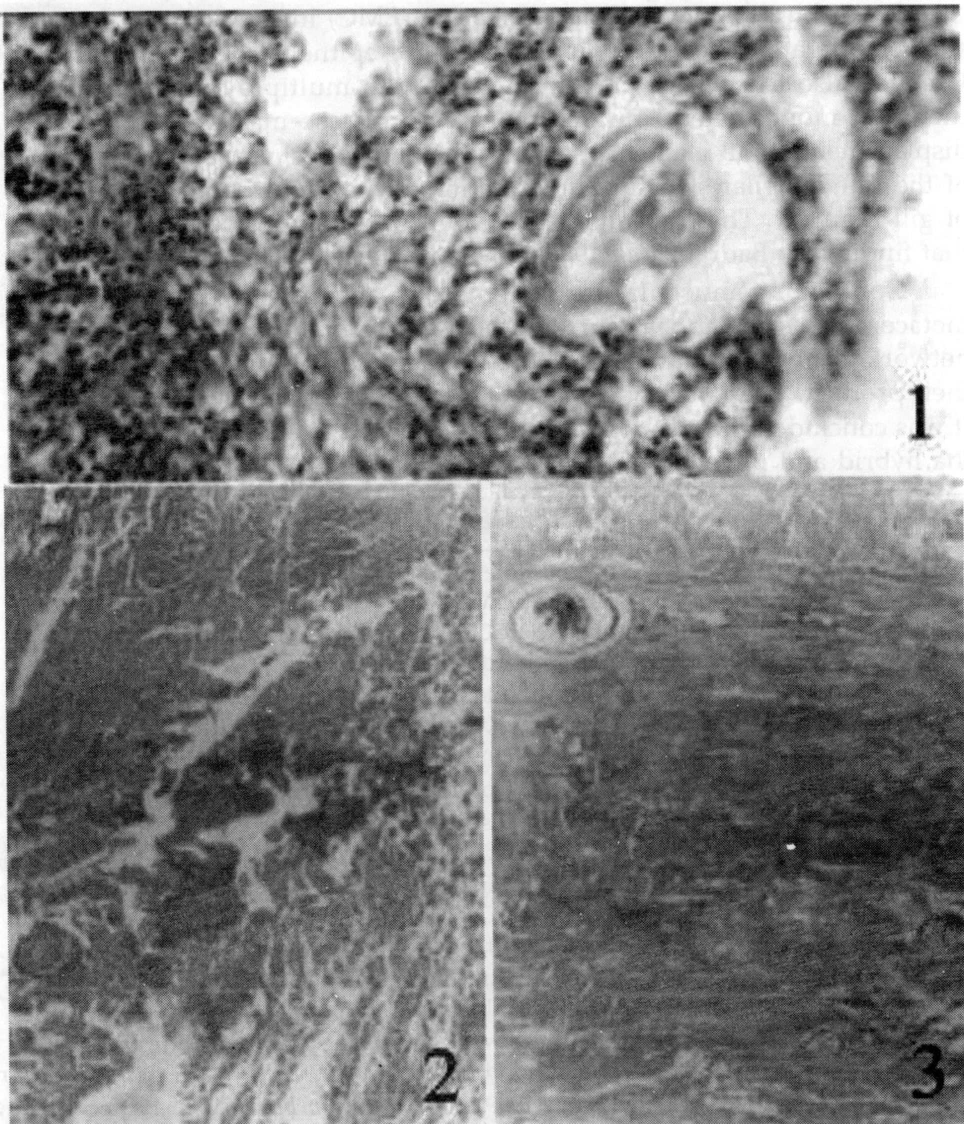

Plate 2.2: **(1) Encysted Metacercariae Embedded in the Primary Gill Lamellae and Surrounded with Severe Leucocytic Infiltrations (Arrows). Stain (H& E) X 125. (2) Dorsal Musculature Deeply Containing Cysts Invaded with Few Leucocytes (Arrows). Stain (H & E) X 125. (3) Encysted Metacercariae Embedded in Tilapia Musculature and Surrounded with Oedema (arrows). Stain (H& E) X 125**

Regarding to encysted metacercariae (EMC) infestation in Tilapia sp show moderate to severe hyperplasia of gill epithelial of the primary gill lamellae also the cysts were surrounded with multiple cellular reactions included mononuclear inflammatory cells. These may be attributed to displacement of gill filament tissues by the EMC which accompanied by loss of the fine lamellar structure deformation and even atrophic degeneration of gill filament. These results nearly similar to that recorded agreed with that finding by Badran *et al.*(1996), Osman (2001), and Ibtsam (2004).

Concerning musculature oedematous and infested with encysted metacercariae was appear surrounded with serous fluid which contain a network of fibrin. It may be attributed to irritation of infective parasite and their product. These nearly were similar to that recorded by Soliman (1997). It was concluded that monosex were less exposed to encysted metacercaraie tha hybrid and phyenotypic *o.niloticus.*

REFERENCES

1. Amany Abbass, A. A. R. (1997): Role of Fish as an Intermediate Host of Some Trematodes in Birds. Ph.D. Thesis, Fac. Vet. Med. (Moshtohor), Zagazig Univ., Egypt Drury, A. A. and Wallington, E. A. (1980): Carleton's Histological Technique. 5th Ed., Oxford University press, New York, Toronto.
2. Badran. A.F.; Aly S. A.M.; and Abd El- Aal A.A. (1996): Studies on Skin Parasitic Diseases of Hybrid Tilapia. Assiut, Vet. Med. J., Vol. 35, No. 70, July 1996.
3. Drury, A.A. and Wallington, E.A. (1980): Carleton's Histological Technique. 5th Ed., Oxford University Press, New York, Toronto.
4. Eissa, I.A.M. (2002): Parasitic Fish Diseases in Egypt. Dar El- Nahda El- Arabia Publishing, 23 Abd El- Khalak Tharwat St. Cairo, Egypt.
5. Eissa, I.A.M.; A.S. Diab and A.F. Badran (1996): Studies on Some Internal Parasitic Diseases Among Wild and Cultured Oreochromis Niloticus Fish. 7th Sci. Cong., 17-19. Nov. 1996, Fac. Vet. Med., Assiut, Egypt.
6. Eman, K.A. Bazh (2003): Epidemiological Studies on Some Fish Borne Parasites. M.V. Sc. Thesis, Fac. Vet. Med., kafr El-Sheikh, Tanta Univ.
7. Farris, E.J. (1967): The Care and Breeding of Laboratory Animals. 7 Ed., pp. 182-201. John Wily & Sons, Inc. New York, London and Sydney.
8. Gado, M.S.M. and El-Bahy, N.M. (1999): *Euclinostomum heterostomum* Affection of Cultured *Oreochromis niloticus* in kafr El-sheikh governorate.Vet. Med. J. Vol., 11(1), Suez Canal University.
9. Kabata, Z. (1985): Parasites and Diseases of Fish Culture in the Tropics. Printed in Great Britain by Taylor and Franks (Ltd. Basingstoke Hants). pp. 127-161.
10. Kruse, G.O.W. and Pritchard, M.H. (1982): The Collection and Preservation of Animal Parasites. University of Nebraska Press, United States of America. pp. 135.
11. Ibrahim, T.B.E (2000): Studies on Metacerarial Parasitic Infestation in Some Fresh Water Fishes. M.V. Sc., Thesis, Fac. Vet. Med., Cairo Univ.
12. Ibtsam, E.B.E.D. (2004): Studies on Some Prevailing Parasitic Diseases Among Cultured Tilapia Fish. Ph.D. Thesis, Fac. Vet. Med., Suez Canal University.

The increase of liver function enzymes in case of LOTA and HOTA doses may be due to the toxic effect of toxin in liver cells. Moreover the liver used to be the site of detoxification of the OTA to 4(*R*)-and 4(*S*) - hydroxyochratoxin A (Stormer and Pederson, 1980). In the same time the level of liver enzymes in case of OTA plus yeast were less than OTA only. This may be indicated that yeast decreased the toxic effect of OTA on liver and in the same time increase liver function.

The increase of creatinine and uric acid in serum of ochratoxicosis fish my be attributed to renal disturbance associated with damage of proximal tubules and thickening of the glomerular basement membrane caused by OTA which lead to reduce the ability of kidney to produce concentrated urine (Marquadret, 1996). Moreover, kidney is the main target organ of OTA genotoxicity, where induced DNA single-strand breaks and DNA adducts in kidney (Pfohl-Leszkowicz, et.al, 1993).

Saad (2002) found that in case of OTA on acute and chronic toxicity in *O. niloticus* causes severe destruction of the proximal tubules of the posterior kidney and hydropic degeneration of the tubular epithelium.

Creatinine is a protein produced by muscle and released into the blood hence removed by the kidney and the increase of creatinine levels indicated to decrease of kidney function (Zotti *et al.*, 2008).

The histopathological alteration which confirmed in case of LOTA and HOTA in the form of activation of melanomacrophage centers in liver and spleen atrophied of hepatic cells, severe fatty changes, and cellular degeneration of kidneys could be attributed to the toxic effects of OTA (Saad 2006).

Similar results obtained by Manning *et al.*, (2003) in case of catfish fed dietary concentrations of 2.00 to 8.00 mg OTA/kg which revealed increase incidence and activation of MMCs centers in hepatopancreatic tissue and posterior kidney.

Orrenius and Bellomo (1986) demonstrated that lipid perox idation which caused by OTA may be an early event in hepatotoxicity, which results in structural changes in the cell membrane and allow an influx of cellular calcium to cause changes in metabolic activity within the cell and ultimately cause cell necrosis.

Also the activation of the MMCs considered as indicative on the degree of the tissue damage (Roberts, 2001).

Regarding to addition of yeast to diets of ochratoxicosis fish elimenate the drastic effects of OTA on hepatopancreas. Also spleen in LOTA dose didn't affected but in HOTA dose spleen showed mild activation of MMCs.

Addition of whey to toxicated fish diets affects the histological findings as follow; Hepatopancreas in LOTA dose are congestion and hydropic degeneration. Meanwhile, with HOTA dose the alteration appeared as mild fatty changes, focal lymphocytic aggregation, enlargement and hyper activation MMCs. Posterior kidney in LOTA dose showed acute cellular swelling of tubular epithelial lining with mild MMCs infeltiration. The effect of HOTA dose on posterior kidney appeared as focal tubular necrosis replaced by inflammatory cells. In spleen the alteration is activation of MMCs in both OTA doses but severity increased with HOTA dose.

The histopathological examination results concluded that yeast more effective than whey in minimize the destructive effect of ochratoxin in the most affected organs (hepatopancreas, kidney and spleen) especially at the LOTA dose.

Moreover, yeast reduce the presence of potentially pathogenic bacteria by competitive exclusion and causes intestinal microbial balance of the host organism and confer various beneficial effects include immunostimulation and enhance disease resistance (Gatlin *et al.*, 2006).

The detoxification effect of yeast on OTA may be revealed to the ability of yeasts to secrete an enzyme related to carboxypeptidases which convert OTA to OTá (non toxic form) (Péteri *et al.*, 2007) by the cleavage of the peptide bond between isocoumarin and phenylalanine in OTA moiety (Marquardt, 1996). Furthermore, yeast cell wall was an effective adsorbent for OTA (Ringot *et al.*, 2007) which may reduce OTA absorption from the fish gastro intestinal tract and excluded with feces.

Molnar *et al.* (2004) found that yeast strain of the genus *Trichosporon* from the hindgut of the termite, refers to important characteristics to detoxify mycotoxins such as OTA. Since, fish gastric microorganisms able to transform mycotoxin to non toxic form in various environmental conditions (Guan *et al.*, 2009). Moreover, yeast showed antagonistic effects to OTA production and growth of OTA producing fungi (Petersson *et al.*, 1998 and Masoud & Kaltoft, 2006).

In conclusion, OTA proved to produce drastic effects on physiological and pathological levels of *O. niloticus.* Meanwhile, active yeast and Sweet whey were successed to neutralize the drastic toxic effects of OTA.

REFERENCES

1. Abdel-Tawwab, M., Abdel-Rahman, A.M. and Ismael N.E.M. (2008a). Evaluation of Commercial Live Bakers' yeast, *Saccharomyces cerevisiae* as a Growth and Immunity Promoter for Fry Nile tilapia, *Oreochromis niloticus* (L.) Challenged *in situ* with *Aeromonas hydrophila*. Aquaculture, 280: 185-189.
2. Abdel-Tawwab, M., Mousa, M.A.A. and Mohammed, M.A. (2008b). Effect of Yeast Supplementation on the Growth Performance and Resistance of Galilee Tilapia *Sarotherodon galilaeus* (L.) to Environmental Copper Toxicity. 8th International Symposium on Tilapia in Aquaculture, 459-474.
3. Abdel-Wahhab, M.A., Hassan, A.M., Aly, S.E. and Mahrous, K.F. (2005). Adsorption of Sterigmatocystin by Montmorillonite and Inhibition of its Genotoxicity in the Nile Tilapia (*Oreochromis niloticus*). Mutation Research, 582: 20-27.

4. Anderson, D.P. and Siwicki, A.K. (1995). Basic Haematology and Serology for Fish Health Programmes. In: Diseases in Asian Aquaculture II. M. Shariff, J. R. Arthur and R.P. Subasinghe (Eds). Fish Health Section, Asian Fisheries Society, Manila, Philippines, pp. 185-202.
5. Anderson, D.P., Siwicki, A.K. and Rumsey, G.L. (1995). Injection or Immersion Delivery of Selected Immunostimulants to Trout Demonstrate Enhancement of Nonspecific Defense Mechanisms and Protective Immunity. In: Shariff, M., Arthur, J.R., Subasinghe, R.P. (Eds.), Diseasesin Asian Aquaculture: II. Fish Health Section. Asian Fisheries Society, Manila. 413-426.
6. Badran, A.F. (1990). The Role of Adjuvants in the Immune Response of the Fish. Zagazeg Veterinary Medicine Journal. 18: 126-136.
7. Carlye-Rose, D.V.M. (2002). Evaluation of Hypoalbuminemia. HCVMA Newsletter, February. 1-2.
8. Chang, C.F., Huff W.E. and Hamilton. P.B. (1979). Aleucocytopenia Induced in Chickens by Dietary Ochratoxin-A. Poultry science. 58: 555-558.
9. Coles, E.H. (1986). Veterinary Clinical Pathology. 2nd Ed. W. B. Saunders Company, Philadelphia and London.
10. Culling, C.F. (1983). Handbook of Histopathologic and Histochemical Staining. 3rd Ed., Buterworth, London.
11. Duncan, D. B. (1955). Multible Range and Multible F test. Biometric, 11: 1-42.
12. Easa, A.A.M. (1997). Effect of *Aspergillus ochraceus* Mould and its Metabolites on some Cultured Fresh Water Fishes in Egypt. M.V. Sc. Faculty of Veterinary Medicine. Cairo University.
13. Elaroussi, M.A., Mohamed, F.R., El Barkouky, E.M., Atta, A.M., Abdou, A.M. and Hatab, M.H. (2006). Experimental Ochratoxicosis in Broiler Chickens. Avian Pathology, 35(4): 263-269.
14. Elkafoury. M.A. (2006). Comparative Studies Between *Oreochromas niloticus* and Monosex Tilapia from Immunological and Pathological Aspect of View. M.V.SC. Faculty of Veterinary Medicine. Alexandria University.
15. Engstad, R.E., Robertsen, B. and Frivold, E. (1992). Yeast Glucan Induces Increase in Activity of Lysozyme and Complemente Mediated Haemolytic Activity in Atlantic Salmon Blood. Fish Shellfish Immunol, 2: 287-97.
16. Fuchs, R., Appelgren, L.E. and Hult, K. (1986). Distribution of 14 C-ochratoxin A in the Rainbow Trout (*Salmogaidneri*). Acta pharmacologica et toxicologica, 59: 220-227.
17. Fuchs, S., Sontag, G., Stidl, R., Ehrlich, V., Kundi, M. and Knasmüller, S. (2008). Detoxification of patulin and ochratoxin A, Two Abundant mycotoxins, by Lactic Acid Bacteria. Food and Chemical Toxicology, 46 (4): 1398-1407.
18. Gatlin III, D.M., Li, P., Wang, X., Burr, G.S., Castille F. and Lawrence, A.L. (2006). Potencial Application of Prebiotics in Aquaculture. En: Editores: L. Elizabeth Cruz Suarez, Denis Ricque Marie, Mireya Tapia Salazar, Martha G. Neito Lopez, David A. Villarreal Cavazos, Ana C. Puello Cruzy Armando Garcia Ortega. Avances en Nutricion Acuicola VIII. VIII Simposium International de Nutricion Acuicola. 15-17 noviembre. Universidad Autonoma de Nuevo Leon, Monterrey, Nuevo Leon, Mexico. ISBN 970-694-333-5.
19. Guan, S., He, J., Young, J.C., Zhu, H., Li, X., Ji, C. and Zhou T. (2009). Transformation of Trichothecene Mycotoxins by Microorganisms from Fish Digesta. Aquaculture, 290: 290-295.

20. Hesser, E.F. (1960). Methods for Routine Fish Haematology. Progressive Fish Culturist, 22: 164-171.
21. Hichey, C.R. (1976). Fish Haematology, its Used and Significance. New York Fish com. J., 33: 170-175.
22. Horton, B. (1997). The Whey Processing Industry. Into the 21st Century. In: Proceedings of the Second International Whey Conference, Chicago, USA, 27-29 October. International Dairy Federation. pp. 12-25.
23. Jordan, M., Rzehak, K. and Maryanska, A. (1977). The Effect of Two Pesticides; Miedzian 50 and Gtsagard 50, on the Development of Tadpoles of *Rana temporaia*. Bulletin of Environmental Contamination, 17: 349-354.
24. Kawahara, E., Ueda T. and Nomura. S. (1991). In vitro Phagocytic Activity of White-spotted Shark Cells After Injection with *Aermonas salmonicida* Extracellular Products. Gyobyo Kenkyu, Japan, 26: 213-214.
25. Kermanshahi, H. and Rostami, H. (2006). Influence of Supplemental Dried Whey on Broiler Performance and Cecal Flora. International of Journal Poultry Science, 5: 538-543.
26. Khalil, R.H. (1998). Effect of Bayluscide on Some Cultured Fresh Water Fish *Oreochromis niloticus*. Ph. D. Thesis, Faculty of Veterinary Medicine. Alexandria University.
27. Knowles, G. and Gill, H.S. (2002). Immune Modulation by Dairy Ingredients: Potential for Improving Health. In: Shortt C, O'Brien J, Editors. Functional Dairy Products. Boca Raton 7 CRC Press; p. 125-54.
28. Madhyastha, M.S., Marquardt, R.R. and Frohlich, A.A. (1992). Hydrolysis of Ochratoxin A by the Microbial Activity of Digesta in the Gastrointestinal Tract. Archives of Environmental Contamination and Toxicology, 23: 468-472.
29. Manning, B.B., Ulloa, R.M., Li, M.H., Robinson, E.H. and Rottinghaus, G.E. (2003). Ochratoxin A Fed to Channel Catfish (*Ictalurus punctatus*) Causes Reduced Growth and Lesions of Hepatopancreatic Tissue. Aquaculture, 219: 739-750.
30. Manning, B.B., Terhune, J.S., Li, M.H., Robinson, E.H., Wise, D.J. and Rottinghau, G.E. (2005). Exposure to Feedborne Mycotoxins T-2 Toxin or Ochratoxin A Causes Increased Mortality of Channel Catfish Challenged with *Edwardsiella ictaluri*. Journal of Aquatic Animal Health. 17: 147-152.
31. Marquardt, R.R. (1996). Effects of Molds and Their Toxins on Livestock Performance: A Western Canadian Perspective. Animal Feed Science and Technology, 70: 3968-3988.
32. Masoud, W. and Kaltoft, C.H. (2006). The Effects of Yeasts Involved in the Fermentation of Coffea Arabica in East Africa on Growth and Ochratoxin A (OTA) Production by *Aspergillus ochraceus*. International Journal of Food Microbiology, 106: 229- 234.
33. McLaughlin, J., Padfield, P.J., Burt, J.P.H. and O'Neill, C.A. (2004). Ochratoxin A Increases Permeability Through Tight Junctions by Removal of Specific Claudin Isoforms. American Journal of Cell Physiology, 287: C1412–C1417.
34. Molnar, O., Schatzmayr, G., Fuchs, E. and Prillinger H. (2004). *Trichosporon mycotoxinivorans sp.* nov., A New Yeast Species Useful in Biological Detoxification of Various Mycotoxins. Systematic and Applied Microbiology, 27: 661-671.
35. Naghton, P.J., Mikkelsen, L.L. and Jensen, B.B. (2001). Effects of Non Digestible Oligosaccharides on *salmonella typhimuium* and Non Pathogenic Escherichia *in vitro*. Journal of Applied and Environmental Microbiology, August pp. 3391-3395.

36. Nurmi, E.V. and Rantal (1973). New Aspects of Salmonella Infection in Broiler Production. Nature, 241: 210-211.

37. Orrenius, S., and Bellomo, G. (1986). Toxicological Implications of Perturbation of Ca2+ homeostasis in hepatocytes. In: W. Y. Cheung (Ed.) Calcium and Cell Function. p 185. Academic Press, Orlando, FL.

38. Péteri, Z., Téren, J., Vágvölgyi, C. and Varga, J. (2007). Ochratoxin Degradation and Adsorption Caused by Astaxanthin-producing Yeasts. Food Microbiology, 24: 205-210.

39. Petersson, S., Hansen, M.W., Axberg, K., Hult, K. and Schnurer, J. (1998). Ochratoxin A Accumulation in Cultures of *Penicillium verrucosum* with the Antagonistic yeast *Pichia anomala* and *Saccharomyces cerevisiae*. Mycological Research, 102 (8): 1003-1008.

40. Pfohl-Leszkowicz, A., Grosse, Y., Kane, A., Creppy, E.E. and Dirheimer, G. (1993b). Differential DNA Adducts Formation and Disappearance in Three Mouse Tissues After Treatment with the Mycotoxin Ochratoxin A. Mutation Research, 289: 265-273.

41. Pickering, A.D. (1981). Stress and fish. Academic Press, Londo, New York. pp. 149-152.

42. Reyes-Becerril, M., Tovar-Ramírez, D., Ascencio-Valle, F., Civera-Cerecedo, R., Gracia-López, V. and Barbosa-Solomieu, V. (2008). Effects of Dietary Live Yeast *Debaryomyces hansenii* on the Immune and Antioxidant System in Juvenile Leopard Grouper Mycteroperca Rosacea Exposed to Stress. Aquaculture, 280: 39-44.

43. Ringot D., Chango A., Schneider Y. and Larondelle Y. (2006). Toxicokinetics and Toxicodynamics of Ochratoxin A, an Update. Chemico-Biological Interactions 159: 18-46.

44. Ringot, D., Lerzy, B., Chaplain, K., Bonhoure, J., Auclair, E. and Larondelle, Y. (2007). *In vitro* Biosorption of Ochratoxin A on the Yeast Industry By-products: Comparison of Isotherm Models. Bioresource Technology. 98: 1812-1821.

45. Roberts, R.J. (2001). Fish Pathology. Third Edition. Harcourt Publishers Limited 2001.

46. Rutherfurd-Markwick, K.J., Johnson, D., Cross, M.L. and Gill, H.S. (2005). Modified Milk Powder Supplemented with Immunostimulating Whey Protein Concentrate (IMUCARE) Enhances Immune Function in Mice. Nutrition Research. 25: 192-203.

47. Saad, T.T. (2002). Some Studies on the Effects of Ochratoxin-A on Cultured *oreochromis niloticus* and Carp Species. M.V.SC. Faculty of Veterinary Medicine. Alexandria University.

48. Safinaz, G.M.I. (2001). Effect of Phenol on the Immune Response of Tilapia Fish and Susceptibility to Disease. Ph.D. Thesis Faculty of Veterinary Medicine Suez Canal University, Egypt.

49. Sakai, M., Yoshida, T., Atsuta, S. and Kobayashi, M. (1984). Enhancement of Resistance to Vibriosis in Rainbow Trout, *Oncorhynchus mykiss* (walaum), by Oral Administration of *Clostridium butyricum* Bacterin. Journal of Fish Diseases, 18: 187-190.

50. Sakai, M., Taniguchi, K., Mamoto, K., Ogawa, H. and Tabata, M. (2001). Immunostimulant Effects of Nucleotide Isolated from Yeast RNA on Carp, *Cyprinus carpio* L. Journal of Fish Disease, 24: 433-438.

51. Shalaby, A.M.E. (2004). The Opposing Effect of Ascorbic Acid (vitamin C) on Ochratoxin Toxicity in Nile tilapia (*Oreochromis niloticus*). In: Proceedings of the 6th International Symposium on Tilapia in Aquaculture (R.B. Remedios, G.C. Mair and K. Fitzsimmons, eds), pp. 209-221.

52. Smith, J.W. and Hamilton, P.B. (1970). Aflatoxicosis in the Broiler Chicken. Poultry Science. 49: 207-215.

53. Soliman, M.K. (1996). Principals of Fish Disease. Effect of Stress on Immune System of Fish. Faculty of Veterinary Medicine. Alexandria University, pp. 12-23.
54. Sreemannarayana, O., Frohlich, A.A., Vitti, T.G., Marquardt R.R. and Abramson, D. (1988). Studies of the Tolerence and Disposition of Ochratoxin A in Young Calves. Journal of Animal Science, 88: 1703.
55. Stormer, F.C. and Pederson, J.I. (1980). Formation of (4R)- and (4S)-hydroxyochratoxin A from Ochratoxin A by Rat Liver Microsomes. Applied and Environmental Microbiology, 39: 971-975.
56. Tellez, C.E., Dean, C.E., Corrier. D.E., Deloach, J.R., Jaeger, L. and Hargis, B.M. (1993). Effect of Dietary Lactose on Cecal Morphology, pH, Organic Acid and *salmonella enteritidis* Organ Invasion in Leghorn Chicks. Poultry Science, 72: 636- 642.
57. Truckess, M.W. and Pohland, A.E. (2001). Mycotoxin Protocols, in: J.M. Walker (Ed.), Methods in Molecular Biology, Volume 157, Humana Press, New Jersey.
58. Wang, G.H., Xue, C.Y., Chen, F., Ma, Y.L., Zhang, X.B., Bi, Y.Z. and Cao, Y.C. (2009). Effects of Combinations of Ochratoxin A and T-2 Toxin on Immune Function of Yellow-feathered Broiler Chickens. Poultry Science, 88: 504-10.
59. White, D.G. (1986). Evaluation of a Rapid, Specific Test for Detecting Colostral IgG in the Neonatal Calf. Veterinary Record, 118: 68-70.
60. Yoshida, T., Kruger, R. and Inglis. V. (1995). Augmentation of Non-specific Protection in African Catfish, *Clarias gariepinus* (Burchell) by the Long-term Oral Administration of Immunostimulants. Journal of Fish Disease, 18: 195-198.
61. Zotti, F.D., Visonà, E., Massignani, D., Abaterusso, C., Lupo, A. and Gambaro, G. (2008). General Practitioners' Serum Creatinine Recording Styles. Journal of nephrology, 21(1): 106-109.

Diarrhoea in Neonatal baraki kids-goats

Mona S. Zaki*[1]; Nagwa S. Ata[2]; Shalaby, S.I.[3]; Iman M. Zytoun[4]

ABSTRACT

A survey was carried out in 130 kids-goats aged from 2 days to 3 month from different private farms in El Mounofia and Kalubia Governorates. Out of these animals, 100 were suffering from diarrhoea. Bacteriological examination of the faecal samples revealed the presence of *E. coli* (58%), *Salmonella*, (27%), and *Shigella* (15%), as the main causative agents of diarrhoea. They were sensitive to common antibiotics and less sensitive to 10% garlic extract and 40% *Hibiscaus subdarifa.* Haematological studies revealed significant decrease in hemoglobin content (Hb), erthrocytic (RBCs) count. On contrary, haematocrit value (PCV%) showed significant increase in affected animals. A significant decrease was detected in the values of serum total proteins, albumin, iron, copper, and growth hormone. On the other hand, there was a significant increase in cortisol hormone, lactate dehydrogenase (LDH), and alkaline phosphatase

1. Dept. of Hydrobiology, National Research centre. Cairo, Egypt.
2. Dept. of Microbiology and Immunology, National Research centre. Cairo, Egypt.
3. Dept. of Reproduction, National Research centre. Cairo, Egypt.
4. Dept. of Microbiology, Central Lab. Zagazig University, Zagazig, Egypt.

enzymes. We emphasize that the demonstrated diarrhoea caused many harmful clincopathological effects, reduced growth hormone, and caused severe anaemia in kids-goat.

Keywords: Kids-goat - kids - diarrhoea - haemogram - Salmonella - *E. coli* -serum biochemistry - LDH - alkaline phosphatase - hormones - trace elements - garlic extract - *Hibiscous subdarfa*.

INTRODUCTION

With the increasing application of intensive husbandry methods the various causes of ill-thrift in sheep and goats have attracted increasing attention. The results of many investigations have shown that the greatest loss among these species occurs in the neonatal period (Snodgrass and Angus, 1983). Neonatal diarrhoea in kid-goat is a common problem with not very well understood cause (Snodgrass, et al., 1977). This syndrome has been ascribed to a variety of causes such as nutritional imbalance, faulty management and infectious agents (Durham et al., 1979). Infectious diarrhoea affecting kids-goat occurs mainly where intensive systems of breeding which use paddocks, pens and indoor kids-goat sheds are employed. Such systems unless very carefully managed, encourage the progressive build-up of infection (Allan and John, 1987; Aly, et al., 1996 and Angus, et al., 1982).

Aim of the present work to study the cause of diarrhoea, the clinicopathological changes in blood of infected animals and the suitable antibiotic for treatment.

MATERIAL AND METHODS

Animals

One hundred and thirty kids-goat (100 diarrhoeic + 30 apparently healthy as a control group), aged from 2days to 3 months were used in this study. These kids-goats belonged to different localities in El-Mounifia and Kalubeia Governorates and under semi-intensive management system.

Sampling

All animals were sampled once before administration of any treatment.

Bacteriological Studies

Fecal Samples

Two faecal samples were taken directly from the rectum of all animal in the investigation. One sample was taken in a clean dry plastic packs for parasitological examination to detect gastrointestinal parasites (Coles, 1986) and the second using sterile swabs for further bacteriological analysis. These swabs were immediately inoculated on Carry and Blair's transport medium and were cultured on selective and differential culture media at 37°C for 24 hours and the isolated colonies were then identified according to Carter

(1984) sand Baily and Scott (1990) as follows: Isolated colonies from MacConky's agar plate were examined to be either Lactose fermenting or non-lactose fermenting. Lactose fermenting colonies appeared to be rose pink in color and non-lactose fermenting as pale yellow colonies. Isolated colonies were then examined by Gram staining. Colonies, which appeared as Gram negative bacilli were then described for further identification of Gram negative isolates. These were then subjected to biochemical reactions such as indol production, methyl red Gobes Proskauer test (MR/VP), citrate utilization, hydrogen suiphide production, reaction of triple sugar iron agar (TSI), urease production and oxidase test.

Detection of K99 antigen was performed by slide agglutination test (SAT) according to Baily and Scott (1990), with specific antisera Cryptoporidia were examined in faecal smears on glass slides which were air dried, fixed in methanol and stained with Geimsa stain according to Abou-Zaid and Nasr (1995).

Haematological Studies

Whole blood samples with EDTA were obtained form the jugular vein for determination of hemoglobin content, haematocrit (PCV%) value, erythrocytic (RBCs) count and total leukocytic (WBCs) count according to Coles (1986).

Biochemical and Hormonal Studies

Serum samples were used for determination of copper and iron by atomic absorption according to Issac and Kerber (1971). Total proteins, albumin, alkaline phosphatase (ALP), lactate dehydrogenase (LDH) were determined b spectophotomoeter in the rang UV "240 nm". Cortisol hormone was measured according to Kuehn and Burvenich (1986). Growth hormone was measured by special kits according to the method described by Ronge and Blum (1988).

SENSITIVITY TEST

1. Sensitivity test using common antibiotics

The following chemotherapeutic agents were used in testing the isolated micro-organisms:

Gentamycin (10mcg/disc), chloramphenicol (30mcg/disc), rifamycine (30mcg/disc), tetracycline (30mcg/disc), ampicillin (10mcg/disc), streptomycin (10mg/disc), nalidixic acid (30 mg/disc), and colistin (10 meg/disc).

2. Sensitivity test using Garlic aqueous solutions

The isolates were incubated in about 1 0% garlic aqueous solution at 28°C till the colonial broth become evident. The degree of inhibition was compared to control.

3. Sensitivity test using dry *Hibiscus subdarifa* flowers

The flowers were extracted with 75% ethyl alcohol using apparatus Soxhlet till complete exhaustion occurs. Alcohol was then evaporated to obtain a semisolid extract. Dilutions to 40% were obtained by dissolving the extract in distilled water. The resultant dilutions were used to test microorganisms were streaked with 0.4 mm loop on the extract into the gutter avoiding it over flow on the surface.

Statistical Analysis

All data were subjected to statistical analysis using T- test according to Gad and Well (1967).

RESULTS

Kids-goat were divided after, careful clinical examination and bacteriological examination of the faecal samples into three groups as shown in Table (7.1).

Table 7.1: Bacterial Examination of Faecal Samples of Diarrhoeic Kids-goats

The Organism	Number of Isolates	% of Isolates
E. Coli	58	68.84
Salmonella spp.	27	44.68
Shigellaspp.	15	1.05

Clinical Signs

Diseased kids-goats showed severe depression unable to stand or move and some of them showed sternal or lateral body recumbent. Soft to watery of faeces tinged with mucus or occult blood or both and having putrefied odour. Varying degree of dehydration and severe losses of skin elasticity. Contaminated skin of anal region, rough hairs, dry muzzle, increase of body temperature, pulse and respiratory rates.

Bacteriological Studies

Bacteriological examination of the faecal samples of diarrhoeic kids revealed that 100 samples were positive for pathogenic bacteria. The distribution of thee indicated that enteropathogic E. Coil and Salmonella constituted the high incidence while Shigella recorded the very lowerest incidence. The increase in packed cell volume (PCV%) reflected the severity of dehydration occurred in diarrhoeic kids with bacterial enteritis in group 2 (infected with E. coli) and group 3 (infected with Salmonella) than in group 4 (infected with Shigella) and apparently healthy kids (group 1). This reflects the severity of diarrhoea caused by enterotoxins produced by enterotoxigenic bacteria proliferation in the intestine which lead to toxaemia and that in turn aggravates the dehydrations. The most characteristic features in diarhoeic kids faeces was watery and contained mucus or occult blood or both and was having putrefied odour could explain the high incidence of isolated enteropathogenic E. coli and Salmonella. However the presence o other pathogenic bacteria was also suggested but their incidence was very low as Shigella

Concerning sensitivity test; the result indicate that E. coli and Salmonnela were highly sensitive to gentamycine, chioramphenicol, rifamycine, and tetracycline, less sensitive to ampicillin and nalidixic acid and resistant to streptomycin and colistine. Moreover, E. coli was moderately sensitive to *Hibiscous subdarifa* and garlic solution (Table 7.2).

Table 7.2: Results of Sensitivity Test Against Different Chemotherapeutic Agents

Chemotherapeutic Agents	Disc Concentration	E. coli	Salmonella
Gentamycin	10 mcg	+++	+++
Chlorampheni-col	30 mcg	+++	+++
Rifamycine	30 mcg	+++	+++
Tetracycline	30 mcg	+++	+++
Ampicillin	10 mcg	++	+
Streptomycin	l0mcg	+	+
Naildixic acid	30 mcg	++	+
Garlic aqueous solution 10%	l0%	++	++
Hibiscous extract 40%	40%	++	+
Colistine	10%	+	+

+++ 0.58mm ++ = 0.38mm + = 0.23mm

Results of Haematology and Biochemistry

A significant decrease in haemoglobin content (Hb), erythrocytic (RBCs) count while, haematocrit values (PCV%) and the leukocytic (WBCs) count showed significant increase in affected animals with E. coli (group 2) and Salmonelh (group 3) than the control healthy animals (group 1) as shown in Table (7.3).

Table 7.3: Means ± SE of Haemoglobin (Hb) Haematocrit (PCV%) and Erythrocytic (RBCs) Count in Both Healthy and Diarrhoeic Kids-goat

Animals Groups	Number of Animals	PCV%	RBCs (x106/p.i)	Rb (g/dl)
Group I (control)	30	24.25 ± 0.12	10.20± 0.23	9.80± 0.20
Group 2 (E. coli)	58	40.00 ± 0.02 **	8.24± 0.24**	8.00± 0.14**
Group3 (Salmonella)	27	34.00±0.10**	8.10±0.13**	8.23± 0.74**
Group 4 (Shigella)	15	23.24 ± 0.72**	9.42± 0.40	9.03± 0.72

** = Highly significant at Pd ≤ 0.01 SE = Standard error.

As shown in Tables (7.4, 7.5), there were a significant decrease in total proteins, albumin growth hormone, iron, and copper. On the other hand, there was a high level of cortisol hrrnone, lactate dehydrogenase, an alkaline phosphatase in diarrhoeic kids-goat in comparison with the control one.

Table 7.4: Means ± SE of Iron, Copper, Cortisol and Growth Hormones in Both Healthy and Diarrhoeic Kids-goat

Animals Groups	Number of Animals	Iron (mg/dl)	Copper (mg/dl)	Cortisol (ng/dl)	Growth Hormone (ng/dl)
Group 1 (control)	30	250 ± 2.30	185 ± 3.4	0.098 ± 0.73	11.0 ± 0.08
Group 2 (E. coli)	58	178 ± .54**	130 ± 47**	0.130 ± 0.28**	8.0 ± 0.11 **
Group3 (Salmonella)	27	180 ± 3.53**	134 ± 4.0	0.140 ± 0.30**	7.8 ± 0.20**
Group 4 (Shigella)	15	168 ± 4.01**	148 ± 2.0 **	0.150 ± 0.40**	7.1 ± 0.30**

** = Highly significant at Pd ≤ 0.01 SE = Standard error.

Table 7.5: Means ± SE of Total Proteins, Albumin, Lactate Dehydrogenase (LDH) Alkaline Phosphates (ALP) Changes in Both Healthy and Diarrhoeic Kids-goat

Animals groups	Number of Animals	Total proteins (g/dl)	Albumin (g/dl)	LDH (U/l)	ALP (U/l)
Group 1 (control)	30	9.3 ± 0.40	4.90 ± 0.27	252 ± 23	15.3 ± 0.80
Group 2 (E. coli)	58	8.2 ± 0.27**	3.80 ± 0.14**	263 ± 31 **	18.7 ± 0.50*
Group3 (Salmonella)	27	7.0±0.10**	3.40± 0.72**	270± 14**	19.1 ± 60 **
Group 4 (Shigella)	15	6.8 ±0.78**	2.86 ± 0.73**	260 ± 26**	19.0 ± 0.54**

** = Highly significant at Pd ≤ 0.01 SE = Standard error.

DISCUSSION

Infectious diarrhoea is a common condition affecting kids-goat specially those which are bred under intensive system of breeding in this study. Fecal samples screened the presence of the common enteropathogenic organisms E. Coli, Salmonella species and Shigella which causing diarrhoea. E. Coli seems to be the dominant enteropathogen which plays the major role among diarrhoeic kids goat (Tzipori, et. al., 1981; Angus, et. al., 1982; Carter, 1984; Farid, et. al., 1987 and Rodostits, 1992). Isolation of Salmonella species from diarrhoeic kids-goat confirmed the opinion that Salmonellosis is a sporadic cause of enteritis and cause loss in young kids-goat and buffaloe-calves (Bhullar and Tiawana, 1985). E. Coli and Salmonella were sensitive to garlic 10%. *Hibiscou.s sabdorifa* flowers 40% sensitive to E. Coli but less sensitive to Salmonella.

The significant decrease in serum total proteins, albumin, iron and copper, in diarrhoeic kids-goat may be referred to the cause of diarrhoea.

Where, there was significant increase in bacterial enteritis this could be explained by impaired absorption of these trace elements through the damaged intestinal epithelium resulting from enterotoxins produced by these bacteria in the small intestine (Kasari, 1990 and Aly el. al., 1996). Concerning serum protein and albumin, they showed significant decrease in diarrehoeic kids-goat than the cntrol group. Such drastic reduction may be attributed to diarrhoea, which lower the synthetic power of albumin in the liver due to microorganism. This opinion is supported by finding of Aly, et al. (1996). The significant increase in alkaline phosphatase, lactate dehydrogenase was observed in diarrhoeic kids-goat. Similar results were observed by Sadiek (1987).

A highly significant decrease in serum iron was noticed in diarrhoeic kids-goat, this result agreed with those obtained by Aly, et. al. (1996). The decrease of iron was accompanied by decrease of copper and this lead to anaemia (Radostitis, 1992).

Concerning cortisol hormone, an increase of this hormone can be considered as an expression of stress and helps the organism to counteract this stress, bacmatological, metallic and endocrine changes enhanced protein catabolism and gluconeogenesis during endotoxaemia (Dvorak, et al., 1974). Growth hormone concentrations tended to decrease in diarrhoeic kids-goat. An effect which was probably in part mediated by tumour necrotic factor (Walton and Cronin, 1989).

We can conclude that a substantial, bacteriological haematologlcal, biochemical, and hormonal changes occur in diarrhoeic kids-goat when the cause of diarrhoea is enterotoxigenic bacteria. This means that we must interfere quickly with therapeutic plan to put in consideration the decrease in damaged intestinal epithelium and supporting the body immune status during infection along side with the traditional electrolyte therapy.

REFERENCES

1. Abou-Zaid. A. A and Nasr, M.Y. (1995): "Some Studies on Enterotoxaemia in Calves" Alex. J. Sci. 11: 105-111.
2. Allan and John (1987): "Sheep Husbandry and Diseases". Ed. Sheridan House. Inc. USA. 257-268 pp.
3. Aly, A.O.; Zamzam, H.A. Kohilo, KH and El-Sheilch, A.R. (1996): "Some Studies on Clinical, Haematological and Biochemical Changes in Diarrheic Neonatal Buffaloe-calves with Reference to Hygienic Condition". Assiut Vet. Med. J. 35(69): 91-101.
4. Angus, K.; Appleyard, W.T.; Menzies, J.D; Campbell, I.; and Sherwood, D. (1982): "An outbreak of Diarrhoea Associated With Cryptosporidiosis in Naturally Reared Lambs. Vet. Record; 110: 129-130.
5. Baily, W.R. and Scott, E.G. (1990): "Diagnostic Microbiology. Atext Book for The Isolation and Identification of Pathogenic Microorganisms". C.V. Mosby Company, Saint Lowis.

6. Bhullar, M.S. and Tiawana, M.S. (198): "Factors Affecting Mortality Among Buffalo-calve". Indian J. Anim. Sci., 55: 599-601.
7. Cantarw, J.C.; Moeuer, T. and Kleinberg (1985): University Chemistry D.C. Health and Co., Boston, M.A.
8. Carter, G.R. (l984): "Diagnostic Procedures in Veterinary Bacteriology and Myeology'. 1st Ed., Charles, C., Thomas Publisher, USA.
9. Coles, E.H. (1986): "Veterinary Clinical Pathology". 4th Ed., W.B Saunders Co. Philadelphia, London, Toronto, p. 215.
10. Durtbm, P.J.K; Stevenson, B.J. and Farquharson, B.C. (1979): "Rotavirus and Corona Virus Associated Diarrhoea in Domestic Animals". N.Z. Vet. J., 27: 30.
11. Dvorak, M.; Lebduska, J. and Oplish M. (1974): "Adrenocortical Response to E. Coli Endotoxin in Mediated and Non-mediated Calves'. Acta. Vet. Brno 43: 23-32.
12. Farid, A.F.; Nashed, S.A. and Marcell, K.S. (1987): "Salmonellosis in Bufaloe- calves in Upper Egypt". J. Egypt. Vet. Med. Ass. 47(182): 153-160.
13. Gad. W. and Well G. (1967): "Statistical Methods". 6th Ed. the Iowa stat Univ. Press Iowa, USA.
14. Issac. RA. and Kerper, I. (1971): American Madison; 17.
15. Kasari, T.R. (1990): 'Metabolic Acidosis in Diarrhic Calves: "The Importance of Alkalinizing Agents in Therapy". Vet. Clin. of North America: Food Animal Practice, 6: 29-43.
16. Kuchn, C. and Burvenich, C. (1986): "Cortisol and Thyroid Hormones After Endotoxin Administration in 1actatiiig Goats". Arch. Int. Physiol. Biochem. 94: 37-386.
17. Rodostits, O.M. (1.992): Proc. Aust. Assoc. Conference. Addlaides, p. 153. Cited in Vermunt, J. (1994). Rearing and Management of Diarrhoea in Calves to Wearing Aust. Vet. 3. (7), 2: 33-41.
18. Ronge, H. and Blum, LW. (1988): "Somatomedin C and Other Hormones in Dairy Cow Around Parturition, in Newborn Calves and Milk". J. Anim. Nutr. 60: 168-1 76.
19. Sadiek, A.H. (1987): "Clinical and Some Biochemical Blood Changes Accompanying Alimentary and Respiratory Manifestations Among Fattening Buffalo-calves". M.V.Sci. Thesis Fac. Vet. Med. Assut Univ.
20. Snodgrass, D.R and Angus, K.W. (1983): "Diseases of Sheep". 1st Ed, Blakwell Scientific Publications, London, 43-48 pp.
21. Snodgrass, D.R; Herring J.A.; Linklater K. A. and Dyson, D. A. (1977): "A Survey of Rotaviruses in Sheep in Scotland". Vet. Rec., 100: 344.
22. Tzipori, S.; Angus, K.W.; Cambell, and Clerihew, L.W. (1981): "Diarrhea due to Cryptosporidium Infection in Artificia11y Reared Kids-goat". J, Clin, Micro., 14: 100-105.
23. Tzipori., S.; Larsen, 3.; Smith and Luefi., R. (1982): "Diarrhoea in Goat Kids Attributed to Cryptosporidium Infection". Vet Rec. 111: 35-36.
24. Walton P. and Cronin, M. J. (1989): "Tumour Necrosis Factor-alpha Inhibits Growth Hormone Secretion from Cultured Anterior Pitutitary Cells. Endocrinol'. 125 925-929.

8

Effect of *E. coli* 0H157 on Baladi Broiler Chicken and Some Biochemical Studies

Mona S. Zaki*[1]; Olfat Fawzy[2]; M.H. Osfor[3]

ABSTRACT

Forty Chicken 4 weeks old and 800-1000 g average body weight were used. They kept in a balanced diet to study some performance, and clinicopathological changes under *E.coli* 0157:H7 infection. Ten chickens kept as control and 30 were infected with *E. coli* 015,: H7 by dose 0.05m1 (x 10^7 CFU) inoculated intramuscularly. Body weight were recorded, blood samples were collected at 7, 15, 30 days post infection, serum was separated for determination of AST, ALT, *Total* protein. Albumin, urea, creatinine, calcium phosphorous, sodium, potassium and cortisol hormone. The biochemical analysis showed increase in AST and ALT and a significant change in protein. Hypoalbuminemia, was observed, increase of serum urea, creatinine, hypocalcaemia, hyperphosphatemia, and decrease in level of potassium, sodium and cortisol hormone in areas. Blood examination revealed pancytopenia. This indicates that *E. coli* 0157: H7 causes deleterious effect on the Hematopoietic system.

1. Department of Hydrobiology, National Research Center Dokki, Cairo, Egypt.
2. Department of Biochemistry, National Research Center Dokki, Cairo, Egypt.
3. Department of Nutrition, National Research Center Dokki, Cairo, Egypt.

Key words: *E. coli;* Baladi Broiler Chicken; AST, ALT; Biochemical analysis.

INTRODUCTION

Infection with *E. coli* 0157: H7 presents with a wide spectrum of clinical manifestations, including severe abdominal cramps with little or *no* fever and watery diarrhea that often progresses to grossly bloody diarrhea (Levin, 1997). Infection can be asymptomatic or can present with only nonbloody diarrhea (Belongia *et al.,* 1990). Extraintestinal involvement, including cardiac and neurologic manifestations, has been reported, and infection can be associated with the hemolytic-uremic syndrom and thrombotic thrombocytopenic purpura. The disease can be fatal (Karmali *et al., 1985*).

Esherichia coli comprises a group of bacteria found in the intestines of humans, animals and birds, E. coli 0157:H7 strain produces potent toxins and can cause food born pisones to person transmitted disease after ingestion of very low numbers of microorganism E. coli 0157:H7 was first identified as a human pathogen in 1982 (Riley et al., 1983).

Griffin and Tauxe, (1992), a recorded reported that strain of E. coli infection is more often reported in the young, illness signs are bloody diarhreae, severe abdominal pain, low grade of fever and vomiting. The major source of food born E. coli 0157:H7 ciated disease is undercooked grand beef. Roast beef, roast chicken, raw milk and water an out break of the disease in persons who had eaten fast food in these restaurant chain. Marks and Robert, (1993), reported that the cytotoxins of E. coli 0157:H7 production seems to be important factors in the pathogenesis of disease. These cytotoxins are among the most potent bacterial toxins. These toxins in active host cell ribosomes disrupting protein synthesis and causing cell death Obrien et al. (1992).

Prevention of illness is especially critical in addition to strategies designed to prevent food born illness. Controlled production of live animal, meat processing relatively little information is available on clinicopathological changes in experimental animals with this disease. The present work designed to study some serum biochemical changes after experimental infections of chicken with E. coli 0157:H7.

MATERIAL AND METHODS

E. coli strain

E. coli 0157: H7 strain was used for the experimental infection for 40 chicken 4 weeks old as well as 800-1050 gm average body weight. Bird proved to be free from pathogenic bacteria and parasitic infection. I/M with 0.05 * 107cfu colony forming unit ml of viable organisms of E. coli 0157:H7.

Blood Samples

Two blood samples were collected from wing vein the first blood sample was collected into dry clean tube containing dipotassium. Ethylene diamine tetracetate (EDTA) as anticoagulant to covering out the hematological studies including red blood cells counts (RBCs) hemoglobin, (H) packed cell volume (PCV), mean corpuscular. Hemoglobin (MCH) and mean corpuscular hemoglobin concentration (MCIIC) were calculated from these hematological parameters according to Jain, (1986).

Second blood samples were collected from wing vein and serum was separated and used for the determination the activity of asparatate aminotransferase. (AST) and alamine aminotransferase (ALT) according to Reitman and Frankel, (1957). Total protein and albumin according to Doumas and Biggs, (1972). Urea according to Sanders, (1980) creatinine was estimated according to Bartels, (1971), calcium was determined according to Sarkar and Chankan, (1967), phosphorous was measured according to Goodwin, (1970), Na, K were determined by atomic absorption. Serum cortisol was analyzed by means of a gammacoat 125 I cortisal radioimunassay kit according to the method described by Campbell and Coles, (1986). Also at the time of scarification feaces from these birds are cultivated on sorbitol MaConkey agar medium for bacteriological examination according to Ratnam and March, (1986).

Statistical analysis according to Snedecor and Cochran, (1967).

RESULTS

Bacteriological results recorded fail to ferment sorbitol can be recognized as colorless colonies. Further confirmation we made by agglutination test with anti-serum against the flagella antigen H7 it give positive results.

In Table (8.1) there is a significant decrease on body weight at 7, 15, 30 days and mortality rate is increase in the 1" week after infection, signs of infection appears in the form of depression, loss of body weight, bloody diarrhea and ascites.

Table (8.3) revealed a significant decrease in RBcs count Hb concentrations PCV, MCV, MCH, McHc also TLC such decrease was very highly significant on days 30 of infection ($P < 0.01$).

In Table (8.4) there is a significant increase in ALT and AST if compared with control group $P < 0.05$. Total protein and Albumin showed highly significant decrease if compared with control group. Concerning cortisol the result showed highly significant increase if compared with control group.

Table (8.5) revealed a significant increases in serum urea and creatinine and Hyperphosphatemia in d15 and d30 .p<0. 01. also there is a significant decrease in serum level sodium,potasium and Hypocalcemia in d15 and d30 p<0.01.

Table 8.1: Changes in Body Weight in Infected Baladi Chicken with E coli

	7 days	15 days	30 days
Control	860 ±0.72	880 ± 0.13	1000 ± 0.40
Infected	800 ± 0.70	700 ± 0.75*	708 ± 0.56**

*P<0.05 **P<0.01

Table 8.2: Composition of the Basal Diets (According to National Research Council)

Ingredients (%)	Started Diet	Grower-Finisher Diet
Yellow corn ground	67.40	72.90
Soyabean meal (44%)	21.30	18.30
Fish meal (72%)	4.00	3.00
Meat meal (60%)	5.84	4.30
Bone meal	0.08	0.10
Dicalcium phosphate	0.15	0.10
Limestone ground	0.79	0.94
Salt	0.71	0.17
Methionine	0.12	0.04
Premix *	0.15	0.15
Calculated analysis		
Crude protein (%)	2150	19
ME (Kcal/kg)	2989	3040
C/P ratio	139.02	160

Broiler premix furnishing the following ingredients per kg of feed vit. A 12000 IU, vit D_3 2000 IU, Vit E 10 mg, folic acid I mg vit Niacin 20 mg, pantothenic acid 10 mg, vit K 2 mg, vit B_1 1mg, vit B2 4 mg, vit B6 1.5 mg vit B12 10 μg, iron 30 mg, copper 10 mg, Zinc 55 mg, Mn 55 mg, Iodine 1 mg, Se 0.1 mg, choline chloride 500 mg.

Table 8.3: Hematological Values (Mean Values ± S.E of Normal and Affected Baladi Chicken by E. coli

Groups	R.B.C.S 106 μL	HB gm/dl	P.cv%	M.cv	MCH pg	M.CH.C% * 103 μl	TL.C
Control	2.2 ± 0.23	8.4 ± 0.16	28.9 ±0.43	117.5 ± 11.8	40.1 ± 1.72	37.3 ±	31.2 ± 0.21
7 days	2.6* ± 0.20	8.7 ± 0.32	25.9 ±0.73	114 ± 6.2	35.4 ± 0.23	34.1 ± 0.16	24.2 ± 0.70
15 days	2.1 ± 0.84	7.60 ± 0.57*	21.8±0.11*	105.5 ± 4.13*	33.6 ± 0.25*	22.4 ± 0.26*	22.2 ± 0.23*
30 days	1.74 ± 0.62*	6.80 ± 0.70*	21.0±0.70*	100.0 ± 2.20*	21 ± 0.64*	20.4 ± 0.13**	20.2 ± 0.13**

Table 8.4: Changes of Liver Function Test and Cortisol Hormone in Baladi Chicken Infested with E coli 0157: H_7

Pavameter	A S T µ/d	A L T µ/d gm/dl	Total Protein gm/dl	Albumin	Cortisol µg/dl
Control	26.0 ± 0.12	15 ± 0.24	5.0 ± 0.12	2.50 ± 0.04	0.08 ± 0.11
Infected 7 days	27 ± 0.12	17 ± 0.17	4.8 ± 0.80	2.56 ± 0.19	0.11 ± 0.64
Infected 15 days	37 ± 0.12	20 ± 0.20	3.8 ± 0.56*	1.93 ± 0.13*	0.10 ± 0.65*
Infected 30 days	46 ± 0.27*	28.8 ± 0.66**	3.6 ± 0.70	1.00 ± 0.70	0.17 ± 0.90**

* P<0.05 ** p<0.01

Table 8.5: Renal Function in Chicken Infested with E coli 0157:H_7

Parameter	Urea mg/dl	Creatinine mg/dl	Calcium mg/dl	Phosphorous mg/dl	Sadium Meg/l	Potassium Meg/l
Control	3.17 ± 0.72	1.45 ± 0.76	9.00 ± 0.12	6.19 ± 0.23	155 ± 0.62	8.0 ± 0.13*
Infected 7 days	4.00 ± 0.12*	2.1 ± 0.10*	7.70 ± 1.00*	6.12 ± 0.248*	140 ± 0.7*	7.0 ± 0.2*
Infected 15 days	4.82 ± 0.21*	2.8 ± 0.30	7.14 ± 0.21*	7.00 ± 0.11	130 ± 0.20*	5.8 ± 0.9*
Infected 30 days	5.60 ± 0.72**	2.98 ± 0.90*	6.1 ± 0.12*	8.1 ± 0.80	122 ± 010*	5.00 ±

** P 0.01 * P< 0.05

DISCUSSION

Hemorrhagic colitis caused by E. coli 0157:- H7 is a clinical syndrome that consists of abdominal cramps; diarrhea that progresses to become bloody; radiologic or endoscopic evidence of clonic mucosal edema, erosion, or hemorrhage; and the absence of conventional enteric organisms in the stool.

The present study shows a significant decrease in RBcs count, Hb concentration and PCV in the affected birds indicate anemia of microcytic hypochromic as showed by the erythrocytic indices that were proportionally correlated with the severity of infection of *E. coli.* This result is in accordance with Jain, (1986).

The increase in serum AST levels in this work could be due to liver damage produces by the infected bacteria. Campell and Coles, (1986); mentioned that the increased of the activity of.AST has been associated with hepatocellular damage in birds.

Concerning ALT in chicken some studies reported elevation of ALT *it* birds infected with bacteria. (Bokori and karasi, 1969). Our result agrees with Omaima (1987), who observed a significant increase in (AST & ALT; in chicken infected with *E. coli.* The significant change in total protein anc albumin in the present work could be due to liver and kidney damage whicl could be associated with bacterial infection.

Similar findings were previously mentioned by Riley *et al.,* (1983) Pai, (1984); Campbell and Coles, (1986) and Ostroff *et al.,* (1989).

The increase in Urea and creatinine could be due to the effect of th+ micro-organisms and its Toxin on the kidneys. Our results is completely agree with Pai *et al.*, (1986); Tzipori *et al.*, (1987) and Obrig *et al.*, (1987) who reported increased creatinine, urea level in case of renal disease.

Hypocalcaemia, and. Hyperphosphatemia could be due to decreas calcium resorption by damaged renal tubules and associated wit: Hypoalbuminemia as reported by Campell and Coles, (1986); Beer *et al.* (1985) and Marks and Robert, (1993).

The decrease of potassium and sodium level in serum could be due t renal disease as reported by Campbell and Coles, (1986). Also th metabolism of Calcium and Phosphorus is closely linked in the body an hypocalcaemia always accompanied with hyperphosphatemia concernin serum cortisol level, the significant increase of serum cortisol level may t attributed to the activation of Hypothalamus piutitary axis due to stress. Oi result agree with Ghanem, (1986) and Campbell and Coles, (1986).

In conclusion infection of chicken with *E. coli* 0157: H7 injured live, and Kidneys. The change in liver and kidney function were more severe in days of infection.

REFERENCES

1. Bartel, H. (1971): Determination of Serum Creatinine. Clin. Chem. Acta 32:81.
2. Belongia, E.; MacDonald, K.; Partham, G.; White, K ; Korlath J. Locato M.; Strand, S.; Casale K. and Ostertholm M. (1991): An Outbreak of E. coli O157:H7 colitis Associated with Consumption of pre-cocced Meat. J. Infect. Dis.: 164: 338-343.
3. Beery, J.; Doyle, M. and Schoeni, J. (1985): Colonization of Chicken Cecae by Escherichia coli Associated with Hemorrhagic Colitis. Appl Environ Microbiol.11 :335-42.
4. Blake, P. and Cohen, M. (1983): Hemorthagic Colitis Associated with a rare E. coli Serotype. New Engl J Med 1983: 308: 681-685.
5. Bokori, J. and Karasi, F. (1969): Enzyme Diagnostic Studies of Blood from Geese and Ducks, Healthy and with Liver Dystrophy. Acta vet. Acad Scienc. Hung., 19: 269-279.
6. Campbell, T. and Coles, E. (1986): Avian Clinical Pathology,' in "Veterinary Clinical Pathology". 4th Ed., W.B Saunders Company. Philadelphia. London and Toronto.
7. Doumas, B. and Biggs H. (1972): Standard Methods of Clinical Chemistry, Vol. 7, Academic Press New York.
8. Ghanem, I.A. (1986): Epidemiological Studies on Pasteurellosis in Dukes: Duks. Ph.D. Thesis, Dept. of Poultry and Fish Diseases, Dept.of Poultry and Fish Diseases. Fac. of vet. Med. Zagazig Univ.
9. Goodwin, J.F. (1970): Determination of serum phosphorus. Clin. Chem.: 6 (9): 776-780.
10. Griffin, B. and Tauxe, R. (1992): The Epidemiology of Infections Caused by *Esherichia coli* 0157:H7, Other Enterohemorrhagic E. coli and the Associated Hemolytic Uremic Syndrome. Epidemiol rev; 13:60-98 Jain, O.W. (1986): «Schalm's Veterinary Haematology > th Ed., Lea and Febiger, Philadelphia, USA.

11. Karmali M.; Petric, M.; Lim, C.; Fleming, P.; Arbus, G. and Lior, H (1985): The Association Between Hemolytic Uremic Syndrome and Infection by Verotoxin-producing Escherichia coli. J infect Dis: 151: 775-782.
12. Levine, M.M. (1997): Escherichia coli that Cause Diarrhea: Enterotoxigenic, Enteropathogenic, Enteroinvasive, Enterohemorrhagic and Enteroadharent. J. Infect. Dis. 155: 337-89
13. Mark. S and Robert, T. (1993): E. coli O157:H7 Ranks as the Fourth most Costly Foodborne Disease. Food Review USDA/ERS: 16:51-59.
14. O'Brien, A.; Tesh,. V.; Donohue Rolfe, A.; Jackson, M.; Olsnes, S.; Sandvig, K.; Lindberg, A. and Keusch, G. (1992): Shiga Toxin: Biochemistry Genetics, Mode of Action, and Role in Pathogenesis. Curr Top Microbiol. Immunol. 1992: 180: 65-94.
15. Obrig, T.; Del Vecchio, P.; Karmali, M.; Petric, M; Moran, T. and Judge, T. (1987): Pathogenesis of Haemolytic Uraemic Syndrome (Letter). Lancet. Vol. 2, 687-689.
16. Omaima, A. R. (1987): Liver Function Tests in Relation to Some Bacterial and Viral Diseases in Chickens. MVSc, of Biochemistry- Faculty of Vet. Med. – Zagazig University (Benha branch).
17. Ostroff, S.; Kobayashi, J. and Lewis, J. (1989): Infections with Escherichia coli 0157:H7 an Emerging Gastrrointestinal Pathogen. Results of a One-year, Prospective, Population-based Study. JAMA. pp. 262: 355-359.
18. Pai C.; Gordon R.; Sims, H. and Bryan, L. (1984): Sporadic Cases of Heraorrhagic Colitis Associated with Escherichia coli 0157:H7. Clinical. Epidemioloic and Bacteriologic Features. Ann Intern Med. 101: 738-742.
19. Pai C.; Kelly J. and Meyers, G. (1986): Experimental Infection of Infantabbits with Verotoxin-producing Escherichia coli. Infect Immunol. 51:16-23.
20. Ratnam S. and March S. (1986): Sporadic Occurrence of Hemorrhagic Colitis Associated with Escherichia coli 0157:H7 in Newfoundland. Can Med. Assoc. J. 1986, 134:43-9.
21. Reitman, S. and Frankel, S. (1957): A Colorimetric Method for Determination of AST and ALT. Am. J. Clin. Path. 25:56.
22. Riley L.; Remis R.; Helgerson S.; McGee H.; Wells J. and Davis, B. et al. (1983).: Hemorrhagic Colitis Associated with a rare Escherichia Coli serotype. N. Engl.. J. Med. Vol. 2 pp. 132:135.
23. Sanders, G.T. (1980): Determination of Serum acid. Clin. Chem. Acta., 101: 299-303.
24. Sarkar, B. and Chanhan, U. (1967): Determination of Serum Calcium. Anal Biochem, 50:155.
25. Smith, H.; Rowe, B.; Gross, R.; Fry, N. and Scotland, S. (1987): Hemorrhagic Colitis and Vero-cytotoxin-producing Escherichia coli in England and Wales. Lancet. 1: 1062-1064.
26. Snedecor, G. and Cochran, W. (1967): Statistical Methods, 6th Ed., Iowa State Univ., Press. Ames. Icwa, U.S.A.
27. Tzipori, S.; Wachsmuth, I.; Chapman, C.; Birden, R.; Brittingham, J. and Jackson, C. (1987): The Pathogenesis of Hemorrhagic Colitis Caused by Escherichia coli 0157:H7 in Gnotobiotic piglets. J. Infect. Dis.154: 712-716.

9

Some Studies on Lead Toxicity in Marino Sheep

Mona S. Zaki*[1]; Susan Mostafa[2]; Isis Awad[2]

ABSTRACT

The problem of lead toxicity originated in a private farm in *El- Katta* "Giza governorate", due to ingestion of plant polluted with lead. About 8 out of 50 Marino sheep animals showed lead toxicity. The animal's age was 6 months. The animals suffered from depression, pressing head against objects, dilatation of eye pupils, total blindness (in 2 cases) with normal light reflex in both eyes, edema in briskets, enteritis with bloody diarrhea and pupil dilation. Also there were lacrimation, pale dirty mucous membrane and sunken eyes. Serum analysis from these animals revealed high lead concentration. In addition too, significant decrease in the levels of testosterone, LH, FSH. PCV, haemoglobin, R.B.C.s and total proteins were also decreased. Highly degeneration of kidney, and liver accompanied with elevation of AST, ALT, Urea, creatinine, cortisol, sodium, and potassium. Moreover, *S.epidermidis* and *S. Aeruginosa* were isolated. We conclude that the cause of animals morbidity and mortality

1. Dept. of Hydrobiology, National Research Center,Cairo, Egypt.
2. Dept. of Biochemistry, National Research Center, Cairo, Egypt.

in this farm was not due to bacterial infections but due to lead toxicity and we can say that polluted environment, especially with lead, can cause severe harm to animal health, in addition to serious danger on human health, by eating food polluted with lead.

Keywords: Lead toxicity in Marino sheep, environmental pollution, biochemical and microbial changes.

INTRODUCTION

Lead is a major environmental pollutant and its toxicity continues to be a major public health problems, and there is a growing consensus that lead cause toxic injury to human at a level of exposure that was considered to be safe only a decade ago. As the chronic exposure to lead, even at low levels, can result in slow progressive, in most of time, irreversible damage to haematopoeitic, nervous and renal systems [1]. Recent researches predicted that high levels of toxic metals in scalp hair, due to environmental pollution, in addition to deficiency in trace metals, play a role in the development of heart diseases [2].

In recent years, research efforts are directed towards quantification of the impact of lead exposure on human health, particularly from environment. The diagnosis based on blood lead levels doesn't always give an accurate estimate of total body burden of lead, so it's important to detect subcellular damage using reliable sensitive biomarkers [3]. Animals are very good indicator of the environmental pollution, as they inhabit the same space as humans and are exposed to the action of the same pollutants, for that reason, it's appropriate and advantageous to evaluate the negative impact of the polluted environment by heavy metals, and their influences load on human health by parallel evaluation of their load on animals [4, 5], so measuring of lead in blood animals [6], in cows and especially in lactating one, proved to be a good indicator of environmental contamination and also for food contamination from polluted animal [7].

MATERIAL AND METHODS

Animals

8 young Marino sheep of 6 months old were used in the present study. They were obtained from a private farm in *El-Katta* "Giza governorate". The animals suffered from depression, pressing head against objects, dilatation of eye pupils, total blindness (in 2 cases) with normal papillary light reflex in both eyes, edema in briskets, enteritis with bloody diarrhea and papillary dilation. Also there were lacrimation, pale dirty mucous membrane and sunken eyes.

Haematological Studies

Blood samples were collected from the jugular vein on EDTA as anticoagulant for determination of Hb, PVC, ESR, RBC's count, and WBC's count, according to [8].

Biochemical and Hormonal Studies

The activities of aspartic aminotransferase (AST) and alanine aminotransferase (ALT) as well as cholesterol, urea and creatinine levels were determined according to the method of Varley *et al.*,[9] by using commercial kits (Bio Merieus, France).

Total serum protein was estimated according to Drupt [10]. Serum cortisol was analyzed by a Gamma counter using 125 I cortisol radioimmunassay kit (Baxter Health Care Corporation USA) according to the method described by Pickering and Pottinger [11]. Potassium, Sodium and lead concentrations were determined by atomic absorption spectrophotometry.

Bacteriological Studies

Swabs from internal organs (liver, kidney, intestine and lungs) were collected under aseptic condition. The inoculated plates were incubated at 37°c for 24-48 h. The suspected colonies were picked and purified by further subculturing after which they were stained with Gram stain, for further biochemical identifications, the subjected isolates were classified according to Buchman et al., [12] and Wilson & Miles [13].

Soil Forage

The lead content of the soil and forage was measured by atomic absorption according to the method of Rodrigues and Castellon [14].

Statistical Analysis

The obtained data were subjected to the student t-test according to Gad and Well [15].

RESULTS

In the present study, haematological examination showed significant decrease in haemoglobin, PCV, and RBC's count and significant increase was found in ESR and W.B.C's count in all animals (Table 9.1).

Biochemical results detected significant increase in AST, ALT, urea, creatinine, cortisol, sodium, potassium and lead (Table 9.2). While, there was significant decrease in total protein level (Table 9.2). Serum LH, F.S.H, and testosterone hormones were significantly decreased (Table 9.3).

The lead content was found to be 293.72 p.p.m in the polluted soil and 164.3 p.p.m in forage (Table 9.4).

Bacteriological results revealed that the most predominant isolated micro-organisms was *S. epidermis and S. Aeuroginosa* (Table 9.5).

Table 9.1: Effect of Lead Toxicity on Some Hematological Parameters (Mean values ± SE) in Marino Sheep

Parameters	Control (8)	Marino Sheep (8)
P.C.V	32 ± 1.2	32 ± 1.4
E.S.R	2.1 ± 0.01	2.8 ± 1.3*
R.B.C's count 10^6/ml	7.33 ± 0.28	5.4 ± 1.24*
W.B.C's count 10^{3-}/ml	9.35 ± 0.23	10.03 ± 0.49*
HB g/dl	9.1 ± 0.01	8.13 ± 0.14*

*P <0.01

Table 9.2: Effect of Lead Toxicity on Some Biochemical Parameters (Mean values ± SE) in Marino Sheep

Parameters	Control (8)	Marino Sheep (8)
AST U/l	132 ± 1.23	173 ± 2.45*
ALT U/l	32 ± 1.46	63 ± 1.62*
Total Protein g/dl	11.4 ± 1.68	9 ± 0.27*
Urea mg/dl	2.80 ± 0.62	3.01 ± 0.82*
Creatinine mg/dl	0.97 ± 0.03	1.8 ± 0.02*
Cortisol ng/dl	0.8 ± 0.01	1.77 ± 0.23*
Na^+ M.E.Q	98 ± 2.2	124 ± 3.3*
K^+ M.E.Q	4.8 ± 1.3	6.3 ± 1.9*
Lead p.p.m	0.88 ± 0.12	1.78 ± 0.10*

*P <0.01

Table 9.3: Effect of Lead Toxicity on L.H, F.S.H, and Testosterone Hormones (Mean values ± SE)

Parameters	L.H (mu/ml)	F.S.H (mu/ml)	Testosterone (ug/dl)
Control	3.24 ± 0.32	5.5 ± 0.32	5.2 ± 0.042
Affected Animal	2.2 ± 0.14*	4.2 ± 0.42*	3.9 ± 0.23*

*P <0.01

Table 9.4: Mean Level of Lead in Soil and Vegetables in the Studied Area

Samples	Polluted Area Concentration of Lead in p.p.m	Control Area
Soil	294.72 ± 32.24*	75.23 ± 9.12
Forage	165.3 ± 6.32*	65.01 ± 6.23

*P <0.01

Table 9.5: Bacterial Determined in Internal Organs Liver and Kidney in Marino Sheep

Bacterial Isolated	Degree of Presence
Streptococcus sp.	30%
S. epidermidis	70%
S. aeurogenosa	25%

DISCUSSIONS

From our results, we noticed a decrease in the level of hemoglobin, PVC, and R.B.C's count, owing to the fact that lead intoxication causes a documented defect in haem synthesis. The results obtained agreed with several authors [16, 8] because lead pollution has an inhibitory effect on globin synthesis, inhibits iron to form haem and inhibits delta amino levulinic acid dehydratase in red cells.

Moreover, we can conclude that lead toxicity has dangerous effect on animals in the studied areas where the lead content of soil measured was about 293.73 p.p.m, and in contaminated pasture was 164.3 p.p.m, the lead poisoning in the studied Marino sheep may be due to grazing this contaminated pasture which may be due to their contamination by industrial wastes [17]. Hob & Kirn [18] reported that, lead concentration in plants was 80-160 p.p.m and in soil was 100-300 p.p.m which was considered as toxic level. Referring to the FAO-WHO[19] recommendations, the acceptable daily lead intake is 0.05 p.p.m. and our finding agreed with that of Bryant and Rosc [20]; Fayed and Abdallah [21]; Zaki et al., [22]

Bacterial microorganism e.g. Streptococcus Sp, S. Epidermis and were isolated from internal organs, similar finding were reported by Fingold & Martin [23] and Ducan & Prasse [24] who stated that bacterial microorganism are present in animals and birds suffering from high pollution with lead due to immunological suppression.

Both clinical signs and ocular changes, which were observed in the present work, might be attributed to the toxic effect of lead on the C.N.S as mentioned by Krameller-Froetcher, [25] and Schlerka [26], this toxic effect was characterized by severe cerebral disturbances leading to blindness in some cases which may be due to cerebrocoritcal oedema, or may be also due to associated optic neuritis and optic atrophy. We can concluded, that all the clinical symptoms reported in the studied Marino sheep might be due to acute lead intoxication, as mentioned by Ozmen and Mor [27].

The biochemical results detected in Table 9.2, showed significant increase in AST, ALT, while there was significant decrease in total protein level (Table 9.2). These findings agreed with those found by Swarap et, al [28], as the as the elevation in transaminases activities and the decrease in total protein level may be attributed to the liver injury, so the exposure to lead in polluted environments alters serum biochemical parameters indicative of liver functions. The biochemical results, detected in table 9.2, showed significant increase in urea and creatinine, which are indicative of abnormal kidney functions, agreed with those of Goswami and Gachhui [29]. The disturbed liver and kidney functions have been seen on the last stage of lead toxicity, this agred with Zaki et al., [22]. The hormonal results, detected in Table 3, showed significant decrease in L.H., F.S.H. and testosterone, which are affected in the early stages of lead poisoning [30 and 31].

In conclusion lead toxicity cause atrophy of liver, kidney, gonads blindness, in addition to the locomotor disturbances. And the cause of animal morbidity and mortality in this farm was not due to bacterial infections but due to lead toxicity. We can also say that polluted environment, especially with lead, can cause severe harm to animal health, in addition to serious danger on human health, by eating food polluted with lead.

This work supported from internal project belonging to N.R.C 10/8/5 (P.I Dr. Mona S. Zaki).

REFERENCES

1. Silbergeld E.K. 1997: Preventing Lead Poisoinning in Children, Ann Rev. Public Health; 18: 801-810.
2. Afridi H.I., T.G. Kazi, G.H. Kazi, M.K Jamali., G.O. Shar, (2006): Essential Trace & Toxic Element Distribution in the Scalp Hair of Pakistani Myocardial Infarction Patients, Biol.Trace elem. Res. 113(1): 11-34.
3. Endo G., S. Honiglechi, I. Kiyota, (1990): Urinary NaG in Lead Exposed Workers, J Appl. Toxicol, 10: 235-38.
4. Korak M., E. Kralova, P. Sviatko, J. Bilek, A. Bugarsky, (2002): Study of the Content of Heavy Metals Related to Environmental Load in Urban Areas in Slovakia. Bratsil Lek. Listy; 103 (7-8): 231-7.
5. Rashed M.N. and M.E. Soltan, (2005): Animal Hair as Indicator for Heavy Metal Pollution in Urban & Rural Areas, Env. Monit Assess; 110 (1-3): 41-53.
6. Zadnik T., 2004: Lead in Top Soil, Hay, Silage & Blood of Cows from Farm Near a Former Lead Mine & Current Smelting Plant Before and After Installation of Filters. Vet. Hum. Toxicol.; 46(5): 287-90.
7. Swarp D., R.C. Patral, R. Naresh, P. Kumar, P. Shekhar, (2005): Blood Lead Levels in Lactating Cows Reared Around Polluted Localities; Transfer of Lead into Milk. Sci Total Environ.; 347 (1-3): 106-110.
8. Jain S.D. (1986): Evaluation of Haemogram in Healthy and Diseased Sheep. Res. Vet. Sci. 33, 21.
9. Varley H., A.H. Gwenbek and M. Bell, (1980): Practical Clinical Chemistry Vol. I Genera] I top-'scomnoner test 5s1 ed. London, William Medical Books Ltd.
10. Drupt, F., (1974): Estimation of Total Protein, Pharm Biol, 9, 77.
11. Pickering, A.D. and J. Pottinger, (1983): Analysis of Hormone, Gen Comp Ender. 49, 232.

12. Buchman R.E, W.E Gibbuns and R.Y Stajner (1975): Bergeyes Manual of Determinative Bacteriology, Ed. Millions and Wilkins co Baltimore.
13. Wilson G.S. and A.A. Miles, (1975): Topley and Wilsonies Principles of Bacteriology and Immunity 6th Ed, Edwards and Annald, publishers LTD, London.
14. Rodrigues MF and Castellon (1982): Lead and Cadmium Levels in Soil and Plants Near Highways and Their Correlation with Traffic Density. Environ. Pollute. (B) 4: 281-290.
15. Gad W. and G. Well (1976): Statistical Methods 6th Ed the lowa State Univ, Press Iowa U.S.A.
16. Soliman, M.N. (1983): Toxicity Resulting from Lead Compounds in Veterinary Practice. Ph.D. Thesis, Cairo University Egypt.
17. Lemos R.A., D. Driemeier, E.B. Guimacaes, I.S. Dutra, A.E. Mori and C.S. Barros, (2004): Lead Poisoning in Cattle Grazing Pasture Contaminated by Industrial Waste, Vet Hum Toxicol, 46 (6) 326-8.
18. Hob and Kirn (1988): Elevated Levels of a Lead and Other Metals in Roadside Soil and Grass and Their Use to Monitor Heavy Metal Depositions in Hong Kong. Environ. Pollut.,49: 34-51.
19. FAO/WHO 1983: 6th Joint Expert Committee on Food Additives, Evaluation of Mercury, Lead, Cadmium and the Food Additives Diethyl Pyrocarbonate and Acetyl Gallate, WHO Food Additivitie Ser. No. 4.
20. Bryant SL and RW Rose, (1985): Effect of Cadmium on the Reproductive Organs of the Male Ram "Australian Journal of Biological-sciences, 28(3); 305-311-15.
21. Fayed A.H and E.B. Abdallah, (1997): "Technique for Studying the Morphology of Mammalian Spermatozoa which are Eosinophilic in a Different Live/Dead Stain. J. Report. Fertile; 29; 443.
22. Zaki M.S., A.M Haman and F.S Bayaumi and M.N Shalaby, (2001): Some Clinicopathological and Microbial Studies in Lead Toxicity on Cows, Egypt Comp Path & Clinic Pathology Vol, 14 29-35.
23. Fingold S.M. 1982: Diagnostic Microbiology, 6th ed., Mosby co. st. Lowis, Toronto, London.
24. Ducan J. and K.W. Prasse (1986): Vet Laboratory Medicine-clinical Pathology, 2nd ed. Iowastate Univ., Press. Ames; Iowa U.S.A.
25. Krametter-Frooestscher R., F. Tataruch, S. Hauser, M. Leschnick, A. Url and W. Baumgartner, (2007): Toxic Effects in Herd of Beef Cattle, Following Exposure to Ash Residue Contaminated by Lead and Mercury. Vet. J.174 (1): 99-105.
26. Scherleka G., F. Tataruch, R. Krametter-Frooestscher, A. Url, D. Kossler, S. Hogler and P. Schmidt, (2004): Acute Lead Poisoning in Cows due to Feeding of Lead Contaminated Ash Residue, Berl Mumch Tierarztl Wochenschr, 117 (1-2): 52-6.
27. Ozmen O. and F. Mor (2004): Acute Lead Intoxication in an Old Battery Factory, Vet Hum.Toxicol. 46 (5): 255-6.
28. Swarp D., R. Naresh, V.P. Varshney, M. Balgangatharathilagar, P. Kumar, D. Nandi and R.C. Patral, (2007): Changes in Plasma Hormone Profile and Liver Functions in Cows Naturally Exposed to Lead and Cadmium Around Diffirent Industrial Areas, Res. Vet. Sci. 82 (1): 16-21.
29. Goswami K., R. Gachhui and A. Bandopadhyay, (2005): Hepatorenal Dysfunction in Lead Pollution. J. Environ. Sci. Eng.: 47 (1)75-80.

30. Gorbel F., M. Boujelbene, F. Makni Ayadi, F. Gucimazi, F. Croute J.P Soleilhcvoup and A.l. El-Feki, (2002): Cytotoxic Effects of Lead on the Endocrine & Exocrine Sexual Function of Pubescent Male & Female Rats. Demonstration of Apoptotic Activity, C.R Biol; 325 (9): 927-40.
31. Srivastava V., R.K. Dearth, K.J. Hiney, L.M. Ramisez, G. Bratton and W.L. Dees, (2004): The Effects of Low Level Pb. on Steroidogenic Acute Regulatory Protein in the Pubertal Ratovary, Toxicol Sci 77(1): 35-40.

10

Some Biochemical Studies on Friesian Suffering from Subclinical Mastitis

Mona S. Zaki*[1]; Nabila El-Battrawy[2]
Susan, O. Mostafa[3]; Olfat M. Fawzi[3]; Iziz Awad[3]

ABSTRACT

The present study was conducted to investigate the effect of subclinical mastitis on clinicopathological changes in Mastitic friesian. A total of 400 individual milk samples from clinically normal udder quarters of 100 diary friesians were examined microbiologically as well as by using California mastitis test (C.M.T.) for detection of subclinical mastitis and designing rapid diagnostic tests for other infection. Blood samples were analysed for hemogram, cortisol, alanine aminotransferase, asparate aminotransferase, total protein, inorganic phosphorous and calcium. Also L.DH in milk was detected. The results indicated that there is a significant elevation of cortisol, Sgot, p.cv, L.DH activity in milk while a notable decrease in total protein, serum calcium and Hemogram. was observed. However; Serum phosphorous level did not exhibit obvious changes.

Key words: Microbiology of mastitis, Pathology of mastitis, Enzymes in mastitis, changes in blood

1. Department of Hydrobiology - National Research Center, Cairo, Egypt.
2. Department of Hydrobiology - animal Institute of Reproduction, El-Haram, Cairo, Egypt.
3 Department of Biochemistry National Research Center, Cairo, Egypt.

INTRODUCTION

Mastitis is the most frequent, disease responsible for early culling of milking animals, this culling sometimes takes place before the animal reaches the age of maximum production. The colonization of mamary gland by pathogenic microorganisms results in series events which lead to major alteration in the composition of milk, and on the disease set in inflamatory reactions takes place for several days (Elsagheer *et al*, 1992). Preacute coliform mastitis is of great economic importance in the dairy industry since the infection with coliform organisms and the following production of endotoxin leads to high mortality. Akira (1989) reported that when diagnosis of preacute coliform mastitis is given by clinical signs and hematological hematobiochemical findings only misdiagnosis on the prognosis is common. Thus the presence of endotoxin in blood plasma should be checked for the precise diagnosis of bovine preacute coliform mastitis.

This is characterized by severe quarter Inflammation (Schalm *et al*, 2006). Stress in the form of muscular exertion causes alterations in the different blood constituents (Agarwal *et al*, 1984; Bhasrekar *et al*, 1984 and Cabona *et al*, 1990). This work was intitiated so as to investigate clinopathological changes among infected friesian. The aim of the present work was also to study the bacteriological incidence of subclinical mastitis among friesian and to find the relationship between clinicopathological changes and mastitis in subclinical mastitic friesian.

MATERIAL AND METHODS

For conducting this work 400 milk samples were aseptically collected for clinically normal quarters of friesian selected from Mounofia governorate. Samples were examined using the following tests:

(a) California mastitis test C.M.T. according to the procedure described by American Public Health.

(b) Microbiological examinations which include cultivation of milk sediment. The milk sediment obtained by centrifugation of 10 ml of the samples for 20m at 3000 rpm was seeded on a plates of nutrient agar, blood agars, Edward medium, Mackonkey's agar and subarouds dextrose agar.

Examination of Incubated Milk

Loopfuls from the incubated samples over night at 37° were streaked on the same forementioned media and inoculated plates were incubated at 37° for 48hr except sabarouds agar plates which were incubated at 25° and checked daily for the growth of fungi for 3 weeks. Suspected colonies appearing on different media were examined microscopically and ^identification was carried out according to Ajello *et al.* (1966) and El-Sagheer *et al.* (1992).

Blood samples from friesian were collected by jugular venepuncture in test tubes with or without EDTA.

Serum was harvested by centrifugation at 3000 rpm. Calcium, Inorganic phosphorous, total protein Sgot, Sgpt were determined in serum using kits from Diamond Diagnostica company, Egypt and measured by spectrophotometer in the UV range (240 nm). Cortisol was assayed by R.I assay technique using kits from Diagnostic Products Coporation, Los Angles USA, according to method of Kowalaski (1976). A complete blood picture was manually performed as outlined by Jain (1986).

LDH Assay

L.D.H in milk was measured by specials kits according to methods of Kachmar and Moss (1976).

The samples were processed by centrifugation to remove fat and pellet and intermediate layers obtained were further centrifuged at 30,000 Xg for min essentially according to the method of Bagin *et al.* (1977). The supernatent obtained was filtered through filter paper and used as the enzyme source.

LD.H activity was assayed spectrophotometrically at 340nm by special kits according to Kachmar and Moss (1976).

RESULT

The results obtained from Table 1 revealed that out of 100 lactating friesian 14% were infected with *E.coli* 6% infected with S.*agalactia* 3.5% S. *aureus &* 1.5% *Pseudomonas aeruginosa.*

From the Table 10.1 it was obvious that C.M.T. reaction is positive for friesian with preacute coliform mastitis. Further prognostic diagnosis have commonly been done based on clinical symptoms and hematological & biochemical examinations.

Table 10.1: Bacteriological Examination of Infected Friesian

100 lactating friesian	14% infected with E. coli	6% S. Agalactia	3.5% Pseudomonas Aeruginosa	1.5% S. Aureus

The Hemogram showed a significant decrease in R.B.Cs, P.C.V. and hemoglobin while there was a significant increase in E-SR & W.B.C.S ($p<0.01$) (Table 10.2).

Cortisol Levels

The present investigation (Table 10.3) indicated that mastitic cows had significant elevation of serum Cortisol levels as compared with non mastitic cows ($p<0.01$).

Liver Junctions

Enzymatic Activity

Sgot values were significantly ($p < 0.01$) higher in mastitic cows while Sgpt values revealed no obvious changes as compared with control group.

Table 10.2: Effect of Mastitis on Hemogram of Infected Cows

E. coli	Hemoglobin g/dl	P.C.V%	R.B.C.S 10^6/wd	W.B.C.D 10^3/wd	E.SR mrn/2hrs
Control	9.10 ± 0.23	31 ± 0.32	8.10 ± 0.18	10.35 ± 0.64	1.03 ± 0.092
Infected	8.60 ± 1.94*	27.5 ± 0.62	6.33 ± 0.90	12.27 ± 0.053*	1.83 ± 0.045**
Streptococcous agalactiae					
Control	9.9 ± 0.20	32 ± 0.67	9.3 ± 0.74	10.00 ± 0.26	1.00 ± 0.35
Infected	7.80 ± 0.58**	31 ± 0.070*	8.8 ± 0.80*	13.00 ± 0.63*	1.72 ± 0.072**
S. oureus					
Control	9.45 ± 0.05	34 ± 0.69	9.00 ± 0.07	10.57 ± 0.71	1.23 ± 0.021
Infected	7.94 ± 0.08**	28.00 ± 0.23**	8.40.09*	14.00 ± 0.53**	2.2 ± 0.052**
Pseudomonas Aeruginosa					
Control	9.3 ± 0.13	32 ± 0.72	9.00 ± 0.74	10.00 ± 1.83	1.00 ± 0.64
Infected	7.00 ± 0.69	30 ± 0.93*	8.03 ± 0.33*	12.00 ± 0.77*	2.0 ± 0.0.82**

** $p < 0.01$ * $p < 0.05$

Calcuim and Inorganic Phosphorous

Slight non significant decrease were recorded in calcium level while inorganic phosphorous revealed no obvious changes.

Total Protein

T.P. values were significantly lower in mastitic cows ($p < 0.01$). *L.DH in milk*

L. DH level in milk were significantly higher in mastitic cows ($p < 0.01$).

DISCUSSION

Subclinical mastitis is of great economic importance *ixy* the dairy industry since the infection with coliform organism leads to high mortality. When diagnosis is given by clinical signs only Ederhart (2007) suggested further investigations including hematological and biochemical investigations for confirmation. It is clear that incidence of subclinical mastitis among examined dairy cows is relatively high with reduction in milk yield which causes a heavy economic losses. The colonization of mamary glands by pathogenic microorganisms results in a series of events which lead to major alterations of milk compositions secreted from cells. Therefore C.M.T is a suitable measure for use on large scales monitoring programmes. Elsagheer *et al.* (1992) suggest that application of C.M.T. leads to early detection of subclinical infected quarters and aids in the selection of dairy animals for either segregation or therapy for less than costs of the disease including the large losses in milk production for cows with preacute coliform mastitis. The level of LDH seems to increase in mastitic milk, (Kerumori *et al*, 1989).

Table 10.3: Effects of Subclinical Mastitis on Biochemical Changes and Cortisol Hormone Level of Infected Cows

E. coli	Total Protein	L.DH Activity U/ml	Cortisol mg/dl	Sgot U/L	Sgpt U/L	Calcium mg/dl	Phosphorous mg/dl
Control	7.95 ± 0.73	57.3 ± 2.23	0.93 ± 0.32	75.3 ± 0.64	13.23 ± 0.37	8.93 ± 0.74	6.94 ± 0.78
Infected	6.33 ± 0.27	10.14 ± 0.62**	l.34 ± 0.23	16.3 ± 68**	L5.00 ± 0.26*	7.10 ± 1.09*	6.74 ± 0.53
Streptococous agalactia							
Control	7.84 ± 0.14	67.00 ± 0.40	0.70 ± 0.13	80 ± 0.62	12.00 ± 0.074	8.00 ± 0.52	7.00 ± 0.35
Infected	6.10 ± 0.37*	127 ± 17**	1.83 ± 0.29**	1.94 ± 54**	14.00 ± 0.19**	7.33 ± 0.34**	6.89 ± 0.92
S. aureus							
Control	7.90 ± 1.23	50 ± 0.27	0.90 ± 0.54	94 ± 0.40	13.00 ± 1.23	8.73 ± 0.51	7.5 ± 0.68
Infected	6.59 ± 0.22*	134 ± 16**	1.91 ± 0.82**	158 ± l3**	14.3 ± 1.73*	7.10 ± 0.14**	6.8 ± 0.88
Pseudomonas aeruginosa							
Control	7.97 ± 0.62	73 ± 0.48	0.83 ± 0.34	0.94 ± 1.20	14.00 ± 0.73	8.51 ± 0.27	7.00 ± 0.23
Infected	6.83 ± 0.33	178 ± 50**	1.93 ± 0.33**	139 ± 1.00*	1.48 ± 1.70*	7.85 ± 0.34*	7.79 ± 0.40

** $p < 0.01$ * $p < 0.05$

Prognostic diagnosis have commonly been done on clinical symptoms and the hemotological and biochemical examinations blood. Biochemical analysis of mastitic animals may help in diagnosis of subchemical abnormalities and become a helpful means for practice under field conditions (Rose, 1987). The present results in mastitic cows fell in the range given by Jain (1986) and Koneko (1989).

As shown in Table 10.1 the significant changes in hemogram and other biochemical values are due to infection with mastitis. The highly significant increases detected in Sgot values & Cortisol are in line with the results of Sloss & Dufty (1980), Symons *et al.* (1974). Agarowal *et al.* (1984) however attributed these changes to stressful conditions. In the present study we have shown that L.D.H activities were enhanced in mastitic milk. The enhancement can be at least partly explained by the participation of leucocytes which have L. DH activity at the 1,000 U/mg protien level in mastitic milk (Kasumori *et al.*, 1989). Protien concentration as well as somatic cell count and L. DH is increased when compared to normal milk.

In the present investigation we have also measured L. D.H of 4 species of bacteria which were isolated from the mastitic milks used in the present study and the activity was detected in the extracts of *E. coli, S. aureus, S. agolacaltiae & Pseudomonas aeroginosa.* The enzyme activities were much higher in case of the infected udders as compared to the control.

We could not determine the pattern of mastitic udders because the udders contained large number of leucocytes by washing small pieces of udder tissue with mechanical shaking.

Conclusively in mastitic animals the application of C.M.T. leads to early detection of subclinically infected quarters and aids in the selection of dairy animals for either segregation or therapy. Also we conclude that mastitis causes anemia in cows detected by dercrease of hemoglobin, R.B.C.S, and P.C.V. L.D.H activity in milk increases, as well as Cortisol, Sgot and calcium in serum.

REFERENCES

1. Agarwal, S.P., Agarwal, V.K., and Dwaraknoth, P.K. (1984) Effect of Graded Work Load on Circulating Levels of Cortisol and Thyroid Hormones Incros Bred Bullocks. Nat. Anim. phsiol. Research work conf. Thiland A.P. 4.
2. Akira, A. (1989) Detection Endotoxin in Affected Milk from Cows with Coliform Mastitis, Japanese J. Vet Science 41 (4) 845.
3. Ajella, L., George, L.K., Kaplow and Houfman (1966) Laboratory Manual for Medical Mycology, M.S. Dept of Health Education and Walfor Georgia.
4. American Public Health Association APH (1978) "Standard Methods for Examination of Dairy Products" 14th ed., Amer public health Ass. Washington.
5. Bagin, E., Zin Advidor, J., Rivetz, B., Gordin, S. and Saran (1977) Distribution of lactate dehydrogenase isoenzymes in Normal and Inflammed Udders and Milk, Res. Vet Sci. 22, 198.

6. Bhasrekar, M.R., Parage, M.S., Jashi, B.M., and Mangurkar, B.R. (1984) Draftability of Crossbed Bullocks in Comparison to Local Bullock, Nat Animal Physiology Research Work Conf. Thialand A.P. 8.
7. Cabona, E.M., Adriano, E.A. and Encarnacion, R.O. (1990) Hematologic Observations on Swamp Buffallow Harvested to Increased on Pulling, Lods Buffallow Bull. 9, 27.
8. Ederhart, R.J. (2007). Am. Vet. Med. Assoc. 206, 1973.
9. Elsagheer, M.A., Ahmed, Liala Ali and Hegazi, A.G. (1992) Proc. Inter. Meet work Animal, 134.
10. Join, W.C.(1986) "Schalm's Vet Hematology" 4th ed lee and Febiger Philedelphia U.S.A.
11. Kerumori, K., Kanae, M. and Mario, K. (1989) Contribution of leucocytes to the Origin of lactate dehydrogenase by isoenzymes in Milk of Bovine, Mastitis Japanese Journal of Vet. Science, 530.
12. Koneka, J.J. (1989) Clinical Biochemistry of Domestic Animals 4th ed Academic Press in New York U.S.A.
13. Kowalaski, A. and Paul, W. (1976) Determination of Serum Cortisol, Clin Chemistry (5) 1152 p.
14. Rose, R.J. (1987) Poor Performance Syndrome Investigation and Diagnostic Technologies in Current Therapy in Equine Medicine, (Ed) W.E Robinoson, Philadelphia W.B. Saunders.
15. Schalam, O.W., Caroll, E.J. and Jain, W.C. (2006) Bovine Mastitis Febriger philadephia.
16. Sloss, V., and Dufty, J.H. (1980) Hand Book of Bovine Obstetrics. Williams and Wilkins Blathimore, London.
17. Sndecor, C.W., and Cochran, W.B. (1976) "Statistical Methods". 6th ed Iowa State University Press Iowa U.S.A.
18. Symons, D.A. and Wright, L.J. (1974) Changes in Bovine Mamary Gland Permeability After Intramamary Exotoxin Infusion, J. Comp. Pathology, 84, 9.
19. Verma, R. (1988) Studies on Clinical and Subclinical Bovine Mastitis, Indian Journal of Comparative Microbiology Immology and Infectious Disease. 9 (1) 28.

11

Diminution of Aflatoxicosis in Tilipia Zilli Fish by Dietary Supplementation with Fix in Toxin and Nigella Sativa Oil

Mona S. Zaki*[1]; Olfat M. Fawzi[2]; Suzan Omar[2]
Medhat Khafagy[3]; Mostafa Fawzy[1]; Isis M. Awad[2]

ABSTRACT

Mycotoxins are toxic metabolites of fungal origin, they are produced by certain strains of the fungi *Aspergillus flavus* and *Aspergillus parasiticus*. Under favorable conditions of temperature and humidity, these fungi grow on certain foods and feeds, resulting in the production of aflatoxins, which can enter into the human food chain directly through foods of plant origin (cereal grains), indirectly through foods of animal origin (kidney, liver, milk, eggs); however their continuous intake even in microdoses can result in their accumulation. Aflatoxins are hepatotoxic, hepatocarcinogenic and immunotoxic and cause growth retardation in animals and exposed human populations.Fix in Toxin is a kind of pentonite (clay) consists of (sodium calcium aluminosilicate), a non toxic agent and absorbent for a wide variety of toxic agents. It acts as an enterosorbant that rapidly binds aflatoxins in the gastrointestinal tract resulting in

1. Department of Aquaculture, Vet. Division National Research Centre, Giza, Egypt.
2. Department of Biochemistry, National Research Centre, Giza, Egypt.
3. National Cancer Institute, Cairo University, Egypt.

decreased aflatoxin uptake and bioavailability. *Nigella sativa* is a spicy potent belonging to ranunculacea seeds oil showed antibacterial, fungicidal effects.This study was conducted to evaluate the ability of Fix in Toxin 0.2% and *Nigella sativa* oil 1% to diminish the clinical signs of aflatoxicosis in *Tilapia Zilli* fish, and based on this evidence, it's hypothesized that clay based entersorption of Aflatoxin may be a useful strategy for prevention of Aflatoxicosis in human population.60 *Tilapia Zilli* fish were divided into three groups, 20 fish for each group: Group 1 served as control and will be fed on commercial fish diet. Group 2 were be supplied by Aflatoxin contaminated ration with corn 80 ug toxin/kg ration. Group 3 were be supplied by aflatoxin contaminated ration with corn 80 ug toxin/kg ration and treated with 0.2% Fix in Toxin and 1% Nigella sativa oil injected daily I/P. Analysis of hematological parameters, clinical chemistry revealed significant differences between the control groups and the aflatoxicotic groups. administration of Fix in Toxin 0.2% and *Nigella sativa oil* injection 1% of body weight reduced the aflatoxicosis in liver and kidney by improving all liver and kidney enzymes.The dietary HSCAS clay remedy is novel, inexpensive and easily disseminated and proves its efficacy in diminishing the clinical signs of aflatoxicosis in fish, where it acts as an alfatoxin enterosorbant that tightly and selectively binds the poison in the gastrointestinal tract of the fish, decreasing their bioavailability and associated toxicities. In addition the *Nigella sativa oil* has a synergistic effect with Fix in Toxin in diminishing aflatoxicosis in fish. These findings support their use for dietary intervention studies in human populations at high risks for aflatoxicosis, specially in Egypt, where studies have shown that concurrent infection with the hepatitis B virus (HBV) during aflatoxin exposure increases the risk of hepatocellular carcinoma (HCC).

Key words: Aflatoxicosis, *Tilapia Zilli* fish, Fix in Toxin effect, *Nigella sativa oil* effect, Hematological parameters, Clinical chemistry dynamic simulation; model; composting; domestic solid waste.

INTRODUCTION

When certain types of fungus grow on food, they produce minute amounts of toxins called *mycotoxins*. Most fungi-produced mycotoxins are harmless, and even helpful. For example, the antibiotic penicillin came from a fungus, and it is a mycotoxin [Magan N 2005] [1].

The aflatoxins are a group of structurally related toxic compounds produced by certain strains of the fungi *Aspergillus flavus* and *Aspergillus parasiticus*. Under favorable conditions of temperature and humidity, these fungi grow on certain foods and feeds, resulting in the production resulting in the production of aflatoxins, which can enter into the human food chain directly through foods of plant origin (cereal grains), indirectly through foods of animal origin (kidney, liver, milk, eggs) Rojas-Duran T 2006 [2].

The most pronounced contamination has been encountered in tree nuts, peanuts, and other oilseeds, including corn and cottonseed. The major aflatoxins of concern are designated B1, B2, G1, and G2. These toxins are usually found together in various foods and feeds in various proportions [Takatori K 2006] [3]; however, aflatoxin B1 is usually predominant and is the most toxic. Aflatoxin M a major metabolic product of aflatoxin B1 in animals and is usually excreted in the milk and urine of dairy cattle and other mammalian species that have consumed aflatoxin-contaminated food [Martins HM 2007] [4]. These poisons are completely heat stable, so neither cooking nor freezing destroys the toxin. They remain on the food indefinitely. Aflatoxins grow on grains and legumes mostly during storage, so the grains and legumes must be stored correctly to limit this problem [Kabak S 2006] [5]. Aflatoxins produce acute necrosis, cirrhosis, and carcinoma of the liver in a number of animal species; no animal species is resistant to the acute toxic effects of aflatoxins; hence it is logical to assume that humans may be similarly affected. Aflatoxin B1 is a very potent carcinogen in many species, including nonhuman primates, birds, fish, and rodents. In each species, the liver is the primary target organ of acute injury [Gong Y 2004], [Egal S 2005], [Wagacha JM 2008] [6], [7] and [8]. *Nigella sativa* is a spicy potent belonging to ranunculacea seeds oil showed antibacterial fungicidal effects (Akguil, 1989) [9]. Nigella sativa inhibited chemical carcinogenesis, some investigators reported that its antioxidants effect inhibited chemical carcinogenesis. Ascorbic acid and Nigella sativa could reduce aflatoxin induced liver cancer (Newperne *et al.*1999) [10].Fix in toxin is a kind of pentonite (clay) consists of (sodium calcium aluminosilicate) a non toxic agent and absorbent for a wide variety of toxic agents (El-Bouhy *et al.*, 1993) [11]. It acts as an enterosorbant that rapidly and preferentially binds aflatoxins in the gastrointestinal tract resulting in decreased aflatoxin uptake and bioavailability [Phillips TD 2002] [12].

AIM OF THE PRESENT WORK

This study was conducted to evaluate the ability of Fix in toxin 0.2% and Nigella sativa oil 1% to diminish the clinical signs of Aflatoxicosis in *Tilapia Zilli*, and based on this evidence, it's hypothesized that clay based entersorption of Aflatoxin may be a useful strategy for prevention of Aflatoxicosis in human population.

MATERIAL AND METHODS

Experimental Design

60 *Tilapia Zilli* fish (50-100g each) were obtained from Abbassa and were acclimatized to laboratory conditions. They were kept in glass aquaria supplied with dechlorinated tap water at a rate of one liter for each cm of fish body.

The 60 *Tilapia Zilli* fish were divided into three groups, 20 fish for each group:

- Group 1 served as control and will be fed on commercial fish diet.
- Group 2 were supplied by Aflatoxin contaminated ration with corn 80 ug toxin /kg ration.
- Group 3 were supplied by Aflatoxin contaminated ration with corn 80 ug toxin/kg ration and treated with 0.2% Fix in Toxin and 1% Nigella sativa oil injected daily I/P.

The fish were fed by hand twice daily and feed consumption in all groups was recorded daily, also mortality and body weight due to Aflatoxin were recorded.

Samples Analysis

Serum was collected 3 times at 3 months interval and sera were frozen at -20ºC.

Biochemical and Hormonal Studies

The activities of aspartic aminotransferase (AST) and alanine aminotransferase (ALT) as well as cholesterol, urea and creatinine levels were determined according to the method of Varley *et al.*, () [13] by using commercial kits (Bio Merieus, France), total lipids were estimated according to the method of Siesta (1981) [14]. Total serum protein was estimated according to Drupt () [15].

Haematological Studies

Blood hemoglobin was assessed and hematocrit value was carried out by using microhematocrit capillary tubes centrifuged at 2000 P.M. for 5 min according to the method of Drabkin (1964) [16].

Statistical Analysis

Data are collected, summarized then tabulated for st Statistical analysis according to the method of Gad and Weil (1986) [17].

RESULTS

Table 11.1 showed that Aflatoxicosis produce a significant decrease in body weight if compared with the control group.

Tables 11.2, 11.3, 11.4 showed that there is a significant decrease in PCV and Hemoglobin (P <0.01). There is a significant decrease in mean of total protein and a significant increase in AST, ALT. There is a significant increase in urea, creatinine, total lipid, cholesterol and alkaline phosphatase (P <0.01).

Post treatment with Fix in Toxin 0.2% and Nigella sativa oil injection 1% for 3 months. All this parameters return to normal level gradually as shown in Tables 11.1, 11.2, 11.3 and 11.4 if compared with control group.

Table 11.1: Effect of Aflatoxin on Body Weight of Fish during the Course of the Experiment

Groups	1 month	2 months	3 months
Group 1	57 ± 0.21p	68 ± 0.16*	101 ± 0.72*
Group 2	51 ± 0.10	61 ± 0.2*	74 ± 0.13*
Group 3	54.5 ± 0.06	64 ± 0.73*	84 ± 0.64*

* P <0.01

Table 11.2: Effect of Aflatoxin After One Month on Biochemical and Hematological Parameters in Fish and After treatment with Fix in Toxin 0.2% + *Nigella sativa* 1%

Parameters	Group 1 Control N =20	Group 2 Aflatoxin N = 20	Group 3 Aflatoxin + Fix in Toxin 0.2 % *Nigella sativa* 1% N=20
Total protein mg/L	5.5 ± 0.18	3.13 ± 0.73**	4.4 ± 0.71
AST U/L	81 ± 0.24	112 ± 0.05**	103 ± 0.04
ALTU/L	17 ± 0.68	27 ± 0.73**	24 ± 0.75
Urea mg/dl	2.88 ± 0.28	4.4 ± 0.63**	5.2 ± 0.28*
Creatinine mg/dl	0.72 ± 5.5	0.98 ± 0.63**	0.88 ± 0.35
Total lipids cholesterol mg/dl	98 ± 0.98	143 ± 0.24**	104 ± 0.28*
Cholesterol mg/l	188 ± 0.78	210 ± 2.3**	198 ± 0.34*
Alkaline phosphatase mg/dl	18.9 ± 0.38	28.7 ± 0.34**	22 ± 0.14
Hemoglobin mg/dl	8.3 ± 0.24	5.4 ± 0.75**	7.1 ± 1.61
P.C.V%	39.1 ± 64	34.1 ± 0.04*	34.1 ± 0.08

** p < 0.01

Table 11.3: Effect of Aflatoxin After Two Months on Biochemical and Hematological Parameters in Fish and after Treatment with Fix in Toxin 0.2% + Nigella sativa 1%

Parameters	Group 1 Control N =20	Group 2 Aflatoxin N = 20	Group 3 Aflatoxin + Fix in Toxin 0.2 % *Nigella sativa* 1% N = 20
1	2	3	4
AST U/L	84 ± 1.27	121 ± 2.3**	94.6 ± 0.09
ALT U/L	18 ± 0.72	31 ± 0.89**	19 ± 0.16
Urea mg/dl	2.8 ± 0.74	5.1 ± 913**	3.1 ± 0.21

(Contd...)

1	2	3	4
Creatinine mg/dl	0.83 ± 0.26	1.3 ± 0.51**	0.83 ± 0.27
Total protein mg/l	5.7 ± 0.22	3.1 ± 0.14**	4.7 ± 0.27
Total lipids mg/dl	98 ± 0.14	184 ± 13**	99 ± 0.77
Cholesterol mg/dl	186 ± 0.64	239 ± 3.6**	189 ± 2.3
Alkaline phosphates U/L	18.8 ± 0.18	33.9 ± 0.28**	201 ± 0.13
Hemoglobin%	8.6 ± 0.29	4.8 ± 0.73**	7.1 ± 114
P.C.V%	42 ± 0.71	28 ± 0.03**	37 ± 0.28

** P <0.01

Table 11.4: Effect of Aflatoxin After Three Months on Biochemical and Hematological Parameters in Fish and After Treatment with Fix in Toxin 0. 2% + Nigella sativa 1%

Parameters	Group 1 Control N = 20	Group 2 Aflatoxin N = 20	Group 3 Aflatoxin + Fix in Toxin 0.2% *Nigella sativa* 1% N=20
Total protein mg/l	5.7 ± 0.23	3.1 ± 0.44**	5.5 ± 0.76
AST U/L	81 ± 0.18	133 ± 6.3**	82 ± 0.28
ALT U/L	19.1 ± 0.23	25 ± 0.38**	19.3 ± 0.08
Urea mg/dl	2.77 ± 0.23	5.1 ± 0.19**	2.78 ± 0.36
Creatinine mg/dl	0.79 ± 0.47	1.5 ± 0.53**	0.82 ± 0.33
Total lipids mg/dl	96 ± 0.74	189 ± 1.4**	95 ± 0.83
Cholesterol mg/dl	184 ± 0.95	254 ± 2.4**	183 ± 0.74
Alkaline phosphatase U/L	18.6 ± 0.28	35.2 ± 0.92**	18.3 ± 0.33
Hemoglobin%	8.5 ± 0.43	4.7 ± 0.72**	8.6 ± 0.38
P.C.V%	38 ± 0.22	26 ± 0.16**	39 ± 034

** P <0.01

DISCUSSION

Aflatoxicosis is poisoning that results from ingestion of aflatoxins in contaminated food, so humans are exposed to aflatoxins by consuming foods contaminated with products of fungal growth. Such exposure is difficult to avoid because fungal growth in foods is not easy to prevent [Bennett JE 2005] [18]. Aflatoxins produce acute necrosis, cirrhosis, and carcinoma of the liver and also impair immunity which ultimately led to increased susceptibility to disease in a number of animal species; no animal species is resistant to the acute toxic effects of aflatoxins [Pier AC 1987, Pier AC 1999, Wildi Dis J 2004] [19, 20, 21]; hence it is logical to assume that humans may be similarly affected.

Evidence of acute aflatoxicosis in humans has been reported from many parts of the world [Williams JH 2004, Kovacs M 2004, Gong Y 2004, Wagacha JM 2008] [22, 23,6, 8] and there is a positive association between dietary aflatoxins and hepatocellular carcinoma (HCC), especially aflatoxin B1, is potent carcinogens in some animals, In 1988, the IARC placed aflatoxin B1 on the list of human carcinogens.

Studies have shown that concurrent infection with the Hepatitis B virus (HBV) during aflatoxin exposure increases the risk of hepatocellular carcinoma (HCC). As HBV interferes with the ability of hepatocytes to metabolize aflatoxins, This effect is synergistic with the resulting damage far greater than just the sum of aflatoxin or HBV individually (Williams, 2004) [22].

The biochemical results detected in Tables 11.2, 11.3, 11.4, showed significant increase in AST, ALT, while there was significant decrease in total protein level in group 2. These findings agreed with those found by by Jassar and Balwant (1993), Rasmassen *et al.* (1986), Sisk *et al.* (1988), due to liver injury induced by Aflatoxicosis [24, 25, 26]. The elevation of ALP activity comes in consisitence with that mentioned by Jassar and Balwant (1993), Svobodava *et al.* (1999) in chicken due to degenerative changes in the liver causing leakage of enzymes into serum and cause the highest concentration of alkaline phosphatase [24, 27].

The biochemical results, detected in tables 11.2, 11.3, 11.4 showed significant increase in urea and creatinine, which are indicative of abnormal kidney functions group 2, Similar finding were reported by Newperne (1999) [12]. These changes due to necrosis of kidneys reported by Jindal and Mahipal (1994) Mansfeld (1989), Pier (1987) [28, 29, 19]. The lipid metabolism was altered during Aflatoxicosis as judged by increase of total lipid content. In the present experiment, there is a highly elevation of total lipid and cholesterol in serum which agree with Sippel, *et al.* (1983), Sisk *et al.* (1988) [30, 31].

It is obvious that administration of Fix in Toxin 0.2% and Nigella sativa oil injection 1% of body weight reduced the Aflatoxicosis in liver and kidney, group 3. These findings agreed with those found by Harvey RB 1991, Phillips TD 1999, 2002, 2008, Wang JS 2005, Afriyie Gyawu E 2005, 2008 in relation to the dieatry HSCAS clay [32, 33, 12, 34, 35, 36, 37]. In addition the *Nigella sativa oil* has a synergistic effect with Fix in Toxin in diminishing aflatoxicosis in fish due to its antibacterial fungicidal antioxidants effects [El-Bouhy *et al.* (1993)] [11].

The present study showed a significant decrease in PCV, HB concentration in the affected fish that was proportionally correlated with the severity of aflatoxicosis. This result is in accordance with Robert (1989), El-Bouhy *et al.* (1993) [38,11]. They found similar results in broilers chinckens common carp. Fish and this indicates that the toxin causes a deleterious effect on the hemopoeitic system.

In conclusion, based on the present research, the dietary HSCAS clay remedy is novel, inexpensive and easily disseminated and proves its efficacy in diminishing the clinical signs of aflatoxicosis in fish, where it acts as an alfatoxin enterosorbant that tightly and selectively binds the poison in the gastrointestinal tract of the fish, decreasing their bioavailability and associated toxicities. In addition that, *Nigella sativa oil* has a synergistic effect with Fix in Toxin in diminishing this aflatoxicosis in fish These findings support their use for dietary intervention studies in human populations at high risks for aflatoxicosis, specially in Egypt, where studies have shown that concurrent infection with the hepatitis B virus (HBV) during aflatoxin exposure increases the risk of hepatocellular carcinoma (HCC).

REFERENCES

1. N Magen, Aldred D (2005). Conditions of Formation of Occhratoxin Ain Drying Transport and in Different Commodities. Food Addit. Contam, 22 suppl 1:10-6.
2. T Rojas-Duran, Sanchez_Barragan I, Costa-Fernandez IM, Sanz-Medel A (2006). Solid-Supported Room Temperature Phosphorescene from Aflatoxins for Analytical Detection of Aspergillus. Analyst, 131(7); 785-7.
3. K Takatori, Aihara M, Sugita-Knishi Y(2006).Hazardous Food-borne Fungi and Present and Future Approache to the Mycotoxin Regulations in Japan. Kokuritsu Iyakuhin Shokuhin Eisei Kenkyusho Hakoku; 124: 21-9.
4. HM Martins, Mendes Guerra MM, d'Almeida Bernardo FM (2007). Occurrence of Aflatoxins B1 in Dairy Cow Feed Over 10 Years in Portugal (1995-2004). Rev Iberoam Mical.; 24(1): 69-71.
5. B Kabak, Dobson AD, Var I, (2006). Strategies to Prevent Mycotoxin Contamination of Food and Animal Feed Review. Crit Rev Food Sci Nutr. 46 (8): 593-619.
6. Y Gong, Hounsa A, Egal S, Turner PC, Sutcliffe AE, Hall AJ, Cardwell K, Wild CP. (2004). Postweaning Exposure to Aflatoxin Results in Impaired Child Growth: A Longitudinal Study in Benin, West Africa. Environ Health Perspect.; 112 (13): 1334-8.
7. S Egal, Hounsa A, Gong YY, Turner PC, Wild CP, Hall AJ, Hell K, Cardwell KF. (2005). Dietary Exposure to Aflatoxin from Maize and Groundnut in Young Children from Benin and Togo, West Africa. Int J Food Microbiol.; 104 (2): 215-24.
8. JM Wagasha, Muthomi JW.(2008). Mycotoxin Problem in Africa: Current Status Implications to Food Safety and Health and Possible Management Strategies. Int J Food Microbiol. [Epub a head of print].
9. Akguil, (1989) Antimicrobial Activity of Balck Seed (Nigella sativa of Aflatoxin) Essential Oil. *Casi Univ. Eczacilik Fax. Derg.*, 6, 63.
10. PM Newperne (1999) Chronic Aflatoxicosis in Animals and Poultry. *J. Am. Vet.* Med. Assoc., 263, 1269.
11. ZM El-Bouhy, Ali A.A. and Helmy M.S. (1993) Preliminary Studies on Aflatoxicosis in Nile Cat Fish and Trials for Detoxification of Contaminated Food. Zagazig Vet. J. 21. (4), 607.
12. TD Phllips, Lemke SL, Grant PG (2002). Characterization of Clay-based Enterosorbents for the Prevention of Alfatoxicosis. Adv. Exp. Med Biol; 504: 157-71.
13. H Varley, AH Gwenbek and M Bell, (1980): Practical Clinical Chemistry Vol. I Genera] I top-scomnoner Test 5th ed. London, William Medical Books Ltd.

14. D Siesta (1981) *Am. Clin. Biochem.*, 6, 24.
15. F Drupt, (1974): *Estimation of Total Protein, Pharm Biol, 9, 77.*
16. DJ Drabkin, (1946) *Clinc. Chem.* 164, 703.
17. SC Gad, and Weil, C.S. (1986) Statistics for Toxicologists, In Hayes, A.W. (2nd ed). *Principles and Methods of Toxiology*: Raven Press, New York, pp. 273-320.
18. JE Benett (2005). Introduction to Mycosis in Man. Dell Benett, and Dolineds Principle and Practice of Infectious Diseases. 6th ed Philadelphia Churchill Living Stone.
19. AC Pier (1987). Aflatoxicosis and Immuno Suppression in Mammalian Animals. In M.S. Zuber, GB. Lillehoj and B.L. Rsnfor (Ed). Aflatoxin in Maize. pp. 65. Cimmyt, Mexico.
20. AC Pier (1999). Major Biological Consequences of Aflatoxicosis in Animal Production. *J. Anim. Sci*, 70, 3964.
21. SE Henke (2004). Survey of Aflatoxin Concentrations in Wild Bird Seed Purchasedin Texas. J Wildi Dis; 4 D (4): 823.
22. JH Williams, Phillips TD, Jolly PE, Stiles JK, Jolly CM, Aggarwal D. (2004). Human Aflatoxicosis *in* Developing Countries*:* A Review of Toxicology, Exposure, Potential Health Consequences, and Interventions. Am J Clin Nutr; 80: 1106-22.
23. M Kovacs (2004): Nutritional Health Aspects of Mycotoxins. Orv Hetil; 145(34); 1739-46.
24. BS Jassar, and Balwant S (1993). Biochemical Changes in Experimental Aflatoxicosis in Broiler Chicken. *Indian J. Animal Sciene* 63 (8), 784.
25. BH Rasmassen, Larsen K, Hald B, Maller OB and Elling F (1986). Outbreak of Liver Cell Carcinoma Among Salt Water Reared Rainbow Trout Salmo Gairdneri in Denmark. Diseases of Aquatic Organisms 1, 191.
26. DB Sisk, Carlton VU and Curtin TM (1988) Experimental Aflatoxicosis in Young Swine. Am J. Vet. Res., 39, 1591.
27. Z Svobodava, Piskac, A., Havlikova, J. And Groch L (1999). The Influence of Feed with Different Contents of Aflatoxin- B_1 on the Carp Health Condition, Zivocisna Vyroba 27, (11), 811.
28. IV Jindal and Mahipal SK (1994). Toxicity of Aflatoxin B_1 in Broiler Chicks and its Reduction by Activated Charcoal. Research in Vet. Science 56. 37.
29. R E Manseld Grunert, and Kautna, J (1989) Mycotoxicosis-a problem of Dairy Cowherds. Monatsheft fur Veterinary Medizin 44 (12), 409.
30. WI Sippel, Burnside, JC and Atwood MB (1983) A Disease of Swine and Cattle Caused by Eating Mouldy Corn. Proc. 6th Ann. Meet. Am. Vet Med. Assoc. pp. 174-181.
31. Sniezko S (1974): The Effect of Environmental Stress on Outbreaks of Infectious Diseases in Fish. Journal of Fish Biol., 6, 197-208.
32. RB Harvey, Kubena LE, Phillips TD, Corrier DE, Elissaide MA, Huff WE (1991) Diminution of Aflatoxin Toxicity to Growing Lambs by Dieatary Supplementation with Hydrated Sodium Calcium Aluminosilicate. Am J Vet Res. 52(1): 152-6.
33. TD Phillips (1999) Dietary Clay in the Chemoprevention of Aflatoxin Induced Disease. Toxicol Sci. 52 (2 suppl): 118-26.
34. TD Phillips, Afriyie Gyawu E, Williams J, Huebner H, Ankrah NA, Ofori-Adjel D, Jolley P, Johnson N, Taylor J, Marroquin Cardona A, Xu L, Tang L, Wangs JS (2008). Reducing Human Exposure to Aflatxin Through the Use of Clay; A Review. Food addit Contam; 25(2) 134-45.

35. JS Wang, Luo H, Billam M, Wang Z, Guan M, Tang L, Goldstone T, Afriyie Gyawu E, Lovett C, Griswold J, Brattin B, Taylor RG, Huebner HJ, Phillips TD (2005). Short Term Safety Evaluation of Processed Calcium Clay (Novacil) in Humans. Food addit Contam; 22(3) 270 -9.
36. E Afriyie Gyawu, Mackie J, Dash B, Willis M, Taylor RG, Huebner HJ, Tang L, Guan M, Wang JS, Phillips TD (2005). Chronic Toxicological Evaluation of Dieatary Novacil Clay in Sprague – Dawley Rats. Food Addit Contam; 22(3) 259-69.
37. E Afriyie Gyawu, Ankrah NA, Huebner HJ, Ofosuhene M, Kumi J, Johnson NM, Tang L, Xu L, Jolley P, Ellis WO, Ofori-Adjel D, Williams J, Wang JS, Phillips TD (2005). Novasil Clay Intervention in Ghanaians at High Risk for Aflatoxicosis 1. Study Design and Clinical Outcome. Food addit Contam; 25(1) 76-87.
38. RA Robert (1989) Fish Pathology. Second Edition, Ballier Tindall, London. Philadelphia., Sydney, Tokyo, Toronto.

Natural Cases of Rickets in Baraki Goat Kids

Mona. S. Zaki*[1]; Awadalla. I.M[2]; Mohamed. M.I[2]
Iman. M. Zytaun[3]; Sami Shalaby[4]; Nagwa Atta[5]; Suzan.O. Mostafa[6]

ABSTRACT

Rickets was evaluated in 6 kids out 100 from different farms in Monofia Governorate of both sex, under 8 months of age. Clinical signs included anorexia stunded growth arched back, joint enlargement and abnormal, curvature of fore limb bones of the kids. Fed consisted of yellow corn 60% and dried trifolium Alexandrun 22% they housed in door, the main biochemical serum analysis recorded were hyperphosphatemia hypocalcemia and decrease the activities of Alkaline phosphatase significant increase of cortisol hormone. Urea, creatinine, glucose. P.C.V, and hem-oglobin in blood. The results indicated that rations containing high level of com caused decreased digestion coefficient of all nutrients for both growing goat kids (healthy and Rickets). Also Rickets disease

1. Hydrobiology of Department, National Research Center, Egypt.
2. Animal Nutrition Department. National Research Center, Egypt.
3. Department of Microbiology and Internal medicine. Central lab Zagazig University, Egypt.
4. Department of Reproduction, National Research Center, Egypt.
5. Department of Microbiology and Immunology, National Research Center, Egypt.
6. Department of Biochemistry, National Research Center, Egypt.

decreased digestibility, and nitrogen balance for kids fed two experimental rations. This study recommended that using balanced diets affect decreased significantly in digestion coefficient, feed intake and nitrogen balance.

Keyword: Natural Cases, Rickets, Baraki, Goat Kids.

INTRODUCTION

Rickets is among the most devastating vrippling disease that affect lambs & kids young animal fed diet def-icient in Vit.D and rich in phosphorous and haused in doors without exposure to ultraviolet irradiation develop Rickets, calcium defficiency, also will result in Rickets because of the failure to maintain an adeqate ion product of serum calcuim and phosphorous at (he zone of mineralization is bones enlarged of joints in a typical signs of rickets it involves lung bones and is usually accompanied by lateral or medical deviation. Julb et al (1993) Eruption of teeth is delayed and irregular severe deformity of chest h-one - and chronic ruminal tympany R-adostits et al (2000).

The most consistent clinicopatho-logical finding in Rickets is change in serum sodium serum calcium phosp-horous with hematological alteration hyperphosphatemia and drop of se-rum Alkaline phosphatase (Elsayed & Siam 1992).

* Aim of the present work: this work was conducted to study some Nutritional & clinicopathological findings in naturally affected kids in monofia governorate. to avoid the occuirence of this disease and correction of diet offered to kids.

MATERIAL AND METHODS

Out of 100 kids under 8 M. age were included in this work, 6 kids showing clinical signs of Rickets, this study was conducted in Manrofia governorate. and 6 apperentely healty control kids of same age.

All animals were examined clinically and blood samples were collected from jugular vein with & without EOT A. Blood samples were collected for determination of Hemoglobin, P.C.V volume were made, according to Hunger "ford (1989) serum total protein, sodium, potassium, chloride, Urea. Creatinine, glucose, the activities of alkaline phosphatase and lactate dehydrogenase. L.D.H, calcium, phosphorous were measured colorimetrically by using commerical available test kits supplied by Bio Merieux lab. Reagent and inistruments France. Coitisol hormone was measured according to Kuehen and Burvenich (1986). Statistical analysis: statistical analysis of the obtained data were statistically analysed by T. test according to Petrie & Waston (1999).

Twelve growing goat kids (6 normal and 6 Rickets Kids), 8-9 months old with an average bodv weight of 18.23 1.87 kg were randomely assigned to examine the effect of Rickets and high level of corn in the experimental rations on digestion coefficint. and Nitrogen utilization by normal and Rickets Kids. Animals of each (normal and Rickets disease kids) were divided. Randomly into two equal groups. Animals of the first group were fed complete feed mixt-ure ration (R_1, control), the second group was fed in a complete feed mixture containing high level yellow corn (R_2) Tables (12.1) and (12.2) showed "Ihe composition of experimental ra-tions and its chemical composition. The animals are belonging to farm in monofia governorate to the sheep and goats research unit. El- Bostan -Nubaria, Animal Production. Dep. National" Rsearch Center. Cairo, Egypt. Animals were individually placed into 12 metabolic cages and adapted for 21 days as a preliminary, period followed by 7 days as a collection period. Faeces and urine were collected and sampled properly. Rations and water were available ad libitum. Samples from the residuals, faeces and urine were analysed for proximate analysis by A.O.A.C (1980).

Table 12.1: Ingredients of Experimental Ratios Used

Item	Exp. Complete Feed Mixtures	
	R_1 (Control)	R_2
Yellow corn	22	60
Wheat bran	25	5
Undecorticoated colton seed cake	20	10
Barssem hay	30	22
Lime stone	1.9	1.9
Common salt	1.0	1.0
Minerals mixtures	0.1	0.1
Vit & minerals mixtures	498	600
Total	100	100
Price of 1 ton. L.E	584	670

Product of RoviGypt Contain: 70g manganese, 20g copper, 50g zinc. 0.25 selenium, 4.0g iodine, 1.0g cobalt, I2x 10^6 IU vit. A, 2 x 10^6IU vit D3 . l5xl0 1U vit E in 3.0 kg calcim earbonate.

Table 12.2: Chemical Composition of Experimental Ration Used

Item	DM	% as DM Basis					
		OM	CP	CF	EE	NFE	ASH
R_1 (Control)	93.6	92.77	13.63	15.61	2.90	60.63	7.23
R_2	92.8	94.03	12.25	1 1.22	2.27	68.29	5.97

The data of nutritional parameters were analysed according to SAS (1993) procedures. The significancy among means was tested by pie rang test (1959).

RESULTS AND DISCUSSION

There was a significant decrease in total protein and alkaline phosphatase. in groups (2) sodium, potassium, chlorine, and calcium and significient increase in serum Urea, creatinine, glucose, phosphorous and cortisol level. In diseased animal th-ere was also significant increase in P.C.V & Hemoglobin as show in Table (12.3). A common cause of rickets is grain over lood in support of this carbohydrate over lood has been a reliable way to reproduce Rickets and housing indoors. In this study several reports of naturally occuring rickets Crowely (1961), Elsayed and Siam (1992) in this work clinical Rickets was evidenced by anorexia, arched backs, stiffness in gait joint enlargement, similar signs were rec-orded by Charyrabarti (2000) Radostities et al (2000) Smeth (1996) and Sonnenrirth & Jaratte (1580) enlarge of joints are the most charachterisitic features in our diseased kids.

Table 12.3: Some Biochemical & Hematological Parameters in Diseased and Control Kids Animal Groups

Parameters	Control Kids	Diseased Kids
Alkaline phosphatase U/L. 216.2 10.24	216.210.24	189.2 9.47*
Total protein g/dl.	8.23 0.14	6.14 0.17*
Urea mg / dl	7.79 0.84	8.94 0.14*
C reatinine mg/dl	0.83 0.03	1.2 0.17*
Glucose mg/dl	6.70 1.79	7.84 0.80*
Sodium m. Eq/L	157.08 0.89	138 0.98*
Potassium m. Eq/L	2.70 0.54	1.98 0.64*
Chloride mmol/1	76 0.78	60 0.13*
Cortisol Hormone ug/dl	0.98 0.03	1.94 0.45*
p.c.v.%	32.9 0.78	40.2 1.70*
Hemoglobin g/dl	10.23 0.33	13.27 0.84*
L.D.H u/l	228.5 63.4	398 48.33*
Calcium ma / dl	1 1.33 9.78	9.24 0.54*
Phosphours. mg/dl.	8.94 0.27	12.42 0.13*

* $P< 0.01$

Sonnenrirth & Jaratte (1980) reported that phosphorous deficiency has commonly been in animal as major factor in the cause of Rickets sometimes alone or in association with Vit D deficiency our study disagree with this opinion. In this investigation there was no evidence of Hypophosphatemia, serum Kypocalcemia. and decrease in serum Alkaline phosphatase. This opinion agrees with. Agag et al (2002) in serum phosphate & serum calcium but disagree in serum alkaline phosphatase. The most prodominents Biochemical finding in this study. The significant hyperphosphatemia was the results of elevated dieatry phosphorous this observation was previously recorded by Mahin in et al (1984) and Haward (1982) in lambs fed diets rich in cereal, and wheat bran respectively. Hurgerfood (1989) and Agag et al (2002) they described that concentrate which are particulary rich in posphorous and poor in calcium will cause bone abnormality and joint tranlules. The observed hypoprotemenia in our work, could be attributed to prolonged anorexia, our study agree with Agag et al (2002), this indicated by increase P.C.V & Hemoglobin coneentration this finding attributed to loss of plasma water through large intestine of kids because of anorexia and adipsia. (Beech 1994). Hyperglycemia in diseased kids was probably due to hydrocortisone which has been indentified as the major free plasma keneta (1989). Field et al (1975) glucocorticoid Rickets mentionened that increased hydrocortisone was probably responsible to some degree of leukocyte changes and the hyperglycemia Somth (1996) Nislet et al (1966).

The elevated value of serum urea, creatmine and change in soduim and potassium value in disease kids may attribute to dehydration, glumerulo-nephrities, and medullary mecrosis Mahim et al (1984) Koneka (1989). L.D.H, the significant increase in L.DH value may be due to hepatocellular changes from endot-oxin delivered in portal circulation of secondry bacterial invasion due to immunolgical suppression this result confirmed the result of jull (1993) who mentioned that there were muscular and hepatic disorders associated with inmmunological suppression in animals suffered from Rickets. Concerning electrolyte changes were similar, to those reported by Agag (2002) A marked hypochloremia was recorded in diseased animal the obta-ined results may attributed to severe dehydration caused by excessive loss of fluid electrolytes this observation supported the results that, recorded by. Oviisten (1964) Koneko (1989). We can concluded from this study that Rickets in kids is a complex disorder and despite our best effect to prevent treatment of diseased kids by offered a.balanced ration rich in mineral and put them in sun shine for at least 5-6 H every day it is often featal to kids and treatment should be given as soon as possible after clinical sign develop or preferably before, the best policy is to use high quality of raughge and to supplement with minimum grain.

Apparent Digestibility and Nutritive Values

Results in Table (12.4) indicated that rations containing high level of corn with normal kids did not affect the apparent nutrients digestibilites. While the apparent digestibility (%) of DM. OM, CP, CF and NFE of experimental rations fed to the Rickets Kids were significantly (P<0.05) decreased for both rations and increasing level of corn (R_2) decreased the apporent digestibility than Rickets kids fed (R_1, control) however, either extract digestibility was not significantly affected nither by Richets disease or by high level of corn in the experminetal rations. The si-gnificant reduction of nutrient digestibilites (DM, OM, CP, CF and NFE) as a result of high level of corn and Rickets disease by (CFin Rl = 15.61) and (CF in R2 = 11.22) was related to the increasing percentage of CF content of R_1 (Blaxter, 1967). Contrariwise, the DCP% increased (P<0.01) for experimental ration (R_1, control) con-taining high level of CP perentage (13.63% US 12.25%).

Table 12.4: Apparent Nutrients Digestibility and Nutritive Value of the Experimental Ration Fed to Growing Goat Kids

Item	R_1		R_2		Significance
	Normal Kids	Rickets Kids	Normal Kids	Rickets Kids	
DM	"7-2.27 2.31a	68.33 1.23	70.26 1.22	66.82 1 .42	*
OM	71 .90 1.76	66.17 2.14	71.22 2.36	63.19 1.97	*
CP	70.81 1.11	67.12 1.26	70.96 1.86	64.89 1 .62	*
CF	71.66 1.92	66.71 1.55	71.12 1.01	62,37 2.67	*
EE	72.18 2.27	70.12 2.18	70.86 2.36	68.12 1 .06	NS'
NFE	70.73 1.27	65.56 0.99	71.36 1.26	61. 16 1.49	*
TON	'-'68.44 1.41	63.89 1.17	68.93 1.27	60.19 0.09	**
DCP	9.66 0.56	9.15 0.27	8.69 0.15	7.95 0.17	**

A.b.c values in the same row with different superscripts are significantly different
*(P<0.05) **P<0.01
1. Apparent digestibility, %
2. Nutritive values. %

Highest nutritive value as TDN was observed for the control ration with normal kids followed by ration 2 with normal kids also. The results revealed also that TDN more affec-ted by kids health, the lowest TDN was recorded by Richets kids with RI followed by Rickets kids with R2. These results proued that Rickets disease of kids was reduced the total digestible nutrients intakes which consequen-tly causing a reduction in TDN values recorded by Rickets kids. The due to the lower feed intake by Rickets kids and lower CP and CF content in R2 than in Rl.

Nitrogen Utilization

Results in Table (12.5) indicated that ni-trogen intake expressed as (g/h/d) were significantly (P<0.05) affected among rations. Wherease, high level of corn in R_2 decrease significantly (P<0.01) the nitrogen intake from control ration (R1). This difference could mainly due to the high level of corn and its lower contents of CP (El- Shaer and Kandil, 1990). For the above reason nitrogen losses in both faeces and urine were followed the same trend of nitrogen intake. Rickets kids fed experimental rations. Showed significant (P<0.01) differences in nitrogen retention compa-red to the healthy kids fed the same rations. Nitrogen balance as percent of nitrogen intake (NB/NI) value for healthy kids fed control ration (R_1) was significantly (P<0.01) higher than the other goat kids groups fed the control ration (Rickets kids) or highly corn in the other ration (R_2). (Normal and Rickets Kids) due to the rickets disease and the higher nitrogen intakes from rations.

Table 12.5: Nitrogen Utilization (g/h/d) of Growing Goat Kids Fed Experimental Rations

Item	R_1		R_2		Significance
	Normal Kids	Rickets Kids	Normal Kids	Rickets Kids	
BW, Kg	17.9 1.26	18.0 1.47	18.6 1.13	18.4 0.97	*
DMI, g	530 0.13	480 0.37	505 0.80	440 0.43	*
DMI/BW, %	3 0.86	2.7 0.74	2.7 1.10	2.4 0.85	*
Faecal, N.	3.36 0.11	3.44 0.26	2.87 0.46	3.03 0.47	*
Urinary, N	4.67 0.66	517 1.16	4.81 0.70	4.13 1.11	NS'
N-balance	3.52 0.23	1.86 0.30	2.22 0.66	1.46 0.14	*
NB of NI, %	30.48 1.26	17.77 1.23	22.42 1.11	16.94 0.80	**
Nitrogn I, g	11.55 0.17	10.47 0.37	9.90 0.44	8.62 0.31	*

A, b, c values in the same row with different superscript, are significantly different (p<0.05).
* p<0.05 ** p<0.01 NS = non = significant

In conclusion, under conditions of this study, data indicated that ration containing normal level of corn and balanced diet was the best ration for healthy kids to obtain satisfy digesion coefficient and nitrogen balance and reduced feeding cost. Rickets disease decreased digesion coefficient for all nutrients and nitrogen balance. In the two experimental rations.

REFERENCES

1. A.O.A.C. (1980). Association of Official Agriculture Chemists. Official Methods of Analysis". 13th ed, Washington , DC.', U.S.A.
2. Agag B.I, Naima A Afify and El Seidy I.A. (2002) Egypt Comp. Clinical Pathology Vol 15 No. 141-148.
3. Blaxter, K.L. (1967). The Energy Metabolism of Ruminants. 2nd Ed. Hutchinson and Co. Ltd. London.
4. Charkrabarti A (2000): Text Book of Clinical Veterinary Medicine "Deprint of the 2nd Ed. pp. 392-393 Taj "Press A - 3514 Maja Puri, Phase-1 New Delhi.
5. Crowly J.P (1961) Veterinary Record 73; 295 by Bannivell et al (1988).
6. Duncan, D.B (1955). Multiple Range and Multiple F-test. Biometrics, 11.1.
7. El-Sayd R.F and Siam A.A (1992) Clinical and Biochemical Aspects Assoicated with Rickets in Young Goats. Assuit vet. Med J 27 (54): 162-167.

8. El-Shaer, H.M and Kandil H.M. (1990). Compartive Study on the Nutritional Value of Wild and Cultivated Atriplex Halimus by Sheep and Goat in Sinai: Com. Sei. And Dev. Res., 29 81.
9. Field A.C., Suttle N.F and Nibest D.J (1975) Effects of Diets Law in Calcium and Phosphorous on the Development. of Growing Lamb J dge 85: 435.
10. Howard J. LC (1982) the South-western Veterinarian 34: 88 Cited by Hahin et al (1984).
11. Hungerford T.G (1989) Diseases of Livestak. 8lh Ed pp. 1045-1046 Me grow Hill Book Company Sydney.
12. Juble, K.V, Kennedy P.C, and Pulmer N. (1993): Pathology of Domestic Animals 4th ed. Vol. 1 pp. 67-77 Academic Press. Inc U.S.A.
13. Kaneko J. (1989) Clinical Biochemistry of Domestic Animals 4lh ed, pp. 699-730 Academic Press In. San Diega.
14. Kuehm and Burvenichic (1986) Cortisol and Thyroid Hormones After Endotoxin Administration in Lactading Goals Arch Int. Physiol. Biocher 94, 37, 386.
15. Mahind. L.ghaldi M. and Marrou A (1984) Osteody Strophying Growing lambs Feat a Diet Rich in Wheat Bran vet Rec. 115: 355-357.
16. Nisbet D. Buttler E.J and Robertson J.M (1966). Osteodystraphic Diseases of Sheep, Osteomolacia and Asteprasis in Lactating Ewes in West Scotland Hill Farms. J. Comp. Path 80: 535-542.
17. Petrie A. and Waston P. (1999) Statistics for Veterinary and Animals Science T Ed pp. 90 99 the Black well Science. Td united Kingdom.
18. Radostits O.M, Blood D.C, and Goy C.C (2000) Vet. Mediune 8th ed, pp. 1435-1438 Bailliere Traindall, London.
19. SAS (1993). SAS User's Guide: Statistics, SAS Inst. Inc. Gary. NC. Rel. Eigh.
20. Smith B.D (1996): Darge Animal Internal Medicine 2nd Ed P 1263-1264 Masly Yeurbook In New York, U.S.A.
21. Smith. M.C and Sherman D.M (1994) Goot Medicine pp. 99-100 leu and Feliger Philadelphia.
22. Somenwith A.C and Jarette L. (1980): Gradwal's Clinical Laboratory Methods. and Diagnosis Vol 1, 8lh Ed. pp. 258-259. The C.V Moshy Cost louis Toronta. London.

13

Effect of Mercuric Oxide Toxicity on Some Biochemical Parameters on African Cat Fish *Clarias gariepinus* Present in the River Nile

Mona, S. Zaki*[1]; Nabila, Elbattrawy[2]
Olfat M. Fawzi[3]; Isis Awad[3]; Nagwa, S. Atta[4]

ABSTRACT

The effect of dietary carbohydrates and mercuric oxide on haematalogical profile, blood chemistry and hormonal level was studied in African cat fish (*Clarias gariepinus)*. Fish were divided into 3 groups (n = 10), exposed to different doses of mercuric oxide and carbohydrate. Group (1) was served as control. Group (2) was fed with carbohydrate and mercuric oxide (10 mg Kg^{-1} diet ration). Group (3) was fed with carbohydrate and mercuric oxide (1 5 rng Kg^{-1} diet ration). There is a significant decrease in hemoglobin and P.C.V in group (3). There is a significant increase in serum corlisol, cholesterol, AST, ALT, urea, creatinine and alkaline phosphorous in group (3). Also there is a significant decrease in serum phosphorous, sodium and potassium in treated fish. There is a significant high level of mercuric content in kidney muscles, heart and spleen in

1. Department of Hydrobiology, National Research Centre, Cairo, Egypt.
2. Department of Microbiology, Reproductive institute, Cairo, Egypt.
3. Department of Biochemistry, National Research Centre, Cairo, Egypt.
4. Department of Microbiology, National Research Centre, Cairo, Egypt.

group (3) suggesting toxic effects of mercuric oxide on African cat fish (*Clarias gariepinus)*. The total viable count of bacteria identified higher in fish fed on carbohydrate mercuric. Predominate bacteria were identified as, E. coli, Streptococcous, Pseudomonas, and Fluorscences. We emphasize the finding that an increase carbohydrate concentration causes harmful pathological effect which reduces humoral immure responses and enhances dietary mercuric toxicity.

Keywords: *Clarias gariepinis,* mercuric pollution, haematalogical, biochemical, clinicopathological, Bacteria account.

INTRODUCTION

Fish plays an important role, not only in human food diets but also in animal and poultry rations. It is a palatable and easily digested food which is rich in vitamins, calcium, phosphorous and iodine. In Egyp, fish is considered as a cheap food article if compared with other foods of animal origin. The flesh of healthy fish is considered as a marker for the natural aquatic environment.

In animals, mercuric oxides cause inhibition of certain enzymes, which has several neurological effects. Next to the neurological effects vanadium can cause breathing disorders, paralyses and negative effects on the liver and kidneys. Laboratory tests with test animals have shown that mercuric and vanadium can cause harm to the reproductive system of male animals and rat it accumulates in the female placenta. Vanadium can be found in fishes and many other species. In mussels and crabs mercuric and vanadium strongly bioaccumulates, which can lead to concentrations of about 10^5 to 10^6 times greater than the concentrations that are found in seawater [1-8]

In recent years, much attention had been paid to the possible danger of metals poisoning in human as a result of consumption of contaminated fishes. So, the present study was carried out to elucidate the impact of mercuric oxide on African cat fish (*Clarias gariepinus)*. It's haematological, biochemical and hormonal parameters were studied as well as the bacteriological and clinopathological investigation.

MATERIAL AND METHODS

Experimental Design

Thirty African cat Clarias *gariepinis* were used to assess the effects of mercuric oxide. Fish weighting from 180-250 were obtained from Nile river and were kept in glass aquaria supplied with dechlorinate tap water at rate of one litter for each cm of fish's body. Fish were acclimated to the laboratory conditions for two weeks before the beginning of the experiment, they were fed a commercial fish diet [9], the composition of diet is illustrate in table (13.1), the experiment was determined after 4 weeks. Fish were divided into three groups (n=10) and exposed to different doses of mercuric oxide and carbohydrate. Group (1) was served as control, group (2) was fed with carbohydrate and mercuric oxide (10 mg kg-1 diet rations), group (3) was fed with carbohydrate and mercuric oxide (15 mg/kg^{-1} diet ration).

Mean of the initial body, weight of the each examined fish at the beginning of the experiment then after 2-4 weeks of exposure were determined.

Blood Samples

Blood samples were collected from the caudal vein after 4 weeks of exposure. Each sample was divided into two parts the first one was heparinized for haematological investigations, while the second was centrifuged at 3000 rpm for 5 minutes to obtain serum for biochemical studies.

Hematological Analysis

Haematological studies were performed according to Sandnes *et al.* [10], where blood haemologlobin (Hb) and haematocrit (Ht) values were evaluated.

Biochemical Analysis

The activities of alkaline phosphatase, aspartic aminotransferase (AST) and alanine aminotrarsferase (ALT) as well as cholesterol urea and creatinine level were determined according to the method of Varley *et al.* [11] by using commercial kits (Bio Merieus, France)

Total scrum protein was estimated according to Drupt [12]. Serum cortisol was analyzed by a Gamma counter using 125 I cortisol radioimmunassay Kit) Baxter Health Care Corporation USA) according to the method described by Pickering and Pottinger [13]. Potassium, Sodium and Phosphorous concentrations were determined by atomic absorption spectrophotometer [11].

Tissue Analysis

Liver, kidney and spleen samples were washed with distilled water then dried in hot air oven. sulphuric acid and hydrogen peroxide were added on samples then heated until the mixture became transparent after performing a wet ash digestion according to the method of Issac and Kerber [14].

Identification ion of Bacteria

The liver, kidney, spleen, muscle, stomach and gill from each examined fish were diluted immediately after sampling in sterile 0.9% saline and 0.1 ml volumes of appropriate dilutions and were spread over the surface of the typtic soy agar (oxide).The plates were incubate at 22°C and inspected daily for up to 4 weeks.

The isolates were classified and identified according to Steverson [15] and Quirm *et al.* [16].

The data were evaluated statistically according to Gad-Weil [17].

Water Samples

Two water of samples were collected from River Nile (Hawamdya) as well as two water samples from any heavy metal pollution El-Kasr El-Eini (control) were analyzed for mercuric concentration by atomic absorption spectrophotometer.

RESULTS AND DISCUSSION

Data in Table (13.1) showed that, the mercuric oxide level in Hehvan region was clearly higher than the maximum allowable concentration for human consumption as recommended internationally according to WHO (World Health Organisation). Nadal *et al*. [2] concluded that the occurrence of mercuric in nature and its use in various industrial processes has increased its inputs in the environment. From the present study it is clear that the low mercuric levels were reported in water samples collected from areas far from industrial discharges, while high mercuric levels in the present study may be due to the collection of samples from areas subjected to industrial pollution.

In Table (13.3) there is a significant decrease in body weight in group 3 (fish fed 15 mg/kg diet mercuric oxide for 4 weeks) than in group 1 (control) and group 2 (fish fed l0 mg mercuric), this results agree with that reported by Khalaf-Allah [18].

The results present in Table (13.5) showed the cholesterol levels between different groups. The level was significantly increased in group 3 (fish fed on l5 mg vanadium) than in group 1(control). Hypercirolestremia might be due to necrotic changes occurring in liver with liberation of cholesterol as a byproduct of cell destruction. The present data suggest that impaired liver function lead to increased serum levels of alkaline phosphat, AST and ALT among group 3 (fish fed on l5 mg mercuric) and among group 2 (fish fed 10 mg mercuric) compared with group 1(control). In this concern Khalaf-Allah [8] concluded that ALT and AST enzymes are good indices for the health status of liver parenchymatous, tissue necrosis is considered as the main source of AST and its increase in the serum of African cat fish *(Clarias Gariepinus)* and declared these necrotic changes [18]. In addition, exposure of fish to environmental pollutants might result in stimulation or depression of the enzyme activity depending on the concentration of pollutant and the duration of exposure [19, 20].

Regarding the effect of mercuric oxide on serum cortisol level in African cat fish (*Claias gariepinus)* highest level was obtained in group 3 (fish fed on 15 mg mercuric) then in group 2 (fish fed on 10 mg vanadium) as compared to that obtained in group 1 (control). The significant increase of cortisol level is probably due to the activation of hypothalamus pituitary internal axis [21].

From the data present in Table (13.5), it is clear that elevation of mercuric oxide level in the diets fed to *(Clarias gariepinus)* was positively correlated to hemoglobin (Hb) levels and haematocrit (Ht). A marked decrease in the IIb and Ht was recorded after feeding diet containing 15 mg and 10 mg mercuric, respectively. Reduced Hb reflects metabolic adjustment according to reduced need for oxygen by change in blood PH.

Table 13.1: Ingredients and Proximate Composition of Diets Used in the Experiments with Mercuric Oxide

Ingredients	Diet Control	Diet 2	Diet 3
Fish meal	25	25	30
Meat and bone meal	5	5	10
Wheat bran	20	20	20
Skimmed milk	12	12	7
Yeast	10	10	15
Starch	–	10	15
Cod liver oil	2	2	2
Vitamin premix	1	1	1
Mercuric oxide	–	10	15
Crude protein%	40.35	35.95	38.89
Metabolizable energy k cal/kg]	2205.4	2551.78	2315.4
Ether extract%	4.29	4.21	2.86
Crude fiber%	4.46	3.73	4.27
Ash%	5.56	6.26	10.25
Lysine%	2.13	1.88	2.29
Methionino%	0.62	0.55	0.613

Mineral and vitamin premix per/kg of pellet food

Vit A, 8000 g/u, vit D 900 g/u vit E/u, vit k 4mg, vit B2 3.6 niacin 20mg, pyridoxine 0.2mg Vit B1 25, Mn 70mg, Se 60mg

Table 13.2: Mercuric Oxide Concentration in Water Samples Collected from Two Areas in Egypt.

Areas	Sampe No.	Concentration of Mercuric p.p.m
Hawamdya	12	1.05
	2	1.28
Ak-Kasr El-Aini	3	0.156
	4	0.164

Table 13.3: Changes in Body Weight in African Cat Fish (*Clarias gariepinis*) Fed on Different Levels of Dietery Carbohydrates in Addition to Mercuric Oxide

Weight/Group	Group 1	Group 2	Group 3
Initial body weight (g)	70 ± 0.15	85 ± 0.17	94 ± 0.20
After 2 weeks (g)	100 ± 0.45	102 ± 0.24	97 ± 0.62
After 4 weeks (g)	155 ± 0.26	124 ± 0.64	95 ± 0.60*

Table 13.4: The Mean Mercuric Concentration in the Organs of Fish mg/g Net Weight

Groups	Muscles	Spleen	Heart	Kidney	Liver
Group 1	0.24±0.14	0.52±0.83	0.64±0.49	3.15±0.72	2.11±0.69
Group 2	0.43±0.25	0.51±0.71	0.70±0.41	4.00±0.83	3.11±0.70
Group 3	0.55±26	0.82±0.41	0.83±0.24	6.74±0.74	6.13±0.05

Table 13.5: Some Haematological, Biochemical Parameters in African Cat Fish *Clarias gariepinis* on Different Levels of Dietery Carbohydrates in Addition to Mercuric Oxide

Parameters/Group	Group 1	Group 2	Group 3
Hemoglobin g/dl	36.20 ± 0.26	36.2 ± 0.28	31.5 ± 0.25*
HCT %	0.82 ± 0.22	0.95 ± 0.11	1.40 ± 0.68*
Cartisol ng/dl	9.6 ± 0.62	92 ± 0.26	81 ± 0.77*
Phosphorous mg/dl	122 ± 1.24	111 ± 0.75	103 ± 0.14*
Sodium M.EQ	6.23 ± 0.82	6.02 ± 0.44	61 ± 0.74*
Potassium M. EQ	20.42 ± 3.2	21 ± 0.73	26 ± 0.72*
Alkphosphatase U/L	135 ± 0.41	134 ± 0.88	140 ± 0.23*
AST U/L	23 ± 0.17	25 ± 0.74	36 ± 0.28*
Cholestrol mg	140 ± 0.25	145 ± 0.13	161 ± 0.54*
Total protein g/dl	8.2 ± 0.76	8.02 ± 0.81	7.02 ± 0.72*
Urea mg/dl	2.1 ± 0.78	3.4 ± 0.76	4.8 ± 0.23*
Creatinine mg/dl	0.75 ± 0.23	0.72 ± 0.76	0.90 ± 0.52*

Moyle and Ceeh, Hall and Cliffs recorded actived acetchlinesterase of erthrocytes [22, 23] Further more Pickeringand Dusten [24] concluded that a consistent effect of cortisol was the reduction in the hemoglobin and iron levels as a result of decrease in appetite in rainbow trout fish or more likely to be the direct-result of catabolic effect of cortisol in the fish tissues [24].

The mean phosphorus, sodium and potassium values in the serum of fish of group 3 (fish fed 15 mg mercuric oxide) were significantly increased respectively than those recorded in the group 1 (control). This retention maybe attributed to kidney dysfunction, whereas, the kidney is the normal pass for sodium and potassium.

Kidney dysfunction may also explain the increase in serurn urea and creatinine especially in group3, but little known about the mechanisms involved in this association.

The results displayed also in Table (13.5) showed that there was general decrease in the mean total protein value in serum samples collected from the fish of group 3 and 2, respectively. The mean value of these parameters was lower than in group 1. Jagadeesh *et al.* [25] estimated marked decrease in glycogen in tissues of fresh water fish after exposure to vanadium [25].

This experiment showed that the body weight of the examined fish was significantly decreased than the initial body weight after 4 weeks of exposure to 15 mg mercuric oxide. Also, Hilton and Better [25] recorded a significantly reduced growth and increased mortality among feeding diets of mercuric (0, 10, 100, 1000, 10000mg Kg-') [26]. The increase in muscles and tissue lactic acid (2 fold) in association with decrease in pyruvic acid (72 in muscles +26% in liver) reflect a shift towards an anaerobic metabolism of fish following long term exposure to mercuric [26]

Table (13.6) showed that, the bacterial isolates and counts were increased by feeding the fish with CHO and mercuric. The carbohydrates affect immunity and resistance to infection as recorded by Waagbo et al. [19] Utility of vanadate, mimetic protein phosphate inhibitors to protect fish from microorganism [27]. The increase of bacterial count among the fish fed on mercuric may be related to the increased level of corlisol which decreases the host immunity.

Table 13.6: Bacterial Isolates Recorded from the Examined Fish

Groups	Bacterial Isolates	Site of Isolation	Bacterial Count
Group 3 (n= 10)	-E. Coli	-Muscles	–
	-Streptococcus	-External surface, Stomach	2×10^3
	-E. Coli	Gills	–
	-Aeromonas	Gills, Stomach	6.6×10^4
Group 2 (n= 10)	-Enterbacter	Liver, Kidney	1×10^3
	-Pseudomonas	-Spleen, Muscles	4×10^3
	-Fluroscences	-Stomach	2×10^6
	-Lactobacillus	-Gills	–

In the course of experiment, a high concentration or mercuric levels has been found in kidney, liver, spleen, heart and muscles of cat African catfish *(Clarias gariepinus)* fed 15 mg mercuric (Table 13.4). This suggests that these organs could be useful as a marker for vanadium in the aquatic environment. In this concern Ray et al. recorded a high concentration of mercuric in kidney liver and other organs of African cat fish as the concentration of mercuric in the tissues increased with its concentration in the aquatic environment and exposure time [28].After exposure of fish to increased doses for 4 days, the mercuric content in the muscle then increased in all tissues [20, 25, 26] The capability of mercuric to be present in fish muscle is of particular interest in assessing the exposure of man to environmental mercuric as ingested by food.

Clinicopathological Observations

Abnormal swimming lighting of the skin, scale loss and haemorrhasges, water seen on the external body surface. In addition to congestion of gills, eyes mouth, liver, kidney, spleen, and intestine. This was notice in fish exposed to mercuric oxide 15mg (group 3) but not in fish exposed to mercuric oxide 10 mg (group 2).

In conclusion: we emphasize that, the reported finding increase of carbohydrate concentrations causes harmful physiological effects, reduces hormonal immune response and enhances dietary toxicity.

REFERENCES

1. Copyright @ 1998-2007. Lenntech Water Treatment & Air Purification Holding B.V. Rotterdamseweg 402 M 2629 HH Delft, The Netherlands e-mail: info@lenntech.com
2. Nadal, M., M and Schulmacherand J.L. Dommgo (2007):' Levels of Metals, PCB's PCN's and PAH's in Soils of Highly Industrialized Chemical/Petrochemical Area Chemosphere, 66: 267-76.
3. Bu-Olayan, A.H. and S. Al-Yakoob (1998): Lead Nickel and Vanadium in Sea Food an Exposure Assessment for Kuwait Consumers. Sci. Environ. 2-3: 81-86.
4. Huang, Y.C. and A.J. Ghio (2006): Vascular Effects of Ambient Pollutant Particles and Metals, curr. Vasc. Pharmacol, 4: 199-203.
5. Li, Z., J.D. Carter, L.A. Dailey and Y.C.T. Huang (2004): 4-vanadyl Sulfate Inhibits NO Production via Threonine Phosphorylation of eNOS, Environ. Health Prospect, 112: 201-206.
6. Worle, J.M., K. Kem C. Schelh A.C. Helmy, C. Feldman and H.F. Krug (2007). Nanoparticulate Vanadium Oxide Potentiated Vanadium Toxicity in Human Lung Cells, Environ. Sci. Technol., 41 331-6.
7. Figuero, D.A., C.I. Rodriquez-Sierra and B.D. Jimenez-velez (2006): Toxicol & health, 22:87-99.
8. Bu-Olayan, A.H. and M.N.V. Subranmanyam (1996): Trace Metal in Fish from Kuwait Coast Using Microrvave Acid Digestion Technique. Environ-Inter., 22: 753-758.
9. Waagbo, R., J. Glette, K. Sandnes and G.F. Hemre (1994): J. Fish Dis., 1 7:1 45.
10. Sarndnes, K., Q. Lee and R. Waagatn, 1998. J. of Fish Biol., 31: I19.
11. Varley, H., A. HI. Gwenbek and M. Bell (1980): Practical Clinical Chemistry, Vol. I, General I Top's Comneuer Test 5th ed. London, William Medical Books Ltd.
12. Dmpt, F. (1974): Pharm. Biol, 9: 77.
13. Pickering, A.D. and I. Pottinger (1983): Gen Comp Ender. 49: 232.

14. Issac, R.A. and Kerber, I (1971): Amer. Madison. 17.
15. Steverson P., (1987): "Field Guide Systematic Bacteriology". University of Cuelphontaria, Canada, pp: 280.
16. Quinn, P.J., M.E. Carter, B.K. Makey and G.R Carter (1994): "Clinical Veterinary Microbiology", Wolf Publishing Mosby, Year Book Europe Limited.
17. Gad, S.C. and C.S. Weil, (1986): Statistics for Toxicologists. In, Hages A.W. (2nd ed.), "Principles and Methods of Toxicology", Raven Press, New York, pp: 273-32.
18. Khalaf-Allah, (1998) Screening the Effect of Water Pollution with Some Pesticides on the Immune Response in *Oreochromis nilolicus* Fish. Vet. Mid. J. Giza., 46: 883-393.
19. Venberg, F.G. and W.B. Venbcrg, (1974): Pollution and Physiology of Marine Organisms. Academic Press New York, pp: 59.
20. Edel, J. and E. Sabioni (1993): Accumulation and Distribution of Mussel Myails Edulis and the Gold Fish Carassits Auratus. Sci. Total-Envilon. 133: 139-151.
21. Carballo, M.J., M.J. Torroba, C. Munoz, D.V. Sanchez, I.D. Txazora and J. Dominguez (1992) J. Fish and Shell Fish Immunology, Z. 121.
22. Moyle, P.B. and J.J. Cech (1982): Blood and its Circulation in Fish-An Introduction to Ichthyology" (Ed. by, P.B. Moyle, J.H. Cech) pp: 52-73 Prentice.
23. Hall, I. and E. Cliffs (1982). Aspects and Energy Response in an Indian Catfish Babachus, Biometais, 11: 95-100.
24. Pickering, A.P. and J. Duston (1983): J. Fish Biol., 23: 163.
25. Jagadeesh K.B., S.A. Shaffi and S. Jeelani, (1989): Acta Physiologia Hungarica 74: 43.
26. Hitton" J.W. and W.G. Bettgeo (1988): Aquatic Toxicology, l2: 63.
27. Evans-Donald L. and L. Jaso. Friedmarur (2001): Protection of *Teleost fish*. Biotclr, Nav., 15: 777.
28. Ray, D., S.K. Panerjeo and M.I. Chattejee, (1999): Bioaccumulation of Nickel and Vanadium in Tissues of Catfish Batracchus. J. Inorg-Biochem., 38: I 69-173.
29. Dunford, D.K.; Salinaro, A.; Car, L.; Serpone M.N.; Harikoshi, S.; Hidaka, H. and Knowland, J. (1997): Chemical Oxidation and DNA Damage Catalyzed by Inorganic Sunscreen Ingredients. FEBS Letters, 418: 97-90.
30. Bann, R.; Straif, K.; Grosse, Y.; Secreton, B.; Ghissassi, F.F. and Cogliano, V. (2006): Carcinogenicity of Carbon Black, Titanium Dioxide and Talc. J. of the Lancet Oncol, 7: 295-296.
31. Ghoropade,V.M.; Desphande, S.S. and Salunkhe, D.K. (1995): Food Colours in Food Additive Toxicology by Joseph, A.M. and Authony,T.Tu, New York. Basal, Hony Kong. Chapter 4, Page 214.
32. Wang, J.; Zhou, G.; Chen,C.; Yu, H. ; Wang, T.; Ma, Y.; Jia, G.; Gao, Y.; Li, B.; Sun, J.; Li, Y.; Jiao, F.; Zhao, Y. and Chai, Z. (2007): Acute Toxicity and Biodistribution of Different Sized Titanium Dioxide Particles in Mice after Oral Administration. Toxicology Letters, 168: 176-185.
33. Leone, J. (1973): Collaborative Study of the Quantitative Determination of Titanium Dioxide in Cheese. J. Assoc. Offic. Anal Chem., 56: 535-558.
34. Mahrousa, M.H. Kandiel (2004): Cytogenetic and Biochemical Effects of Some Food Colours in Rats. Ph. Dr. Thesis Submitted to Animal Production Department, Faculty of Agriculture, Cairo University.

14

Pathological and Biochemical Studies in *Tilapia Zilli* Infected with *Saprolegnia parasitica* and Treated with Potassium Permanganate

Mona S. Zaki*[1]; Olfat M. Fawzi[2]
Suzan Omar Mostafa[2]; Nadia Taha[3]

ABSTRACT

The present study was planned to investigate the effect of *Saprolegnia parasitica* infection in the hematological, serum biochemical and pathological alterations of *Tilapia Zilli*. Forty five fish were divided into three equal groups. Fish of first group served as a control. Fish of group (2 & 3) were infected by *Saprolegnia parasitica*. Fish of group (3) were treated after 7 days of post-infection using potassium permanganate for 10 days. Sampling was done after 1 and 7 days of post-infection (gps 1 & 2) and 10 days of post-treatment (gps 1& 3). The results revealed a non significant changes in the hematological and the biochemical parameters after 1 day of infection, but after 7 days of post-infection and 10 days of post-treatment, a significant decrease in RBCs, Hb, PCV and significant increase in AST, ALT, urea, creatinine, sodium, potassium, cortisol, insulin and glucose were seen. Iron showed a significant decrease at the same period of sampling.

1. Department of Aquaculture, National Research Centre, Giza, Egypt.
2. Department of Biochemistry, National Research Centre, Giza, Egypt.
3. Departmet of physiology, Veterinary medicine, Cairo Univ. Giza, Egypt.

The pathological examination revealed a massive fungal growth resembling a tuft of cotton wool threads was seen in eyes, grills, fins and in localized areas of the skin. Microscopically, the fungal hyphae and spores appeared on eyes, gills, skin and underlying muscles with marked degenerative, necrotic and inflammatory reactions. These reactions were evident, after 7 days of post-infection and the severity of the lesions were markedly decreased after 10 days of post-treatment. It could be concluded that, saprolegnia parasitica infections induced marked tissue alterations as well as some hematological and serum biochemical changes. Although potassium permanganate treated the infected cases and allowed the regenerative processes but it does not progress the hematological and serum biochemical parameters.

Key words: Tilapia Zilli; Saprolegina parasitica; Biochemical changes.

INTRODUCTION

Saprolegnia species are opportunistic facultative parasite either ecrophs or saprotrophs [1]. It causes substantial mortality among fresh water fish and mostly associated with environmental stresses such as overcrowding. Rough handling, transport, low dissolved oxygen, temperature fluctuation, osmotic shock and water pollution [2]. Moreover, saprolegnia may be secondary invader to bacterial infection or parasitic agents [3]. However, the importance of saprolegnia as a primary pathogen is still debatable where some outbreaks with mass mortalities may occur absence of other pathogens [4].

Saprolegniosis in fish usually starts as a cotton wool like, white to dark gray or brownish growth over the head region or dorsal fin and then spread allover the body. The infection may be associated with pathological and hematological alterations as well as biochemical changes [5]. Potassium permanganate is used in protection of fish from ectoparasites and it is reported to be a strong antifungal [6]. The present work aimed to study the effect of *saprolegnia parasitica* on biochemical and clinicopathological findings of infected *Tilapia Zilli* before and after treatment with potassium permanganate.

MATERIALS AND METHODS

Fish

Forty five *Tilapia Zilli* with average body weight of 100-150 gm/fish were obtained from River Nile and transported to the laboratory and reared in 3 equal glass aquaria (115 liter capacity), fed a balanced ration and provided with continuous aireated and renued tap water.

Fish were kept one week for acclimatization and mean time subjected to mycological, bacteriological and pathological examinations.

Fungus

Saprolegnia parasitica was kindly obtained from Mercen Department, Faculty of Agriculture, Ain Shams University.

Chemical: Potassium permanganate was obtained from Nasr. Co., Cairo, Egypt.

Experimental Infection

Fish were divided into 3 equal groups. Fish of group (1) were kept without treatment to serve as a control. Fish of groups (2 and 3) were infected by *Saprolegnia parasitica*. Fish of group (3) were treated after 7 days of infection using potassium permanganate (2.5 mg/L) for 10 days. The challenge infection was done by immersing a manual wounded *Tilapia Zilli* in a zoospore suspension of *Saprolegnia parasitica* (4×10^6 zoop/L) for 10 min. according to Willoughby and Pichering [7]. Infection was indicated by the presence of cottony white patches on the body of fish and diagnosed using G.Y.Ps. agar plates.

Sampling

Blood samples and tissue specimens were taken at first and seventh days of infection (gp2) and also after ten days of treatment (gp3). Sampling was also done at the same tome from control group (gp1). Blood samples were taken in heparinised microhematocrit tube and other tubes to be centrifuged at 3000 r. p. m. for 10 min. for serum separation. The serum stored at 20°C until analysis.

Hematological Examinations

The erythrocytic indices (RBCs, Hb, PCV and MCV) and reticulocytes were determined according to Schalm [8].

Serum Biochemical Analysis

Serum aspirate aminotransferase (AST) and alanin aminotransferase (ALT) also serum urea, creatinine and glucose were estimated using kits supplied from Biomerieux (France). Sodium and potassium were determined by flame photometer according the method described by silversmith[9]. Serum cortisol level was determined using radio immunoassay technique[10]. Insulin was estimated by radioimmunoassay using kits obtained from diagnostic products corporation (Los Angeles, USA). Iron was determined using atomic absorption according to Joseph and Roger [11].

RESULTS

Saprolegniosis, after 1 of day post-infection, induced non significant changes in the hematological and serum biochemical parameters. A significant decrease in RBCs, Hb and PCV was observed in *Tilapia Zilli*, after 7 days of post-infection and 10 days of post-treatment, while MCV and a period of reticulocytes showed a high significant decrease at the same period of sampling in comparison with control. A significant increase in AST, ALT, urea, creatinine, sodium, potassium, cortisol, insulin and glucose was noticed in *Tilapia Zilli* after 7 days of post-infection by *Saprolegnia* and 10 days of post-treatment while iron showed a significant decrease at the same period of sampling in comparison with control.

Clinically, *Tilapia Zilli* infected by saprolegnia showed conspicuous fungal colonies, after 7 days of post-infection that appeared on the mouth, gills, eyes, fins and localized areas of the body surface. The fungal growth appeared white or grey thin threads resembling a tuft of cotton wool. The colour frequently changed to dark by accumulation of debris. Blindness was evident, in some cases, due to eye infection. Later on, some *Tilapia Zilli* swam eradically and vigorously into the side of the aquaria. After 10 days of treatment most of these signs were disappeared.

Grossly, massive fungal growth appeared on the fins, gills and skin. It is accociated with focal areas of hemorrhage, necrosis and ulceration. The internal organs revealed a mild congestion. Small grayish white foci on the liver surface was seen.

Table 14.1: Effect of Saprolegniosis on Some Hematological Parameters of *Tilapia Zilli* Before and After Treatment in Comparison with Control (Mean±SE)

Parameters	Control gp.	Infected gp.		Treated gp. (10 days P.T)
		1 day P.I.	7 days P.I.	
RBC_s ($10^6/mm^3$)	2.72 ± 0.10	2.83 ± 0.07	1.95 ± 0.85*	1.83 ± 0.24*
Hb (gm/dl)	9.03 ± 0.24	9.21 ± 0.04	8.30 ± 0.63*	7.93 ± 0.52*
PCV	20.03 ± 0.74	19.01 ± 0.05	17.01 ± 0.33*	16.01 ± 0.18*
MCV (FL)	36.03 ± 0.04	35.28 ± 0.06	30.10 ± 0.52**	29.01 ± 0.44**
Reticulocytes (%)	1.75 ± 0.04	1.64 ± 0.08	1.33 ± 0.13**	1.65 ± 0.18**

**Significant at P<0.01, P.I. = Post-infection, P.T. = Post-treatment, gp. = group

DISCUSSION

It is apparent that, Nile *Tilapia Zilli* infected with saprolegnia caused a significant increase in glucose and insulin levels only during 7 days of infection and 10 days of treatment with potassium permanganate (2.5 mg/L). It is well known that, any stress factor such as handling, incubation, or anathesia have been shown to cause hyperglycemia followed by hyperinsulinemia [7].

The present work revealed that, serum glucose was elevated during 7 days of infection and 10 days of treatment. One consistent effect of cortisol was the reduction in the haemoglobin, PCV, RBCs and iron level as a result of decrease in appetite in the *Tilapia Zilli* or more likely to be the direct of catabolic effect of cortisol on the fish [12].

Table 14.2: Effect of Saprolegniosis on Some Serum Biochemical Parameters of *Tilapia Zilli* Before and After Treatment in Comparison with Control (Mean ± SE)

Parameters	Control gp.	Infected gp.		Treated gp. (10 days P.T)
		1 day P.I.	7 days P.I.	
AST (U/L)	81.00 ± 0.64	81.00 ± 0.17	126.00 ± 0.40	128.00 ± 0.63*
ALT (U/L)	22.00 ± 0.19	23.00 ± 0.17	33.00 ± 0.18*	38.00 ± 0.14*
Urea (mg%)	3.23 ± 0.34	3.27 ± 0.36	4.25 ± 0.62*	4.93 ± 0.84*
Creatinine (mg%)	0.71 ± 0.21	0.73 ± 0.33	0.93 ± 0.22*	0.99 ± 0.13*
Sodium (mfg/dl)	129.00 ± 0.33	139.00 ± 0.80	151.00 ± 1.12*	165.90 ± 1.82*
Potassium (mfg/dl)	4.00 ± 0.22	4.20 ± 0.40	6.62 ± 0.82*	7.30 ± 0.72*
Cortisol (µg/dl)	0.80 ± 0.18	0.85 ± 0.19	1.62 ± 0.68*	1.91 ± 0.70*
Insulin (µg/dl)	10.20 ± 0.14	11.60 ± 0.70	13.20 ± 0.42*	13.90 ± 0.63*
Glucose (mfg/dl)	61.30 ± 0.34	62.80 ± 0.70	78.00 ± 0.73*	80.80 ± 0.70*
Iron (mg/dl)	220.00 ± 0.17	222.00 ± 1.12	210.00 ± 1.13*	196.00 ± 1.15*

* Significant of $p<0.01$

The experiment showed that sodium (Na) and potassium (K) concentrations were significantly increased, this retention may be attributable to kidney impairment where the kidney is the normal passway for Na and K, this may explain the main cause for elevation of serum creatinine and urea in the treated groups which also microscopically exhibited vacuolar degeneration of renal tubules. This confirms the previous results recorded by Osfor *et al*. [13], Zaki *et al*. [14] and Abdel Aziz *et al.,* [15]. This led to temporal changes in plasma insulin concentration which did not mirror those for glucose. One of the reasons may be the high sensitivity to glucose of pancreatic cells producing somatostatin which in turn inhibits insulin secretion during the initial period after saprolegnia challenge [16]. Saprolegnia infection causes a significant increase of cortisol level which may be due to the activation of hypothalamus pituitary internal axis. These results coincide with those observed by Jauncey and Ross [17] and Zaki et al.,[18]. who stated that, hyphae of saprolegnia may invade deep tissues of the fish and penetrate the vital organs as kidney, liver and even the central nervous system and eye.

Marked elevations were noticed in the activity of (AST) and (ALT). The liver is the primary organ of detoxification as well as a major site for detoxification reaction, therefore, a significant increase in liver enzymes suggests explanations for the presence of the saprolegnia parasitica or its toxins in liver. This picture was confirmed histopathologically by the marked vacuolar degeneration of hepatocytes.

As primary pathogen for stressed fish, this is in agree with Zaki *et al.*,[14] and Badran *et al.*, [19]. Who stated that hyphae of saprolegnia may invade deep tissues of fish and penetrate the vital organs even the central nervous system.

The clinical signs and postmortem lesions that reported among infected *Tilapia Zilli* were similar to those reported by Aly and Ashram [3] and Attia[20] and Ferguson [21].

REFERENCES

1. Cook, R., 2007. The Biology of Symbiotic Fungi. John Wiley. New York.
2. Ahmed, N., 1998. Studies on the Linkage of Fungi with Some Fish Disease in Fish Farms. MVSc., Zagazig Univ., Egypt.
3. Aly, S. and A. El Ashram, 2000. Some Factors Contributing to the* Development of Saprolegniosis in *Nile tilapia (Oreochromis niloticus)*. Alex. J. Vet. Science, 16 (1): 165-174.
4. Noga, E. and M. Dukstra, 1981. Commycetes Fungi Associated with* Ulcerative Mycosis in Menhaden. Brevoorin Tyrannus. H. of fish diseases.
5. Roberts, J., 1989. Textbook of Fish Pathology. 2nd Edn. Bailliere Tindall. Philadelphia, USA.
6. Srivastava, S., N. Singh, A. Srivastava and Ranjana, 1995. Acute Toxicity of Malachite Green and its Effects on Certain Blood Parameters of *Tilapia nilotica, Heteropneuses fossilis*. Aquat. Toxicol., 31 (3): 241-247.
7. Willoughby, L. and A. Pickering, 1977. Viable Saproleinaceale Spores on the Epidermis of Salmonid Fish Salmo Trutta and *Salvellinus alpious*. Transactions of the British Mycology Society, 68:91.
8. Schalm, O., 1986. Schalm's Veterinary Hematology, 4th Edition 524.
9. Silversmit, A.B. Med. 1965. 45: 175.
10. Pickering A.D. and P. Pottinger, 1983. Gen. com. Endocrinol., 49: 232.
11. Joseph, A. and W.G. Roger, 1976. Clinical Chemistry Principal and Procedures, pp. 168-197.
12. Musa, S.O. and F. Omeregie, 1995. Haematological Changes the Mud* Fish Exposed to Malachite Green. J. of Aquatic Sciences, 14: 3742.
13. Osfor, M.H., M.S. Zaki and A.Z. Saleh, 1998. Impact of Low Diatery CHO Diets on Some Nutritional and Clinicopathogical Parameters of *Tilapia nilotica* Infected with *Saprolegnia parasitica* and Exposed to Copper Nitrite Bull. NRC. Egypt, 23 (2): 128-192.
14. Zaki, M.S., M.H. Osfor, F.S. Bayumi and F.N. Aboul Gheit 2003. Impact of Low Dietry Carbohydrate Diets on Some Nutritional and Clinicopathological Parameters of *Tilapia nilotica* Infected with *Saprolegnia parasitica* and Exposed to Copper Sulphate. Bull. NRC., Egypt, 28 (2): 245-257.
15. Abdel Aziz, E.S., A Ayanis and M.M. Ali, 2002. Effect of Water Temperature Upon the Response of Cultured Clarias lazera to Saprolegnia Infection and the Consequent Hematological Changes. Egypt J. Comp. Clinic. Pathology, 15 (2):108-125.
16. Sheridan, M.A., C.D. Eilerston and E.M. Plisetskaya, 1991. Endocrinol., 81:36.
17. Juncey, K. and B. Ross, 1982. A Guide to Tilapia Feed and Feeding* Institute of Aquaculture Univ. of Striling, Scotland.

18. Zaki,M.S., Fawzi,O.M and El-Jacky,J, 2008. Pathological and Biochemical Studies in Tilapia Nilotica Infected with Saprolegnia Parasitica and Treated with Potassium Permanganate. Am-Euras. J. Agric.& Environ. Sci., 3(5): 677-680.
19. Badran, A.F., M. Ezzat and M. El-Tarabili, 1991. Investigation on Saprolegniosis Among *Nile tilapia (Oreochromis niloticus)* with Special Reference to its Control. Zagazig. Vet. J., 19 (1):26-40.
20. Attia, Y., 2000. Studies on Scales of Healthy and Diseased Fish. MVSc,* Zagazig Univ., Egypt.
21. Ferguson, H., 1989. Textbook of Systemic Pathology of fish. 1st Ed. Lowa State Univ. Press., Ames, Lowa, Canada.

15

Reduction of Alfatoxin in Clarious Lazara Catfish by Ginseng Extract and Nigella Sativa Oil

Mona S. Zaki*[1]; Olfat M. Fawzi[2]; Iman M. Zytuun[3]

ABSTRACT

Aflatoxine the major toxic metabolites of fungi which are able to induce chronic liver damages. The antioxidant and hepatoprotective effects of Ginseng extract and Nigella sativa Oil 1% on Alfatoxin was investigated. Alfatoxicosis causes significant increase in liver enzyme SGOT and SGPT, Alkaline phosphatase activity and an increase in the level of cholesterol total lipid, decrease the level of total protein and hemoglobin and P.C.V. Moreover the liver exhibited some clinicopathological changes and decreased body weight. Both Ginseng extract and Nigella sativa Oil 1% reduced the development of hepatotoxicity by Aflatoxin. Nigella sativa showed more improvement of all enzymes of kidney and liver, and also total lipid and cholesterol were reduced and dody weight increased.

Keywords: Aflatoxin toxicity. Nigella sativa oil effect. Ginseng extract effect. Clarious lazara Catfish.

1. Department of Hydrobiology, National Research Center, Dokki, Cairo, Egypt.
2. Department of Biochemistry, National Research Center, Dokki, Cairo, Egypt.
3. Department of Microbiology, Zagazig University, Cairo, Egypt.

INTRODUCTION

Aflatoxin is a toxic compound produced by Aspergillus flavus and A. parasiticus. The molds can grow in improperly stored feeds and feeds with inferior quality of ingredients. Aflatoxins represent a serious source of contamination in foods and feeds in many parts of the world. These toxins have been incriminated as the cause of high mortality in livestock and in some cases of death in human beings (Murjani, 2003).

Aflatoxin is a potent hepatocarcinogen, strong mutagen and a potential teratogen.(Canton,et al. 1998; Bulter and Clifford, 1985). There are four main Aflatoxins: B1, B2, C1,C2. Aflatoxin B1 is known to be the most significant form that causes serious risk to animals and human health. The carcinogenic effect of aflatoxin B1 has been studied in fishes such as salmonid, rainbow trout, channel catfish, tilapia, guppy and Indian major carps (Jantrarotai and Lovell, 1990; Lovell, 1992; Tacon, 1992; Wu, 1998; Chavez et al., 1994; Murjani, 2003). Aflatoxins inhibited RNA synthesis and DNA in liver. (Jindal et al. 1994).

Nigella sativa is a spicy poten belonging to ranunculacea seeds oil showed antibacterial fungicidal (Akguil, 1989). Nigella sativa inhibited chemical carcinogensis. Some investigators reported that its antioxidants effect inhibited Chemical carcinogenesis. Ascorbic acid and Nigella sativa could reduce Aflatoxin induced liver cancer (Newperne et al., 1999).

Panax ginseng C.A. Mayer is an herbal root that has been used for more than 2000 years throughout Far Eastern countries including China, Japan and Korea. Its beneficial effects have bee nanalyzed by extensive preclinical and epidemiological studies (Yun, 2003). Recently, 20-O-(h-D-glucopyranosyl)-20(S)-protopanaxadiol (IH-901), a novel ginseng saponin metabolite, formed from ginsenosides Rb1, Rb2 was isolated and purified after giving ginseng extract p.o. to humans and animals (Hasegawa et al., 1996).IH-901 has been shown to enhance the efficacy of anticancer drugs in cancer cell lines previously resistant to several anticancer drugs (Lee et al. 1999).

AIM OF PRESENT WORK

This study was conducted to evaluate the effect of Aflatoxin and ginseng with Nigella sativa oil 1% on some nutritional status and clinicopathological changes in Catfish toxicated with Aflatoxin and treated with ginseng and Nigella Sativa oil 1%.

MATERIAL AND METHODS

Experimental Conditions

60 catfish clarious lazera were obtained from Abbassa and were acclimatized to laboratory conditions. They were kept in glass aquaria supplied with dechlorinated tap water at a rate of one liter for each cm of fish body. They were fed commercial fish diet were supplied by Aflatoxin contaminated

ration with corn 80ug toxin/kg ration, as shown in Table (15.1). A total number of 60 cutfish were used in this experiment: 20 Fish each group, 20 cotfish control, 20 fed Aflatoxin and 20 treated with Faxatation Nigella Sativa.

Table 15.1: Ingredients and Proximate Chemical Composition of Diets Used in the Experiments

Ingredient	Control	Provimate	Chemical Composition
Hah meal	30	Crude protein Pg%	35.87
Meas meal	8	M.E/kg	2297.21
Bone meal	1	Ether extract g%	2.78
Soya bean	5	Crude liber g%	3.91
Skimnied milk	3	Ash g%	8.735
Wheat bran	20	Calcium mg &	2.069
Wheat flour	20	Lysine mg%	2.105
Yeast	10	Methionine mg%	0.562
Codliver oil	1		
Mincral and premix	2		

The third group Aflatoxin contaminated ration + 0.2 ginseng + Niegella sativa oil injected daily 1/p. the fish were fed by hand twice daily and feed consumption in all groups was recorded daily, also mortality and body weight due to Aflatoxin were recorded.

Samples

Serum were collected 3 times at 3 months interval and sera were frozen at-20. Tested kits supplied from biomerieux, France were used for determination of the activity of serum glutamic pyurvic transaminse and glutamic oxalocetic transaminase as described by Reitman and Frankel (1956), serum creatinine was determined according to Henery, (1968). Enzymatic determination of urea was done according to King (1965).

Blood hemoglobin was assessed by cyame hemoglobin method Hematocrit value was carried out by using microhematacrit capillary tubesrentri fuged at 2000P.M. for 5min according to the method of Drabkin (1946) serum cholesterol according to the method Flegg (1973), total lipids according to the method of Siesta (1981), andstatistical analysis according to the method of Gad and Weil (1986).

Mineral and vit. Premix perlkg of Pellet Food

Vit. A 8000 IU, vit. D 900 IU, vit, E 2 IU, vit, K4mg, B2 3.6mg, niacin 20mg, choline chloride 160mg, pantothenic acid 7mg, pyridoxine 0.2mg, vit, B12, 5ug, Mn 70mg, Zn 60mg, Fe 20mg, Cu 2mg, Co 0.2mg.

N.B.: we added 80Ug polluted corn with Aflatoxin B1, in this ration.

RESULTS

Aflatoxicosis produced a significant decrease in body weight if compared with control group as shown in Table 15.2. statistical analysis revealed effect of Aflatoxin, B1 on erythrogram. There is a significant decrease in P.C.V. Hemoglobin (P<0.01) as shown in Table 15.2. there is a significant decrease in mean of total protein and a significant increase in SGOT, SGOT, Urea, creatinine, total lipid, cholesterol and alkaline phosphatose (P<0.01).

Table 15.2: Effect of Aflatoxin After 1-2 Months on Clinicopathological Changes in Catfish After Treatment with Ginseng and Nigella sativa 1%

Parameters	Control N=(20)	Aflatoxin 1 month N=(20)	Alfatoxint + ginseng +Nigella sativa 1% N=20	Control N=20	2 months Group N=20	Aflatoxint + ginseng +Nigella sativa 1% N=20
AST U/L	82 ± 0.23	133 ± 0.06**	103 ± 0.05	84 ± 1.27	121 ± 2.4**	946 ± 0.09
ALT U/L	17 ± 0.67	27 ± 0.72**	22 ± 0.74	18 ± 0.72	31 ± 0.89**	21 ± 0.18
Urea mg/dl	2.87 ± 0.27	4.6 ± 0.64**	5.2 ± 0.27*	2.7 ± 0.74	5.3 ± 912**	3.3 ± 0.20
Creatininemg/dl	0.72 ± 5.4	0.8 ± 0.23**	0.88 ± 0.34	0.83 ± 0.26	1.3 ± 0.50**	0.83 ± 0.28
Total protein mg/dl	46 ± 0.17	3.5 ± 0.72**	4.4 ± 0.70	5.7 ± 0.22	3.3 ± 0.14**	4.4 ± 0.60
Total lipidscholesterol mg/dl	88 ± 0.99	143 ± 0.23**	104 ± 0.27*	97 ± 0.14	184 ± 1.2**	101 ± 0.74
Cholesterol	178 ± 0.79	212 ± 2.8**	197 ± 0.39*	188 ± 0.64	244 ± 3.6**	191 ± 2.1
Alkaline phosphates mg/dl	16.9 ± 0.37	28.8 ± 0.33**	23 ± 0.18	18.7 ± 0.18	34.8 ± 0.27**	21 ± 0.12
Hemoglobin mg/dl	7.2 ± 0.23	5.4 ± 0.74**	7.1 ± 1.60	8.6 ± 0.29	4.8 ± 0.72**	7.3 ± 11.75
P.C.V%	38 ± 0.63	33 ± 0.05	33 ± 0.05	42 ± 0.71	28 ± 0.02**	37 ± 0.27

P<0.01

Post treatment with ginseng and Nigella sativa oil injection 1% of body weight for 3 months. All this parameters return to normal level as shown in Tables 15.3 and 15.4 if compared with control group.

DISCUSSION

Aflatoxins are hepatotoxins (Pier. 1987, 1999) and also impair immunity which ultimately led to increased susceptibility to disease (Zaki, 1999).the present work demonstrated a severe necrosis in liver of catfish. The liver is the primary site of metabolism of ingested Aflatoxin. (Butler and Clifford, 1985; Ali etal., 1994). The pathological changes of liver observed in the present investigations may be due to primary site of metabolism o ingested Aflatoxins as well as the primary laceratian laceratian of residues and lesions. Similar finding reported by Newperne (1999). The increase of enzyme Urea, creatinine. These changes due to necrosis of kidneys reported by Jindal and Mahipal (1994), Mansfeld (1989), Pier (1987). The lipid metabolism was altered during Aflatoxicosis as judged by increase of total lipid content. In the present experiment, here is a highly elevation of total lipid and cholesterol in serum which agree with Sipple, et al. (1983),Sisk et al.(1988). It is obvious that administration of ginseng and Nigella sativa oil injection 1% of body weight reduced the Aflatoxin in liver, kidney, of infected fish and may protect liver from free radical reactions due to Aflatoxin, also total lipid, cholesterol return to normal level Mona,et al.(2002).

Table 15.3: Effect of Aflatoxin After 3 Months on Clinicopathological Changes in Catfish After Treatment with Gensing and Nigella Sativa 1%

Parameters	Control 3 Months	Aflatoxin 3 Months	Aflatoxin plus ginseng + Nigella Sativa 1% 3 Months
AST U/L	81 ± 0.14	133 ± 6.2**	82 ± 0.27
ALT U/L	182 ± 0.20	25 ± 0.37**	18.3 ± 0.07
Urea mg/dl	2.88 ± 0.22	5.3 ± 0.18**	2.64 ± 0.39
Creatinine mg/dl	0.81 ± 0.46	1.5 ± 0.54**	0.81 ± 03.2
Total protein mg/dl	5.7 ± 0.24	3.1 ± 0.45**	5.4 ± 0.74
Total lipid mg/dl	98 ± 0.78	191 ± 1.4**	94 ± 0.82
Cholesterol mg/dl	184 ± 0.94	254 ± 2.3**	182 ± 0.73
Alkaline phosphatose U/L	18.8 ± 0.27	36.4 ± 0.91**	18.2 ± 0.32
Hemoglobin%	8.7 ± 0.44	4.6 ± 0.72**	8.6 ± 0.37
P.C.V.%	37 ± 0.21	23 ± 0.15**	40.3 ± 0.24

$P<0.01$

Table 15.4: Effect of Aflatoxin on Body Weight of Catfish during the Course of Experiment

Group	1 Month	2 Months	3 Months
Control 20 fish	68 ± 0.21p	98 ± 0.16*	121 ± 0.72
Aflatoxin group (20 Fish)	92 ± 0.10	81 ± 0.2*	74 ± 0.13
Aflatoxint + gensing + Nigella sative (20 Fish)	86 ± 0.06	104 ± 0.73*	134 ± 0.64

*$P<0.01$

The present study showed a significant decrease in P.C.V., HB concentration in the affected fish that was proportionally correlated with the severity of Aflatoxicosis. This result is in accordance with Robert(1989). El-Bouhy et al., (1993). They found similar results in broilers chickens common carp Fish and this indicates that the toxin causes a deleterious effect on the hemopoeitic system.

Regarding the biochemical serum analysis, the noticed decreased in T.P. may be attributed to the improved protein synthesis as a result of liver function due to Aflatoxicosis. (Ali et al., 1994, A kguil 1989, Edds, 1993). The increase in ALT and AST activities recorded by Jassar and Balwant (1993), Rasmassen et al., (1986), Sisk et al., (1988), due to liver affection in case of Aflatoxicosis the elevation of ALP activity comes in consistence with mentioned by Jassar and Balwant (1993), Svobodava et al. (1999), in chicken due to degenerative changes in the liver causing leakage of enzymes into serum and cause the highest concentration of alkaline phosphates. The great increase of alkaline phosphates activity due to damage of liver. The detection of Aflatoxin in the liver tissues explain the liver degeneration. Similar results were described by Kubena et al., (1990), who used ginseng for preventing the absorption of Aflatoxins from gastrointestinal tract.

CONCLUSION

In conclusion, the metabolism of Aflatoxin result in the alteration of various metabolic process within hepatocytes which leads to severe serum biochemical alterations and serious pathological changes which affect fish production but treatment with ginseng and Nigella sativa give an excellent of results.

REFERENCES

1. AH, M.V., Mohi-Eddin, S,M, and Eedy, V.M., (1994) Effect of Dietary Aflatoxin on Cell Mediated Immunity and Serum Protein in Broiier Chicken. Indian Vet. J>, 78, (8) 760.
2. Akgpi!, A, (1989) Antimicrobial Activity of Black Seed (Nigella Saliva of Aflatoxin) Essential Oil. Cast Univ. Eczacllik Fax. Derg., 6, 63.
3. Butler, W.H. and Clifford, J, L (1985) Extraction of Aflatoxin from Rat Liver. Nature, 206 (5), 1045.
4. Canton, J.H., Kroes, R., Van Logkn, MJL and Van Schathorst, M.s (1998) The Careiriogenicify of Aflat Oxih D1 in Rainbow Trout, Fd. Consmet. Toxicol 19, 564.
5. Chavez, S., P. Martinez, M. Osorio, C.A. M. Palacios, and I.O. Mareno. 1994. Pathological Effects of Feeding Young Oreochromis Niloticus Diets Supplemented with Different Levels of Aflatoxin. Aquaculture 127 (1): 49-61.
6. Drabkin, DJ. (1946) Clinc. Chem. 164, 703.
7. Edds, G.T, (1973) Acute Aflatoxicosis: A Review. V.M.AJ.A. 162,4, 304.
8. Fiegg, (1973) Cl«. Chem,, 29, 1075.
9. Gad, S.C. and Weil, C.S. (1986) Statistics for Lexicologists, In; Hayes, A.W, (2nd ed.). Principles and Methods of Tautology : Raveo Press, New York, pp. 273-320.
10. Hasegawa, H., Sung, J.H., Matsumiya, S. and Uchiyama, M. (1996). Main Ginseng Saponin Metabolites Formed by Intestinal Bacteria. Planta Med. 62, 453-457.
11. Jantrarotai, W. and R.T. Lovell. 1990. Subchronic Toxicity of Dietary Aflatoxin B1 to Channel Catfish. J. of Aquatic Animal Health, 2: 248-254.
12. Jassar, B.S. and Balwant, S. (1993) Biochemical Changes in Experimental Aflatoxicosis in Broiier Chicken. Indian J. Animal Science 63 (8), 784.
13. King, J, (1965) Practical Clinical Eazymology. Van Nostrand Co, Ltd. Rpge) 132.

14. Kubena, F,L,» Harvey, B.R., Huff, £., W, and Corrier, E,D. (1990) Ffficacy of a Hydrated Sodium Calcium Aluminosilicate 10 Reduce the Toxicity of Afiatoxiii and T. 2 Toxin, Poultry Science 69, 1078.

15. Lee, S.J., Sung, J.H., Lee, S.J., Moon, C.K. and Lee B.H. (1999). Antitumor Activity of a Novel Ginseng Saponin Metabolite in Human Pulmonary Adenocarcinoma Cells Resistant to Cisplatin. Cancer Lett. 144, 339-343.

16. Lovell, R.T. 1992. Mycotoxins: Hazardous to Farmed Fish. Feed International, 13(3): 24-28.

17. Marisfeld, R,? Graoert, E. and Kautna, J. (1989) Mycotoxieosis-a Problem of Dairy Cowherds. Monatshefl fur Veterinar Medizin 44 (12), 409.

18. Mona, S. Zaki., M.H. Osfor., A. Tohamy and Iman M. Zytuun (2002). Some Clinicopathological and Nutritional Studies on Reduction of Aflatoxin Induced Hepatotoxicity in Clarious lazara Catfish By Fax-Atoxin and Nigella sativa Oil. Egypt. J. Microbiol. 37(2), 185-195.

19. Newperne, P,M. (1999) Chronic Aflatoxicosis In Animals and Poultry, J, Am. Vet. Med, Assoc., 263, 1269.

20. Pier, A.C. (1987) Aflatoxicosis and Immuno Suppression in Mammalian Animals. In M.S. Zuber, GB. Liilehoj and B, L. Rssifor (Ed.). Aflatoxin in Mam, pp. 65. Cimmyt, Mexico.

21. Pier, A.C, (1999) Major Biological Consequences of Aflatoxicosis in Animal Production, J, Artwi. Set, 70, 3964.

22. Rasmassen, B.H., Larscn, K., Hald, B., Mailer, O.B. and Ellng, F. (1986) Outbreak of Liver Cell Carcinoma Among Salt Water Reared Rainbow Trout Saimo Gairdoert in Denmark. Diseases of Aquatic Organisms 1, 191.

23. Reitman, S, and Frankel, S, (1946) Am. J. Clin. PuihoL 28, 26.

24. Robert, RA. (1989) Fish Pailiology. Second Edition, Baiilier Tindall, London. Philadeiphia., Sydney» Tokyo, Toronto.

25. Siesta, D. (1981) Am. Clin. Biochem, 6, 24.

26. Slppei, W.I,, Burnside, J.C. and Atwood, MB, (1983) A Disease of Swine and Cattle Caused by Eating Mouldy Corn. Proc. 6' Ann. Meet. Am. Vei Med. Assoc. pp. 174-181.

27. Sisk, D.B., Ciarlton, V.I.I. and Curtin, T,M, (1988) Experimental Aflatoxicosis in Young Swine. Am J. Vet. Res., 39, 1591.

28. Tacon, A.G. J. 1992. Nutritional Fish Pathology. Morphological Signs of Nutrient Deficiency and Toxicity in Farmed Fish. FAO Fish Technical Paper No. 330. Rome. 75 p.

29. 29. Wu, F.C. 1998. Retention of Diet-related Mycotoxins in Tissues of Channel Catfish. (http: / /www.egsz.or / BilogicalCurrentContent / Zoology?Comparative%2Physiology / TOXICOLOGY.html).

30. Tun, T.K. (2003). Experimental and Epidemiological Evidence on Non-organ Specific Cancer Preventive Effect of Korean Ginseng and Identification of Active Compounds. Mutat. Res. 523-524, 63-74.

16

Effect of Afla-Toxins B1 on Endocrin Status in Cat fish (*Clarious lazera*)

Mona S. Zaki*[1]; Olfat Fawzy[2]

ABSTRACT

The influence of dietary aflatoxins on body weight, immunity, and hormonal profile was studied in catfish. The results revealed that, administration of aflatoxins, and aflatoxins plus fax-A-toxin 0.1% in diet for 4 months decrease body weight, IgM, Insulin, Thyroxine however there were elevation in cortisol hormone level. Afla-toxins may induce an immunosuppressive effect on humoral immune response of tilapia Nilotica in *which* was suggested by reduction of immunoglobulin

Key words: Afla-Toxins; Endocrine; Cat fish; tilapia Nilotica; immunosuppressive.

INTRODUCTION

IgM, is the most important immune factor to neutralize bacteria and render them more succeptible to phagocytosis (Ingram, 1980). It is well known' that in mammals immunoglobulin production is closely related to endocrine status (Berezi, 1989) for example tyroid hormone enhance the production of

1. Department of Hydrobiology, National Research Center Dokki, Cairo, Egypt.
2. Department of Biochemistry, National Research Center Dokki, Cairo, Egypt.

immunoglobulins (Chen 1980). Cortisol intensify, suppress immunoglobulins production (Pottinger 1985). In teolosts cortisol level markedly increased following stressor exposure and elevated cortisol level results in a significant increase susceptibility to infectious. diseases (Pickering and Pottinger, 1985). The purpose of administration of fax-A-toxin particularly with Aflatoxin to know the effect of fax-A-toxin on Aflatoxin in fish. Many studies concerned the effects of cortisol on IgM production (Anderson et al. (1982). However there is no previous reports on the effect of. Aflatoxins on serum IgM and endocrine status. Many authors observed the effect of Afla toxins *on* liverdamage. The liver enzymes are changed with observation of malignant tumours (Ostrawski, 1984; and Evmgton et al. 1994).

The present work was under taken to study the effect of *afla* toxins on endocrine status and immunoglobulin M of tilapia fish, this fish was selected because their wide availability edibility in Egypt and their important ecological role m the River Nile.

MATERIAL AND METHODS

One hundred and twenty Tilapia Niloticus were used in the present study. Their live body weight averaged of 37.5 gram. The fish were healthy and clinically free from external and internal parasites. They were maintained *in* tanks containing well aireated water at atmospheric temperature for two weeks before the xperiments began. Fish were randomly distributed into four groups; each of 30 fish and 2 control groups, the first group fed Aflatoxin-free ration and used as negative control (C) while the second group (AFC) was fed of Aflatoxins contaminated corn (50 ug toxin/kg ration) and used as positive control. The third group fed aflatoxin- free ration with 0.01% fax-A-toxin. The fourth group fed aflatoxin contaminated corn (50 ug toxin/kg ration) with 0.1% Fax-A-toxin for four months daily. Sources of Aflatoxin is contaminented corn 50 lag toxin/kg ration.

The fish were fed by hand twice daily and feed consumption in all groups was recorded daily. Also the mortality rate and body weight of fish due to Afla-toxins were recorded (Table 16.1).

Ration

Ration used during trials contained 16.3% crude protein, 2.5% crude fat and 14% crude fibre, the digestible energy was 26% cal/kg. The diet contained feed additives which included minerals, vitamins and amino acids. Body weight measured every month for four month. Sources of Afla toxins present in corn (50 p.g toxin/kg ration).

Samples

Serum samples were collected 4 times at one month interval and Sera were frozen at -20 for later analysis. Serum cortisol, IgM, T4, and insulin were determined using kits.

IgM Determination

The serum IgM was measured according to Fuda et al (1991).

Preparation of Antisera

Antisera for Tilapia was prepared by immunizing rabbits as described by Hara (1976).

Catfish IgM Antibody

The procedure for labeling antibody fragment with enzyme was performed according to the method of Nagae et al (1993).

EIISA Assay Procedure

Double antibody sandwich Elisa according to the method of Matsubara et al. (1985) and Nsgae (1993)was used for determination of IgM.

Cortisol was estimated using radio immunoassay technique according to the method of Pickering and Potinger (1983) and Wedmyer (1970).

Serum thyroxine was estimated using radioimmunoassay (RIA) using coat (A) count provide by diagnostic product corporation Los Angelos U.S.A. (Deftoff 1979).

Insulin was determined by RIA according to the method described by Sundly (1991).

Statistical Analysis

The difference between the groups were calculated according to Snedecor and Cochran (1967) by t-test.

RESULTS

As shown in Tables (16.1-16.3) and there is a decrease in body weight in aflatoxins and aflatoxins plus fax-A-toxin 0.1% if compared with control groups.

Table (16.2) showed the influence of aflatoxins and aflatoxins plus fax-A-toxin on IgM. Highly significant decrease of IgM levels was detected in treated groups with afla toxin and fax-A-toxin 0.1%.

Table (16.3) showed the serum hormonal changes in infected fish treated with Afla Toxin & Fax-A-Toxin. The results revealed decrease level of insulin, and thyroxine while a highly significant elevation of cortisol level was observed.

DISCUSSION

IgM level was determined to find out information about fish immune system, which was previously investigated in different species by many authors as Matsubara et al. (1985) and Fuda et al. (1991).

Table 16.1: Effect of Aflatoxin on Body Weight of Cat Fish

Group	1 Month	2 Month	3 Month	4 Month
Aflatoxin	41.8	36.1	31.7	31.1
	38.0	34.2	34.0	28.3
	34.1	30.4	30.5	31.5
Aflatoxin + 0.1 Fax A toxin	43.0	40.3	41.2	41.5
	42.5	30.1	37.4	45.5
	35.5	41.2	31.2	32.6
Control	45.2	43.4	46.7	42.5
	46.0	41.1	41.4	51.6
	36.2	41.5	46.6	46.6
0.1% Fax a toxin	43.6	48.0	41.0	41.2
	44.1	41.4	47.8	44.1
	36.7	47.4	51.8	52.7

AF= Aflatoxin 50 μg/Kg c number of fish each group=30 body weight 1 gm

Table 16.2: Effect of Aflatoxin in 1gm μgm/ml in Cat Fish (clarious lazera)

	1 Month	2 Month	3 Month	4 Month
Control	2.86 ± 0.73	2.45 ± 0.30	2.54 ± 0.50	2.00 ± 0.80
Aflatoxin	1.58* ± 1.40	0.94* ± 0.36	0.98** ± 0.50	0.94** ± 0.72
Control + Fax A Toxin	1.54 ± 0.20	2.60 ± 0.14	2.68 ± 1.08	2.30 ± 1.40
A.F + Fax A Toxin	2.05* ± 0.54	2.16* ± 0.73	1.95** ± 0.27	1.76** ± 0.30

AF -> Aflatoxin 50 μg/Kg c number of fish each group = 30 .

In this work the purified IgM revealed a single preciption in this work reacted against specific polyvalent antiserum to catfish IgM a similar result was obtained by Bagee et al., (1993. They found that chum salmon (IgM) was detected by specific anti (IgM) antibodies.

While the lower limit was 5 mg/ml reported, by Fuda (1991) there is a significant decrease in IgM level in fish with afla toxins, if compared with control groups. Anderson et al. (1982) found a relation between cortisol and (IgM) as when cortisol increased (IgM) decrease.

The significant increase of cortisol level in intoxication with Afla to. groups could be attributed to stress factors and the intoxication have examine response of fish to stress factors e.g. crowding, continous handling, infection John et al., 1994, Barton et al., 1980, Strange, 1978 and Wedemger, 1970,reported that the elevation of cortisol with afla toxins and Fax A 0.1% toxin may attributed to intoxication, and continous handling of fish. These observations emphasizes the extreme care needed during design and *analysis* of experiments, involving the (HPI) axis of teleost fish due to extremly sensitive HPI axis. Similar results were reported by pickering and_Pottinger (1983).

Table 16.3: Effect of Aflatoxins on Hormonal Profile in Cat Fish

	Insulin lig/dl				Thyroxine				Cortisol ng/dl			
	1M	2M	3M	4M	1M	2M	3M	4M	1M	2M	3M	4M
Control	13.6 ± 0.31	10.5 ± 2.24	11.00 ± 2.62	13.08 ± 1.70	0.0882 ± 0.05	0.0854 ± 0.077	0.967 ± 0.027	0.950 ± 0.014	0.888 ± 0.16	0.887 ± 0.21	0.921 ± 0.34	0.954 ± 0.73
Aflatoxin	13.2* ± 0.16	12.01* ± 1.20	14.00 ± 1.27	11.08*	0.0640* ± 0.0330	0.0730* ± 0.022	0.0721* ± 0.039	0.0718* ± 0.0549	1.11** ± 0.30	1.42 ± 0.043	1.70** ± 0.027	1.75 ± 0.038
Control + Fax A Toxin	14.1 ± 012	13.50 ± 0.52	13.80 ± 0.23	13.72 ± 0.72	0.0942 ± 0.072	0.0988 ± 0.440	0.0943 ± 0.24	0.0849 ± 0.074	0.988 ± 0.33	0.942 ± 0.10	0.980 ± 0.50	0.962 ± 0.67
A.F. Fa A Toxin 0.1	13.00* ± 0.23	13** ± 0.27	12.00* ± 0.20	13.54* ± 0.21	0.0821* ± 0.069	0.0698* ± 0.023	0.0764* ± 0.0023	0.0804** ± 0.064	1.35* ± 0.83	1.26* ± 0.74	1.24* ± 0.86	1.18 ± 0.34

* P<0.01   A.F -> Aflatoin   ** P<0.05   M -> Month

Serum thyroxine (T4) concentrations in the serum of Tilapia species decreased in the intoxicated groups. It has been shown that intoxication, and chronic stress rin a marked long lasting depression of serum T_4 levels in Tilapia fish (Osborn et al 1978) and Milne and Leatherland, (1980). The response of thyroid gland of telosts fish needs further investigated with particular attention to possible relationship between the H.P.I. axis and pituitary thyroid axis. Milne and Leatherland. (1980), Osborn et al. (1978) and Mooreoud et al. (1977) using histological approach concluded that cortisol reduced thyroidal activity in sock eye salmon. The significant decrease of insulin values may be attributed to aflatoxin which may somehow reduce the metabolic activities in the aflatoxin inttoxicated fishes. The 'decrease in body weight was observed, while detectable agrees with Ostrowski[l] (1984), Hilton et al. (1987) and Sundly et al. (1991) as they observed a detectable decrease in body weight of duck infected with afla-toxin.

The aim of adminitration of Fax-A-Toxin particularly with Aflatoxin to know if Fax-A-Toxin eleminate Afla-toxins in the body of fish. In the present study Fax A Toxin not affect Afla-toxins as the results indicated that IgM, and endocrine status still not corrected or not return to the normal status in Tilapia fish.

In conclusions afla-toxin reduce of the humoral immune response as detected by decrease of IgM level, body weight and cortisol elevation. Suppress IgM, Thyroxine *(T4)* hormone and insulin levels. Fax-A-toxin has no significant effects on afla toxins.

REFERENCES

1. Abdel-Wahhab, M.A. Abdel-Galil, M.M., Hassan, A.M., Hassan, N.H., Nada, S.A., Saeed, A., El-Sayed, M.M. (2007): "Zizyphus Spina-Christi Extract Protects Against Aflatoxin B1-intitiated Hepatic Carcinogenicity" Afr. J. Trad. CAM 4 (3): 248-256.
2. Anderson, D.P.; Roberson, B.S. and Dixon, 0. W (1982): Immunosuppression Induced by Corticosteroid or an Alkylating Agent in Rainbow Trout. Dev, Comp. Immunol. Suppl. 2: 197-204.
3. Bagee, M.; Fuda, HI; Mara, H.; Kawamura, H. and Yamauchi (1993): Changes in Serum Immunoglobulin M (IgM) Concentrations during Early Development of Chum Salman as Determined by Sesitive Elisa Technique, Comp. Biochem. Physiology 106A: 69-74
4. Barton, B.A.; Peter, R.E. and Paulence C.R. (1980): Plasma Cortisol Level of Fingerling Rainbow Traut at rest and Subjected to Handling Continent Transport and Stocking Fish Aqua sci'37, 805-811.
5. Berezi, I. (1989) Immunoregulation by Neuroendocrine Factors Dev, Comp Immunol 13: 329-341.
6. Chen, Y. (1980): Effect of Thyroxine on the Immune Response of Mice invivo and vitro Immunol org 9, 269-276.
7. Defetoff, S. (1979): Thyroid Function Tests Endocrinology Degvoated Philadelphia Crume and Spratton. Vol. 1: 387-428.
8. Diesen, P. (1967): Insulin in Membrane and Metabolism P. Diesen Ed. William and Wilkins Bathmore 259-262.

9. Edvington, T.S.; Harvey, R.B.; and Kulena-D.F. (1994): Effect of Afiatoxins in Growing Lambs Fed Rumminally Degradable or Escapes Protein Sources. Journal of Animal science 72 (1274-1281).
10. Fuda, H.; Sayano, K; Yamaji, F. and Haraj. (1991): Serum Immunoglobulin M (IgM) during Early Development of masu salmon on Corhyrchus masu. Comp. Biochem. Physiol, 99A., 637-643.
11. John, F.; Carragler, and Christine, M.R (1994) : Primary and Secondary Stress Responses in Golden pereh Macquoria ambigua (J. comp. Biochem. Physiol. Vol. 107A No. 1 pp. 40-56.
12. Hara, A. (1976) Iron Binding Activity of Female Specific Serum Proteins Rainbo'' trout salm'o and chum salman Oncorchynchus Journal of Biochem. Physiology 427: 549-557.
13. Hilton, J.W.; Plisetskeya, E.M. and Leatheland, J.F. (1987): Dose oral 3, 5, 3 triiododthyroxine Affect Dietary Glucose Utilization and Plasma Insulin Levels in Rainbow trout. Fish physiol. Biochem. 4: 113-120.
14. Ingram, G.A. (1980): Substances Involved in the Natural Resistance of Fish to Infection. A Review J. Fish Biol, 16: 23-60.
15. Matsubara, A.; Mihara, S. and Kusuda, R. (1985) : Quantitation of Yellow Tail Immunoglobulin by Enzyme-linked Immunosorbent Assay (Flisa) Bull. Japan sac, Sci. Fish 51, 921-925.
16. Mooreoud, M.M, Mazeaud F & Donaldson E.M (1977): Primary and Secondary Effects of Stress Fish Some New Data with a General Review Trans Am Fish Soc 106, 201-212.
17. Milne R.S. and Leatherland J. F. (1980): Changes in Plasma Thyroid Hormones Following Administration of Exogenous Pituitary Hormones and Steroids Hormones to Rainbow Trout, Comp. Biochem. Physiol. 66A 679-686.
18. Nagae, M; Fuda, H; Hara, A. and Hamuchi, A. (1993): Changes in Serum Inunuaglobulin M(IgM) Concentrations during Early Development of churm salmon as Determined by Sensitive ELISA Comp. Biochem. Physiology pp. (69-74).
19. Osborn, R.H.; Sinpson, T.H. and Yaungson, A.F. (1978): Seasonol and Diurnal Rhythms of Thyroidal Status in the Rainbow Traut J. Fish Biol, 12, 531-540.
20. Ostrowski, M. (1984): Biochemical and Physiological Responses of Growing Chickens and Ducklings of Dietary Aflatoxins. Comp. Biochem. Physio. 79:1, 193-204.
21. Pickering, A.D. and Pottinger, P. (1983): Seasonal and diet Changes in Plasma Cortisol Levels of the Brown Trout, Salmo trutta L. Gen. Corn. Endocrinol, 49: 232-239.
22. Pickering, A.D. and Pottinger, T. G. (1985): Recovery of the Brown trout salmo trutta from Acute Handling Stress a Time-course Study J. Fish Biol Sundly 20: 229-249.
23. Snedecor, G.W. and Cochran, W.G. (1967): Statistical Methods Iawa State University press, Ames USA. pp. 327-329.
24. Sundly, A.; =Fliassen, K A. Blom, A.K. and Asyard, T. (1991): Plasma Insulin, Glucogan like Peptide and Glucose Levels in Response to Feeding, Starvation, Life Long Restricted Fed Starvation in Salmonids, Fish Journal of physiol. & Biochem. Vol. 9, No. 3. pp. 253-259.
25. Sundly, A.; Eliassent K,; Refsti T., and Plisetskaya E. (1991): Determination of Plasma Levels of Insulin, Glucogen and Glucogen like Peptide in Solomonids of Different Weights Fish Physiol., Biochem. 9: 223-230.
26. Strange, R.J. (1978): Changes in Plasma Cortisol Concentrations of Juvenile Salmonids during Stress. Ph.D., Thesis Oregan State University U.S.A.
27. Wedemyer, G.A (1970): The Role of Stress in the Disease Resistance of Fishes spec. Publs Am. Fish Soc. 5, 30-35.

Some Studies on Fish Deformity in Freshwater Fish in Egypt

Shawer R.[1]; Safinaz Gomaa[2]; Saleh. W.[3]
Soliman. M.K.[*4]; Khalil R[5]; Mona S. Zaki[6]

ABSTRACT

Fish anomalies are defined as presence of defects in particular parts of the body like vertebral column, mouth and caudal peduncle regions. This study was carried out on 400 fishes showed signs of anomalies (250 cultured, and 150 wild) collected from Alexandria, Kafr El-Sheikh and El-Behera Governorate in the period from June 2006 to May 2008. The clinical signs were in the form of, deformity of vertebral column, mouth and caudal peduncle. Also most fish were emaciated with dark discoloration of the external body. Internally, congestion of some internal organs (spleen, kidney and gills) with enlargement and paleness of liver, watery fluid in abdominal cavity were the main observed signs.

1. General Organisation of Veterinary Services, Egypt
2. National Inst. of Oceanography and Fisheries, Alex. Branch, Egypt
3. Dept. of Microbiology, Fac. of Agriculture, Cairo Univ., Egypt
4. Dept.of Poultry and Fish Diseases, Fac. of Vet. Med., Damanhour Univ., Egypt
5. Dept. Poultry and Fish Diseases, Fac. of Vet. Med, Alex. Univ., Egypt
6. Hydrobiology Dept.,Veterinary Research Division, National Research Center, Cairo, Egypt.

Ration analysis from affected farms was carried out to detect calcium deficiency effect on fish deformity which revealed 17 samples had calcium deficiency from total examined 250 by a ratio of 6.8%. Deformed fish were examined for cytogenetic effect which revealed 6 samples have cytogenetic anomaly. Infection with *Ichthyophonus hoferi* was 68 samples from total number of 250 cultured fish by a ratio of 27.2% and 30 samples from total number of 150 wild fish by a ratio of 20%. Infestation with *Myxosoma cerebralis* was 68 from total examined 250 cultured fish by aratio of 27.2% and 14 samples from total examined 150 wild fish by a ratio of 9.3%. The prevalence of infection with *Ichthyophonus hoferi* and *Myxosoma cerebralis* were higher in Kafr El-Sheikh governorate followed by El-Behera and Alexandria.

The prevalence of infection site with *Ichthyophonus hoferi* and *Myxosoma cerebralis* were higher in liver followed by kidneys, spleen and intestine respectively Histopathological changes of natural infected fish revealed changes of most affected organs as will as presence of cyst of *Myxosoma cerebralis* and spores of *Ichthyophonus hoferi* in many organs. Through this study we found that fish anomaliesproved to be affect fish economically either by low production or marketabilityAlso infectious causes of anomalies were of high percentage, so more studies and researches are of important in this situation to make planning for control.

Keyword: Fish deformity, freshwater.

INTRODUCTION

The aquaculture industry has been considered as one of the fastest growing agribusinesses over the past two decades (*USDA2000)*.

Fish anomalies occur in both freshwater and marine fish. They have bad economical effect, as they affect marketability and during processing the fillets might be very soft slimy and strong with some times off odors *(Reichenbach-klinke, 1965 and Amany 2010)*.

Infectious fish diseases considered as the main cause of reduction of fish farms production and its profitability *Woo (2004) and Ramaiah (2006)*.

Fish anomalies can be attributed to genetic, pathogenic, environmental and/or nutritional may be involved *(Noga, 1996 and Easa,1997)*.

These anomalies may be genetic, resulting from mutation or recombination either epigenetic, acquired during embryonic development or post embryonic acquired during larval or post larval development. *(Noga, 1996)*.

Skeletal anomalies ranging from modification in gill arch structures, fin rays to extreme vertebral deformation have been noted in fish farms polluted habitats *(Sloof, 1982)*.

The type of skeletal deformities differed according to the species of fish and causes *(Easa, 1997)*.

In Egyption study, the prevalence of infection with *Ichthyophoniosis* and *mycobacteriosis* was 32%. Prevalence was higher in cultured (40%) and female fish (44.7%) than for wild (24%) and males (22.6%). *(Nadia Abdelghany et al. 2008).*

This study was aimed to throw the light on the causes of fish deformity among wild and cultured fish in Egypt.

MATERIALS AND METHODS

Naturally Deformed Fish

A total number of 400 fish (250 cultured *Oreochromis niloticus* and 150 wild fish including 2 *Mugil capito,* 2 *Mugil cephalus,*1 *Bighead carp,* 1 *Gold fish and* 144 *Oreochromis niloticus*) were collected from 30 farms from different localities at Alexandria, Kafr El-Sheik and El-Behera Governorates (7 farms from Alexandria, 13 farms from Kafr El-Sheik and 10 farms from El-Behera) Ration samples were obtained from each farm for analysis.

The fish samples were collected during the period from June 2006 to May 2008. The body weight of the obtained fish was ranged from 40-150 g.

A total number of 12 fish were obtained a live from farms in El-Behera Governorate for studying the cytogenetic effect.

Clinical Examination

Clinical and postmortem examination of the collected fish were done according to the methods described by *Amlacher (1970) and McVicar, (1982)* to detect any clinical abnormalities like (Scoliosis, lordiosis, mouth deformity and loss of tail or fins) and any internal lesions.

Bacteriological and Mycological Examination

Samples from affected organs (spleen, liver, kidneys) were used for cultivation of Mycobacterium species on Trypticase soya agar at 32 C for 48 hrs. The suspected colonies was transported to Dorset egg media then incubated at 25C for 2 weeks

Mycological examination was done according to *McVicar (1982)* and Amany (2010) for the fish showing any deformity. Samples were taken by using sterile dissecting needle from the internal organs (liver, kidney, spleen and intestine) and inoculated onto the MEM- 10 and on Sabouraud's dextrose agar with 1% bovine serum. The inoculated plates and tubes were incubated at room temperature for 15 day.

Identification of the isolates was done according to the morphological characters including the hyphal growth and multinucleated spores through the microscopical examination of wet mount and stained preparation *McVicar (1982).* From the nodules appeared in affected organs of naturally infected cases, squash preparations were prepared.

Calcium Analysis

Ration samples were obtained from every farm where fish samples were collected for calcium analysis. The calcium was analyzed according to the method described by *Khoof (1991)* by analytical chemical method and the obtained results were judged according to *N.R.C (1987)*

Diagnosis of *Myxosoma cerebralis*

A fresh fish sample was put between two sterile slides and compressed then examined under light microscope (high power) for refractile bodies (Myxobolus cyst) according to *(Wolf & Markiw 1984)*.

Cytogenetic Analysis in Deformed Fish

The effect of deformity on the somatic chromosomes of *Oreochromus niloticus* was investigated using micronucleus test (MN) as described by *(Hayashi et al., 1998)*.

X-rays examination X-ray technique was carried out for 10 samples of deformed fish.

Histopathological Studies

Fresh specimens were collected from liver, spleen, gills, muscles and vertebral column for histopathological examinations Sections were stained by hematoxyline and eosin (H,E) according to the method described by *Culling (1983)*.

RESULTS

Isolation and Identification of *Ichthyophonus hoferi*

The young culture of *Ichthyophonus hoferi* on SDA + 1% bovine serum showed rupture of multinucleated bodies and release of spores through extra material discharge after 9 days while the, culture of *Ichthyophonus hoferi* on MEM-10 PH 7.0 showed hyphae with different sizes and formation of multinucleated bodies after 8 days of incubation. Localization and fixation of multinucleated bodies (ameaboblast) at the end of each hyphae with rupture of some ameoboblasts were noticed.

At pH 3.5 showed starting of hyphal growth after 24 hours post incubation. The hyphae produced many branches, extending of the hyphae to grow and increased in length, migration of cytoplasm to the apex of hypae after 3 days was noticed.

Rounding up of the apices of the hyphae after 7 days was also observed, finally all the hyphae rounding up to form spherical hyphae terminal bodies after 10 days.

In old culture chlamydo-spores formation around the multinucleated bodies extend to the test of stacked hyphae at 3 weeks were seen.

Culture of *Ichthyophonus hoferi* showing foamy white color of hyphal growth on M E M-10 (Fig. 17.4)

Isolation of *Ichthyophonus hoferi* were from 98 fishes (1 gold fish, 1 big head carp and 96 from *Oreochromus niloticus*)

Calcium Analysis

Analysis of rations obtained from farms in which the fish showed deformities for calcium examination revealed calcium deficiency in 17 samples. The ratio was less than the reported ratio by FAO. According to *N.R.C (1987)*, the ratio was less than 3.8 mg calcium/kg feed considered to be Calcium deficiency.

Identification *of Myxosoma cerebralis*

The examination of gills and vertebral column of affected fish revealed the presence of refractile bodies indicates *Myxosoma cerebralis* spores at different stages in 68 samples. The spores were ovoid in shape contain two polar capsules with sporoplsm of different sizes (Figs 17.5, 17.6, 17.7, 17.8, 17.9).

Cytogenetic Analysis

The genotoxic examination of collected fish revealed that, six samples monosex *Oreochromus niloticus* gave genotoxic effect for deformity (Figs. 17.10, 17.11)

Clinical signs and postmortem lesions of naturally deformed fish due to:

***Ichthyophonus hoferi* Infection**

Clinical signs of the deformed fish were in the form of excessive mucous on the skin, deformity of the vertebral column and congestion of some internal organs with paleness and enlargement of liver in some cases (Figs. 17.2, 17.3, 17.4). There were 68 fish of *Oreochromus niloticus* from the total 250 by ratio of 27.2% in cultured fish, and 30 fishes from the total 150 with a ratio of 20% in wild fish.

Calcium Deficiency

Emaciation and dwarfism, head size was comparatively larger than head region. The rays spin of fins were soft and easily turned down. Internally paleness of most viscera and watery fluid in the abdominal cavity were the main observed signs (Figs. 17.5, 17.6) in case of calcium deficiency samples. There were 17 samples of calcium deficiency from the total 250 with a ratio of 6.8%.

***Myxosoma cerebralis* Infestation**

Emaciation, dark discoloration of external body, deformed mouth and body and internally congested liver, spleen, kidney and gills (Figs. 17.7, 17.8, 17.9) were observed in case of deformed fish associated with *Myxosoma cerebralis* infestation. There were 68 samples from the total 250 with artio of 27.2 % in cultured fish and 14 samples from the total 150 with a ratio of 9.3% in wild fish.

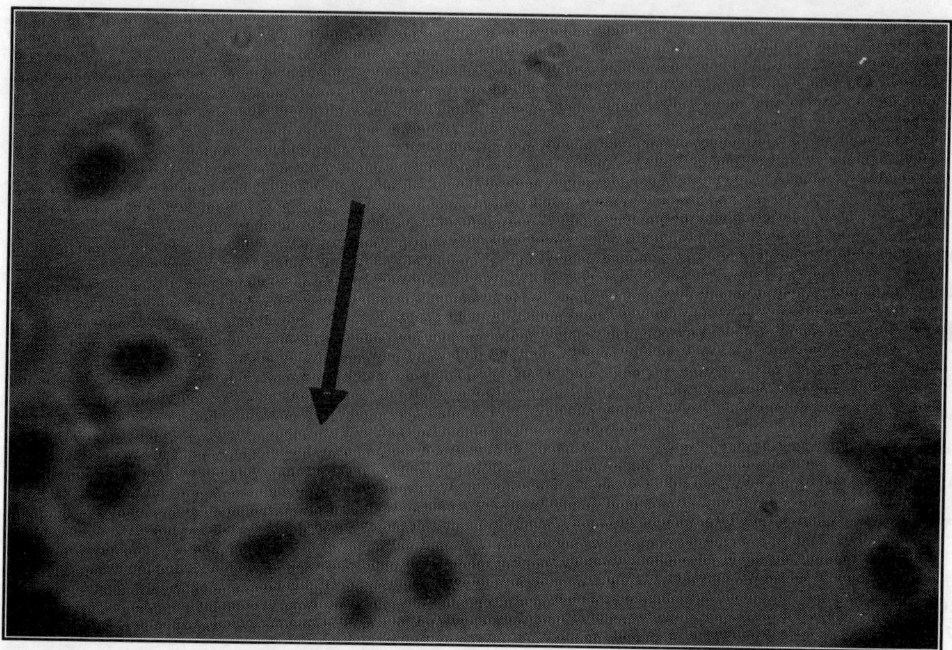

Fig. 17.1: **Peripheral Blood Erythrocytes of *Oreochromus. niloticus* Arrow: Clear Cytoplasm without Micronucleus.Microscopic Magnification X 1000**

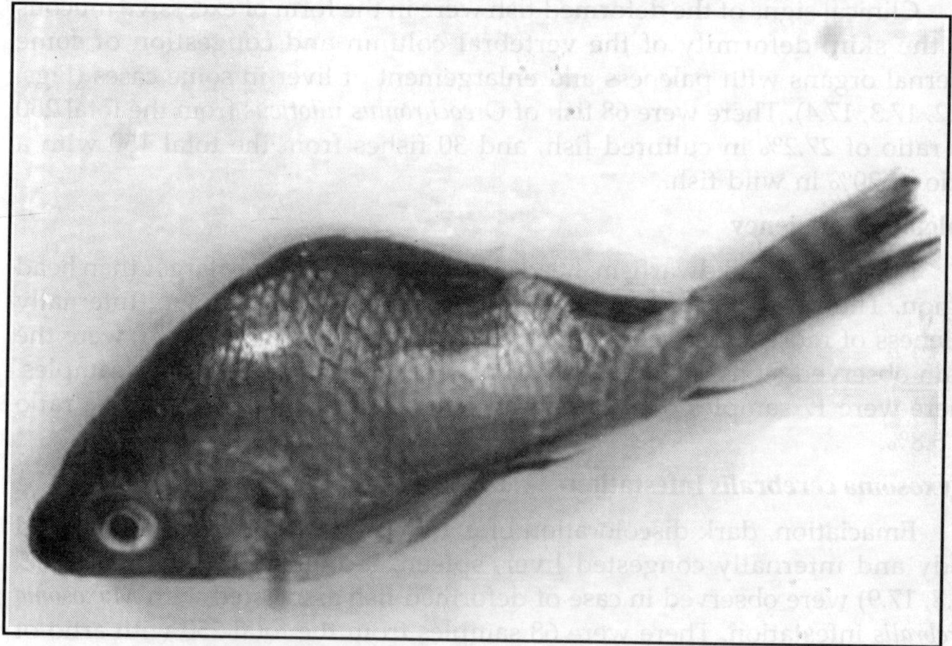

Fig. 17.2: ***Oreochromus niloticus*, Showing Anomalies due to Natural Infection with *Ichthyophonus hoferi***

Fig. 17.3: ***Oreochromus niloticus*, Showing Anomalies due to Natural Infection with *Ichthyophonus hoferi***

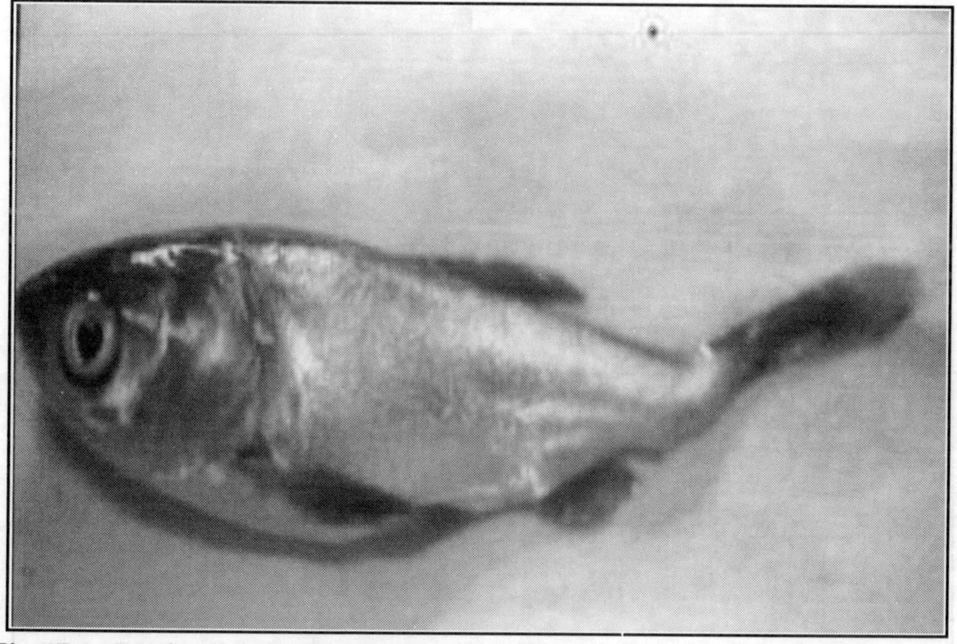

Fig. 17.4: ***Big head carp* Showing Anomalies due to Natural Infection with *Ichthyophonus hoferi***

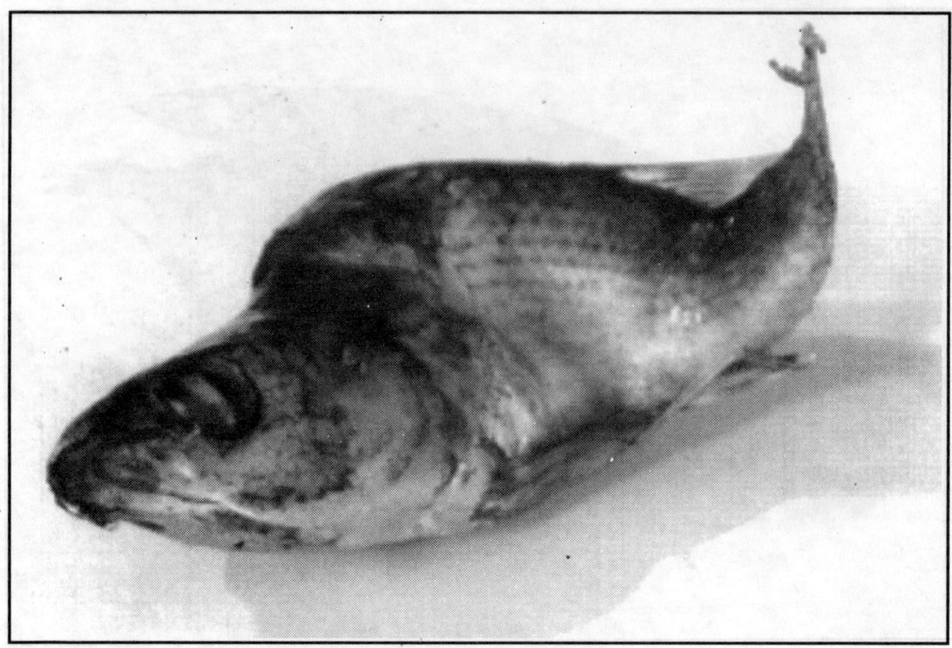

Fig. 17.5: Mmugil capito **Showing Anomalies due to Calcium Deficiency**

Fig. 17.6: Oreochromus niloticus, **Showing Anomalies due to Calcium Deficiency**

Fig. 17.7: Oreochromus niloticus **Showing Anomalies due to Natural Infection with** ***Myxosoma cerebralis***

Fig. 17.8: Oreochromus niloticus **Showing Anomalies due to Natural Infection with** ***Myxosoma cerebralis***

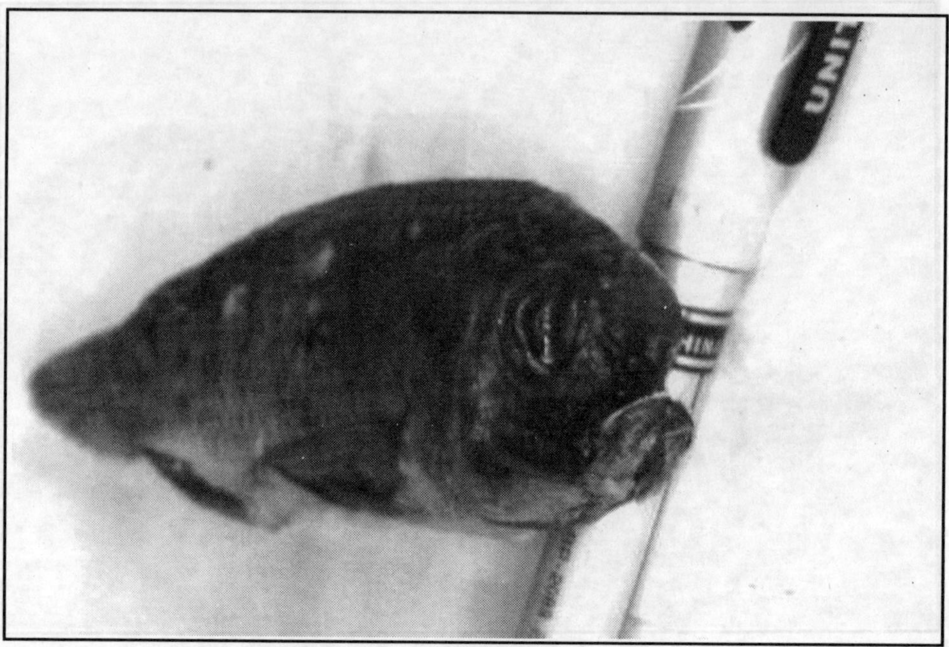

Fig. 17.9: **_Oreochromus niloticus_ Showing Anomalies due to Natural Infection with _Myxosoma cerebralis_**

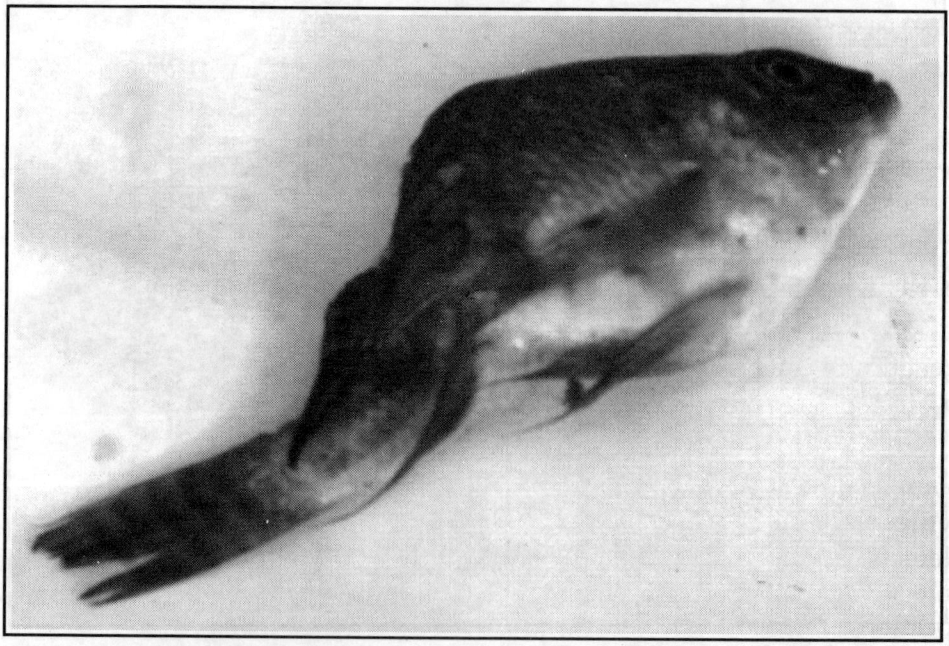

Fig. 17.10: **_Oreochromus niloticus_ Showing Anomalies due to Cytogenetic Effect in the Form of Mouth Deformity**

Fig. 17.11: Oreochromus niloticus **Showing Anomalies due to Cytogenetic Effect in the Form of Tail Loss**

Cytogenetic Deformity

The results of signs which recognized in case of fish with genetic deformity were absence of tail, parrot and bull dog mouth, deformed body and internally congestion of internal organs in some cases. (Figs.17.10, 17.11)

Fish had mixed infection by both of *Myxosoma cerebralis* and *Ichthyophonus hoferi* found to be deformed in body, mouth or tail.

There were 15 wild fish samples found to be deformed in a ratio of 10% from wild examined fish and 3.75% from the total samples.

X-ray Examinations

The X-ray of naturally infested fish by *Myxosoma cerebralis* and by genetically cause showed deformity of vertebral column (Fig. 17.12).

Prevalence of Deformed Fish in Different Localities

Mycological, parasitological examination, nutritional analysis and cytogenetic study of the collected fish revealed the prevalence of infection with *Myxosoma cerebralis*, *Ichthyophonus hoferi*, calcium deficiency and genetic defects among the examined fish. The data revealed that prevalence of infection in cultured fish was higher than in wild fish. With respect to the localities, the fish collected from Kafr- El-Sheikh showed higher infection rate than that obtained from Alexandria and El- Behera Governorates.

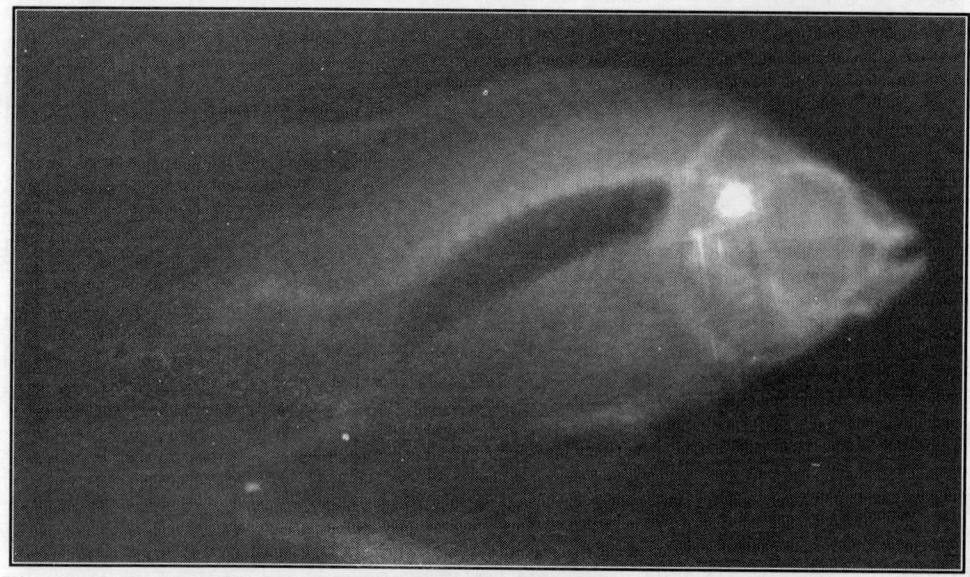

Fig. 17.12: **X-ray Film Showing Deformity of Vertebral Column of *Oreochromis niloticus* Fish due to Cytogenetic Effect**

Seasonal Prevalence of Deformed Fish

Regarding to the seasonal prevalence of *Ichthyophonus hoferi, Myxosoma cerebralis* and calcium deficiency in the examined fish, in the three Governorates the infection recorded in a higher prevalence during Autumn followed by winter and in a lower prevalence during summer in the examined fish.

Twenty random samples were tested for Cytogenetic effect as a cause of deformity and the results revealed six samples were positive for cytogenetic effect as shown in.

Bacteriological Examination

The result of bacteriological examination revealed no bacterial growth on the dorset egg media.

Histopathological Altration

Result of naturally collected samples, proved the presence of resting degenerated spore of *Ichthyphonus hoferi,* in hepatic tissue with severe eosinophilic granular cells (EGCs) infiltration as a tissue reaction against infection. Perivascular severe lymphocytic infiltration with severe hepatic hydropic vacuolation, and diffuse filamentous necrosis were seen. Degenerated spores between muscle bundles with minimal tissue reaction appeared as infiltration of few melanophores adjacent to spores, enlargement and hyperactivation of melanomacrophage centers., multinucleated resting spores surrounded with fibrosis layers of chronic inflammatory cells as chronic tissue reaction were recorded.

DISCUSSION

Lordiosis is one of the most severe deformities developing in reared fish and affect body shape, mostly the posterior abdominal region framed by the anterior and middle base of the pelvic fin. *Shimasaki et al. (2006).*

The present study was carried out on cultured and wild fish from different species morphologically showed signs of anomalies to investigate the main causes of anomalies via cytogenitical, mycological, bacteriological and parasitological examinations in addition to ration analysis.

The results revealed that the fish anomalies due to either *Myxosoma cerebralis* or *Icthyophonus hoferi* were 136 cases from the total number of 250 cultured fish and 44 from the total number of 150 wild fish. These results proved that fish anomalies may be due to infectious or non infectious causes.

Noga (1996) and *Easa (1997)* mentioned that many factors, genetic, pathogenic, environmental and / or nutritional may be causes of fish anomalies.

The clinical signs of naturally infected fish revealed that the shape of anomalies among fish were varied from deformity of vertebral column to dwarfism, emaciation, deformed mouth or absence of tail. These signs were reported by *McCann and Jasper (1972)*. The differences in the shapes of anomalies may be related to fish species and causes of anomalies as well as severity of infection with the pathogenic agent *(Easa, 1997)*.

Ichthyophoniosis is considered as an important newly recorded disease among cultured tilapia species at different localities in Egypt *(Manal Easa 2002)*.

Spanggaard et al. (1996) and *Mellergaard and Spanggaard (1997)* have reported *Icthyophonus hoferi* as a cause of Ichthyophoniosis and deformity among fish.

During this study, *Icthyophonus hoferi* was isolated from different species of fish. The isolated fungus were submitted to complete morphological and cultural examinations.

The young culture of *Icthyophonus hoferi* on SDA+1 %bovine serum showed rupture of multinucleated bodies and release of spores through extra material discharge after 9 days.

Culture on MEM at pH 7 showed hyphae with different sizes and formation of multinucleated bodies after 8 days.

At pH 3.5 showed starting of hyphal growth after 24 hrs post culturing which extend and produce many branches and form spherical hyphae terminal bodies after 10 days.

The growth characters of *Icthyophonus hoferi* were reported by *Ziedan (1999)*.

Regarding to the clinical signs and post mortem lesions of *Icthyophonus hoferi* infection were mainly in form of hemorrhage, congestion of body surface with dark discoloration and emaciation. Internally enlargement of liver, congested kidney and gall bladder, heart with abdominal fluid.

These may be attributed to the effect of quiescent cyst after settled in the different organs and made tissue damage (*Mcvicar and Mclay, 1985).*

Deformity is the most important lesion occur due to *Icthyophonus hoferi* these may be due to migration of quiescent cyst (infective stage) to skeletal muscle around vertebral column. The fish try to localize the cyst which usually occurred by surrounding the cyst by connective tissue which replace the myofibers. The end result will be permanent extension of the muscles which lead to moving the vertebrae from its place and finally the deformity occur *(Chauvier and Mortier- Gabet,1984 and* Amany 2010)

These signs mentioned by *Mcvicar* and *Mclay (1985)* who revealed that the most obvious lesions due to *Icthyophonus hoferi* infection occurred in the white muscle, heart, liver and kidney in herring. In cases of heavy infections normal organ tissue may be replaced by the cyst and C.T. Intern lead to impairing the organ function.

Also *Kocan et al. (2004)* reported that 20% of Yukon river purchased fish were discarded because of muscle tissue damage caused by *Icthyophonus hoferi.*

Myxosoma cerebralis is an important chronic parasitic disease of fish responsible for anomalies especially skeletal deformities *(Wolf et al. 1986).*

In this study *Myxosoma cerebralis* spores revealed high incidence (21%) from examined (82) samples which found harboring *Myxosoma cerebralis* spores in organs.

This result can confirm the role played by *Myxosoma cerebralis* in fish deformity.

In the present study the signs of deformity resulting from *Myxosoma cerebralis* was mainly in vertebral column and mouth. That comes in accordance with the tropism of myxozoan spores to vertebral column multiplication between vertebrae causing deformity and to the upper and lower jaw resulting in deformity of mouth. In addition the emaciation and ascitis may be related to the chronicity of disease which make depletion of many elements of fish body especially protein which come in contact with that described by *(Wolf et al. 1986).*

The deformity which occurred in case of *Myxosoma cerebralis* infestation may be attributed to myxozoan spores multiplication make destruction of the cartilaginous elements of the skeleton leading to the chronic phase of the disease characterized by skeletal deformities especially when the infestation occurred in young fish since the calcium precipitation not completed yet *EL Matbouli et al. (1995)*

Also Stoskoph(1993) and *Noga (1996)* reported that trout infected with *Myxosoma cerebralis* developed misshape of body that mainly in the form of deformed caudal area or curvature of the spine with permanently bent and opened mouth.

In the present study the prevalence of *Myxosoma cerebralis* infestation was 68 samples from the total number of 250 by ratio of 27.2% in cultured deformed fish and 30 samples from the total number of 150 by a ratio of 9.6% in wild deformed fish. This may refer to the role of over-crowded and other aspects of culture systems which make the infestation more easy than wild fish infestation. Moreover, the chance for infestation is quite high.

Calcium deficiency is considered one of the main causes of fish deformity.

During this study the ratio of deformed fish due to calcium deficiency was 6.8% which come in accordance with role of calcium deficiency in fish deformity. The main lesions were softness of fin rays and spins.

The results of ration analysis revealed that Calcium levels were less than 3.8 mg/kg diet. The *N.R.C (1987)* considered Calcium level less than 3.8 mg/kg as Calcium deficiency The negative results of bacteriological, parasitological and mycological examination of deformed fish plus low level of calcium in ration (less than 3.8 mg/kg diet) gave us support to refer these deformities due to calcium deficiency.

Fish deformity due to calcium deficiency was more prevalent in young ages as This may be concerned to the nature of skeletal apparatus of young fish that mainly is gummy and weak so effect will be more and easy for deformity occurrence *Amlacher (1970)*.

Also, in the young fish, the ossification center not closed yet and the precepitation of calcium is week.

Heupel et al. (1999) mentioned that skeletal anomalies are quite common in young fish and may be due to inadequate levels of vitamins, calcium or tryptophan.

Six cases from collected samples were due to genetic causes. These were supported by the genotoxic examination which gave positive results. In the same time the parasitological, bacteriological and mycological examinations were negative which highly supported the causes of genotoxic effect.

This conclusion was supported by *Heupel et al. (1999)* who found that genetic deformities in fish has a minor rank in the risk of aquaculture processes.

Kumar and Thakar (2004) concluded that deformity caused alterations in the chromatin conformation of AR promoter and reduction in its accessibility to DN asel in the brain cortex of adult male mice.

Concerning to localities Kafr-elSheikh Governorate showed higher infection rate with *Myxosoma cerebralis*, *Icthyophonus hoferi* and cases of calcium deficiency than that collected from Alexandria and El-Behera. The possible explanation of higher prevalence in Kafr-elsheikh is that the high number of fish farms which present beside each other using the same water drained from the neighbor farms. Moreover they mainly use fish meal for rations and poultry manure which may contain infective stage of *Icthyophonus hoferi* (quiescent cyst) and infected fish used in feed manufacture *(Lauckner 1984).*

Regarding to the seasonal prevalence of *Myxosoma cerebralis* and *Icthyophonus hoferi* infections in examined fish, the higher prevalence of infections was recorded during the autumn followed by winter, summer and spring seasons respectively.

The possible explanation may be due to the stress effects which caused by low temperature during the winter which interne facilitate the infection with *Icthyophonus hoferi* and infestation with *Myxosoma cerebralis.*

Amany Abdelwahab et al. (*2003*) reported that *Icthyophonus hoferi* proved to be higher during winter (68.1%) in *Oreochromis niloticus.*

In concerning to distribution of *Icthyophonus hoferi* and *Myxosoma cerebralis* in different organs of infected fish showed higher prevalence of infection in liver, kidney, spleen and intestine respectively.

These can be explained that the infection occur mainly in the highly vascular organs with high blood supply. Also, these organs may be the right tropism for these causes.

Faisal et al. (1985) recorded a higher prevalence of infection in liver followed by kidney, spleen and intestine of examined *Claris lazera* infested with *Icthyophonus hoferi* in a rate of 42%, 36%, 14% and 4% respectively.

Also *Noga (1996)* and *Ziedan (1999)* stated that the principle infected organs with *Icthyophonus hoferi* are that rich with blood (parenchymatous organs).

Histopathological changes were mainly in the form of viable multinucleated spores beside degenerated one in hepatic and pancreatic tissues with atrophy and necrotic focci, advanced acute cellular swelling of hepatic cells, perivascular severe lymphocytic infiltration with severe hepatic hydropic vacuolation this may be attributed to the effect of *Icthyophonus hoferi* infection.

Also severe eosinophilic granular cells infiltration of hepatopancreas, degenerated spores between muscle bundles with infiltration of melanophores adjacent to spores of *Myxosoma cerebralis*, degeneration of perichondrial tissue of cartilage these changes can be occurred due to *Myxosoma cerebralis* infestation.

These results refers mainly to the tissue reaction against both *Icthyophonus hoferi* and *Myxosoma cerebralis* spores beside the nature of multiplication through target organs lead to signs of inflammation. At the same time presence of the spores through infected tissues insure the infection.

Rand (1991) detected the resting and germinating spores surrounded by chronic granulomatous reaction with pleocellular infiltration in the infected organs with *Icthyophonus hoferi*. Moreover the positive results of the roles played by *Icthyophonus hoferi* in deformity of vertebral column were proved by X- ray which done for the infected fish.

REFERENCES

Abdelaziz, R.A. (2010): Some studies on Ichthyophonosis in Cultured Fresh Water Fish. M.V.Sc, Facu. of Veterinary Medicine Alexandria University.

Amany, A.A.; Shaheen, A.A.; Ahlam, A. and Manal, E. (2003): Studies on *Icthyophonosis* in Nile Tilapia (*Oreochromis niloticus*). 3rd Int. Sci. Conf. Mansoura. 1123-1140.

Amany, M. (2010): Studies on Some Systemic Mycotic Affections in Cultured Freshwater Fish. Ph.D.V.SC. Fac. of Vet. Med. Alex. Univ.

Amlacher, E. (1970): Textbook of Fish Diseases. P. 117-135. T.F.H. Publication, Neptune, U.S.A.

Cavas, R.C. and Ergene, G.; Richards, R.S. and Bucke, D. (2005): Further Consideration of the Hematology of Proliferative Kidney Disease (PKD) in *Rainbow trout, Salmogairdneri Richardson*. Journal of Fish Disease. 10, 435-444.

Chauvier, G. and Mortier, G.J. (1984): Premiers Observations du pouvoir pathogene d' *Ichthyophonus* pour oiseaux. Annales Parasitologie Paris. 59, 427-431.

Culling, C.F. (1983): Handbook of Histopathologic and Histochemical Staining. 3rd Ed., Buterworth London.

Easa, A.I. (1997): Mycotic Infection in Cultured Fish in Egypt. MVSC Suez Canal Univ.

El-Matbouli, M.; Hoffmann R.W.and Mandok, C. (1995): Light and Electron Microscopic Observations on the Route of the Triactinomyxon-sporoplasm of *Myxobolus cerebralis* from Epidermis into Rainbow Trout (*Oncorhynchus mykiss*) cartilage. J Fish Biol 46: 919-935.

Faisal, M.; Torky, H. and Richenbach-Klinike, H. H. (1985): A Note on Swinging Disease Among the Labyrinth Catfish (*clarias lazera*). J. Egy. Vet. Ass. 45, 1: 53-60.

Halos, D.S.; Alexandra, H.P.H. and Kocan, R. (2005): *Ichthyophonus* in Puget Sound Rockfish from the San Juan Islands Archipelago and Puget Sound, Washnigton, USA. Journal of Aquatic Animal Health. 17: 222-227.

Hayashi, R.; Wergeland, H.I.; Aasjord, P.M. and Endersen, C. (1998): Enhanced Antibody Response in Atlantic Salmon *(Salmo salar L.)* to *Aeromonas salmonicida* cell wall Antigens Using a Bacterin Containing 1, 3.

Heupel, M.R.; Wooster, G.A.; Gethell, R.G. and Timmons, M.B. (1999): Mycobacteriosis Infections of Tilapia (*Oreochromis niloticus*) in Circulation Production Facility. J. of World Aquaculture Soc. 29, 335-339.

Khoof, J.D. (1991): Zebrafish as a Model Host for *Mycobacterial tuberculosis* Pathogenesis. Acta Trop. 91 (1): 53-68.

Kocan, R. and Hershberger, P. (2006): Differences in *Ichthyophonus* Prevalence and Infection Severity Between Upper Yukon River and Tanana River *Chinook salmon, Oncorhynchus tsawytscha* (Walbaum), Stocks. Journal of Fish Diseases 29 (8): 497.

Kumar, J.D. and Thakur, T. (2004): Zebrafish as a Model Host for *Streptococcal* Pathogenesis. Acta Trop. 91 (1): 53-68.

Lauckner, G. (1984): Agents: Fungi. In Diseases of Marine Animals. Vol. IV. Part I. Edited by O. Kinne. Biologische Anstalt Hegoland. Hamburg. pp. 89-0113.

Leah, M.; Lewis, M. and Santosh, P.L. (2007): Effects of Moderately Oxidized Dietary Lipid and the Role of Vitamin E on the Development of Skeletal Abnormalities in Juvenile Atlantic halibut (*Hippoglossus hippoglossus*). Aquaculture 262 (2007) 142-155.

Manal, A.A.E.; Nahla, R.H. El-K. and Easa, M.El-S. (1996): Some Epizootiological Aspects of *Icthyophonosis* in Freshwater Fish from Egypt. 7th Sci. Cong. Vet. Med. Asuit, Egypt., pp. 290-305.

McMann, H. and Jasper, R. (1972): Studies on the Pathogenesis of Bacterial Infection in Cultured Yellow Tails, *Seriola Spp*: Effect of Crude Exotoxin Fractions from Cell-free Culture on Experimental *Streptococcal* Infection. Journal of Fish Diseases. 5, 471-478.

Mcvicar, J.A. (1982): Health Maintainance and Principle Microbial Diseases of Cultured Fishes, 1999 IOW a State University Press, Ames, Iwa-181-209.

McVicar, A.H. and McLay, H.A. (1985): Tissue Response of Plaice, Haddock, and Rainbow trout to the Systemic Fungus *Ichthyophonus*. In: Ellis, A. E. (ed.) Fish and Shellfish Pathology. Academic Press. London, pp. 329-346.

Mellergaard, S. and Spanggaard, B. (1997): An *Ichthyophonus hoferi* Epizootic in Herring in the North Sea, the Skagerrak, the Kattegat and the Baltic sea. Diseases of Aquatic Organisms. Dis Aquat Org. 28: 191-199.

Nadia, A.; Abd-El-Ghany, M.S. and El-Ashram, M.M. (2008): Diagnosis of *Icthyophoniasis* in *Oreochromis niloticus* in Egypt by Polymerase Chain Reaction (PCR). 8th International Symposium on Tilapia in Aquaculture. 1307-1328.

Nadia, A.G. and Hoda, M. Abd-alla (2008): A Trail for Treatment of *Icthyophonosis* in Cultured *Oreochromis niloticus* Using Focus and Neem Plants. 8th International Symposium on Tilapia in Aquaculture pp. 1329-1349.

Noga, P. (1996): Response of Eosinophilic Granule Cells of *Gilthead seabream (Sparusaurata, Teleostei)* to Bacteria and Bacterial Products. Cell Tissue Res. Jan. 287 (1): 223-30.

N.R.C. (1987): Guidline of Animal Ration Content and Ration Quality: Swiz No. 173.

Ramaiah, A. (2006): ICES Identification Leaflets for Diseases and Parasites of Fish and Shelfish. Bacteria of Marine Fish: Leaflet NO. 56.

Rand, T.G. (1991): Studies on the biology of *Ichthyophonus hoferi* (Plehn and Muslow, 1911) from Nova Yellowtail Flounder, *Limandu ferruginea* (Storer). Dis. Abst. Int. Pt. B. Sci. and Eng. Vol. 51, No. 11.

Shimasaki,Y.O.; Suguru, I.; Yoshiyuki, I.; Joon, I.k.; kei, N.; Hisaya, I. and Tsuneo, H. (2006): Effect of Tributyltin on Reproduction in Japanese Whiting, *Sillago japonica*. Marine Environmental Research 62 (2006) S 245-S 248.

Sloof, T.S. (1982): Bacterial Isolation in Marine Fish. Japan Conf. (7): (3): (105-108).

Stoskoph, T.A. (1993): Annu. Rev. Immunol. 2, 283-318.

USDA, (2000): Census of Aquaculture. National Agricultural Statistics Services, Washington, DC.

Woo, P.T.K. (2004): Fish Diseases and Disorders. Vol. 3, Viral. Bacterial and Fungal Infections. CABI Publishing, London, UK.

Wolf, K. and Markiw, M.E. (1984): Biology Contravenes Taxonomy in the *Myxosoma*: New Discoveries Show Alternation of Invertebrate Hosts. Science, 225: 1449-1452.

Ziedan, A.H.H. (1999): Comparative Study Between Hormonal Effect and Hybridization on the Susceptibility of Tilapia to Infection with *Ichthyophonus hoferi* Fungus. M.V. Sc. Thesis (Fish Medicine & Management) Fac. of Vet. Med., Cairo University.

18

Studies on Prevailing Cestodiasis in Wild African Catfish *Clarias Gariepinus* at Kafr El-Sheikh Governorate

Eissa, I.A.M.[*1]**; Viola, H. Zaki**[2]**; Nadia, G.M. Ali**[3]**; Mona S. Zaki**[4]

ABSTRACT

A total number of 200 fish (50 fish in each season) were collected randomly and examined for presence of cestodes. Two species of cestodes were recovered as *Polyonchobothrium clarias* and Monobothria sp. with infestation rate of 50.5% (101out of 200) and 14.5% (29 out of 200) respectively. Seasonally, *P clarias* was prevalent in spring and summer while Monobothria sp. was prevalent in spring, autumn and winter with no record in summer. There was significant decrease in the total serum proteins, albumin and globulin of infested fish comparatively with non-infested fish. The histopathological alterations were manifested as destruction, desquamation and sloughing of affected tissue mucosa with presence of degenerative changes.

Keywords: Cestodes, Clarias gariepinus, Polyonchobothrium clarias, Monobothria sp., histopathology, serum protein, prevalence.

1. Dept. of Fish Diseases and Management, Fac. of Vet. Med. Suez Canal Univ., Egypt.
2. Dept. of Fish Diseases and Management, Fac. of Vet. Med., Mansoura Univ., Egypt.
3. Veterinary Division, Kafr-Elsheikh Governorate, Egypt.
4. Dept. of Hydrobiology, National Research Center., Egypt.

INTRODUCTION

Fish is important as a source of protein with low cholesterol level in the diets of the human and economically as a source of subsistence income (Aken'ova, 2000). Fish not only provide food for immediate consumption but people rely directly or indirectly on fishing for their economic survival and a source of job. In Egypt, parasitic diseases represent about 80% of fish diseases (Eissa, 2006). Parasitic infections in fish cause decreased production and economic losses through direct fish mortality, reduction in fish growth, fecundity and stamina, increase susceptibility of fish to other diseases and high cost of treatment (Cowx, 1992). Under natural conditions 50-90% of freshwater fishes harbor at least one species of parasites (Sineszko, 1979).

The present study was designed to investigate the prevalent diseases caused by cestodes in wild African catfish *Clarias gariepinus* at Kafr El-Sheikh governorate. Besides, determination of total and seasonal prevalence, histopathological alterations and serum proteins were discussed.

MATERIALS AND METHODS

Fish

A total number of 200 *Clarias gariepinus* ranged between 45 to 315 g in body weight and from 18 to 39 cm in total length were collected randomly alive from river Nile at Kafr El – Sheikh Governorate during 2011 as 50 fish seasonally. Fish were kept in glass aquaria and supplied with chlorine free tap water with continuous aeration and filtration according to Innes (1966).

Clinical Picture

Alive fish were examined for clinical signs and postmortem lesions as described by Austin and Austin (1987).

Blood Sampling

Blood samples were collected from the caudal blood vessels and serum was obtained by centrifugation of collected blood at 5000 rpm according to Rowley (1990).

Parasitological Examination

The gastrointestinal tract was separated from the other internal organs then the stomach was separated from the intestine and each part examined. In clean Petri dish, stomach was opened and intestinal mucosa was stripped off by scalpel and washed with normal saline in another clean dry Petri dish. Gall bladder was separated, opened and examined. Cestodes were collected and preserved in alcohol formalin acetic acid and stained with Semichon's acetocarmine stain then the whole mount of collected cestodes was done according to Woodland, (2006). The collected cestodes were identified according to the identification key of Yamaguti (1958, 1959 and 1961).

Serum Analysis

In 20 fish (10 infested and 10 non-infested), serum total proteins were determined according to the method described by Peters *et al.* (1982), serum albumin was determined according to Peters (1970) and serum globulin was calculated by subtraction of albumin value from total protein value as described by Doumas and Biggs (1972). The data of serum protein analysis were statistically analyzed for variance (ANOVA) and least significant difference as described by Snedecor and Cochran (1989) using and (Med Calc. version 11, 2010) computer statistical software. Data were evaluated as significant at P d" 0.05.

Histopathological Examination

The histopathological examinations of affected tissue (intestines, stomach and gallbladder) were performed as described by Drury and Wallington (1980).

RESULTS AND DISCUSSION

The clinical signs appeared on the infested fish were weakness, severe emaciation, anemia, imbalanced swimming, some infested fish showed sluggish movement, loss of condition with paler coloration (Plate, 18.1) which was in agreement with that described by Islam and Woo (1991), Hassen (2002), Eissa (2002), Nadia Ali (2007) and Sabri *et al* (2010).

Monobothrium sp. was isolated from the intestine that appeared hemorrhagic and congested leading to intestinal obstruction (plate 18.1). Monobothria was white in color, elongated. It has large rounded or triangular scolex Plate 18.2 (d). The body length ranged between 7-40 mm and body width ranged between 2.5-4.5 mm. The testis located laterally, appeared as oval follicles, the ovary laterally located in the posterior part of the worm and occupying the two lateral sides (Plate 18.2). The male genital pore opens slightly anterior to the female one. The female genital pore occurred in the middle of the worm. The egg was rounded in shape; these descriptions were similar to that described by Nadia Mahfouz (1991), Mwita and Nkwengulila (2004), Oniye *et al.* (2004) and Oofintoye (2006) who isolated Monobothrium sp. from the intestine of *Clarias gariepinus*.

Polyonchobothrium clarias was isolated from the gall bladder that appeared enlarged with thickened bile duct and containing pale colored watery bile. It was long ranged from 60-100 mm in length, 0.5-1 mm in width. The scolex was elongated, triangular in shape and carries one raw of hooks and bears laterally two shallow bothria Plate 18.1 (h), segmentation begin directly after the scolex with immature stages then mature stages. The ovary is rounded to oval in shape and centrally located in the segment Plate 18.2 (a).The eggs are spherical and containing a mass of rounded cells. The worm attached mainly inside the gall bladder near the neck of bile duct. These findings agree with that recorded by Wabuke – Bunoti (1980) who isolated *Polyonchobothrium clarias* from the gall bladder of naturally infested *Clarias mossambicus*.

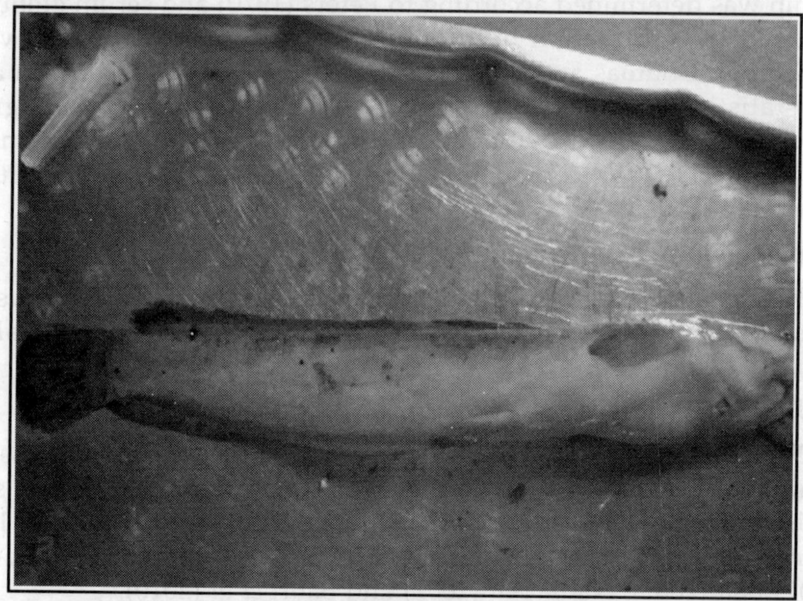

Plate 18.1 (a) Heavily Infested Fish Showing Fading Colouration

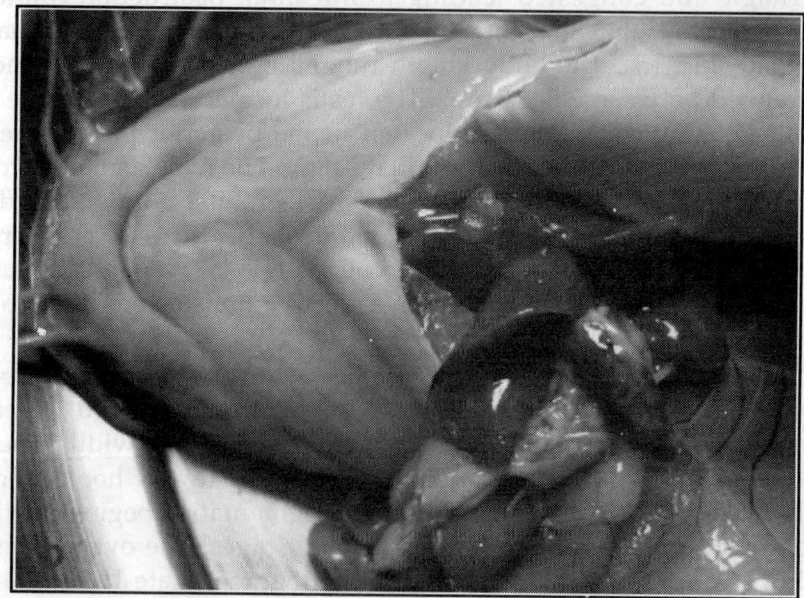

Plate 18.1 (b) Enlarged Distended Gall Bladder Containing *Polyonchobothrium clarias*

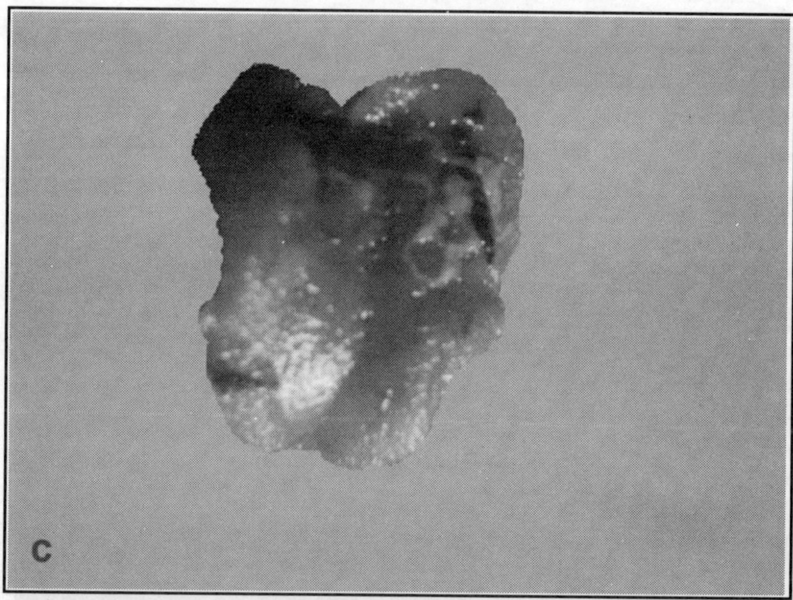

Plate 18.1 (c) Glandular Stomach Containing *Polyonchobothrium clarias*

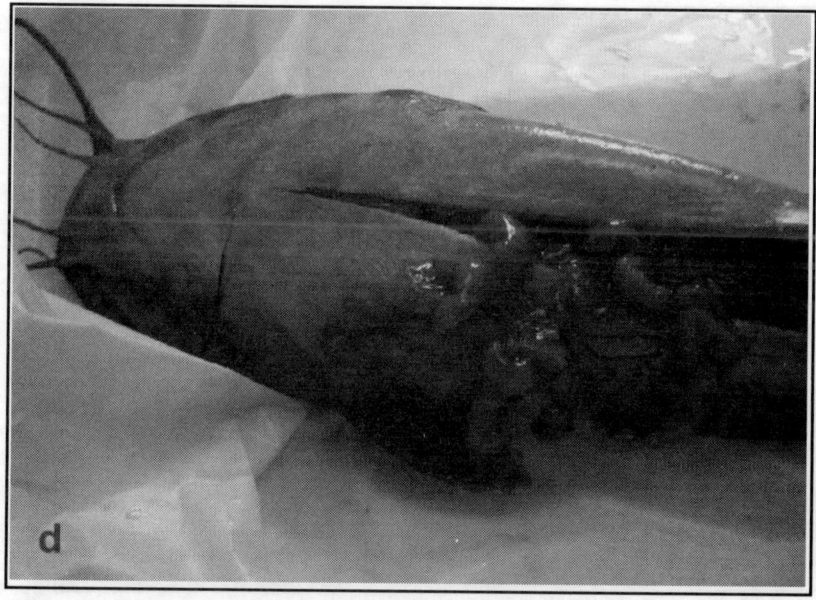

Plate 18.1 (d) Congested Intestine of Infested Fish with Monobothria sp.

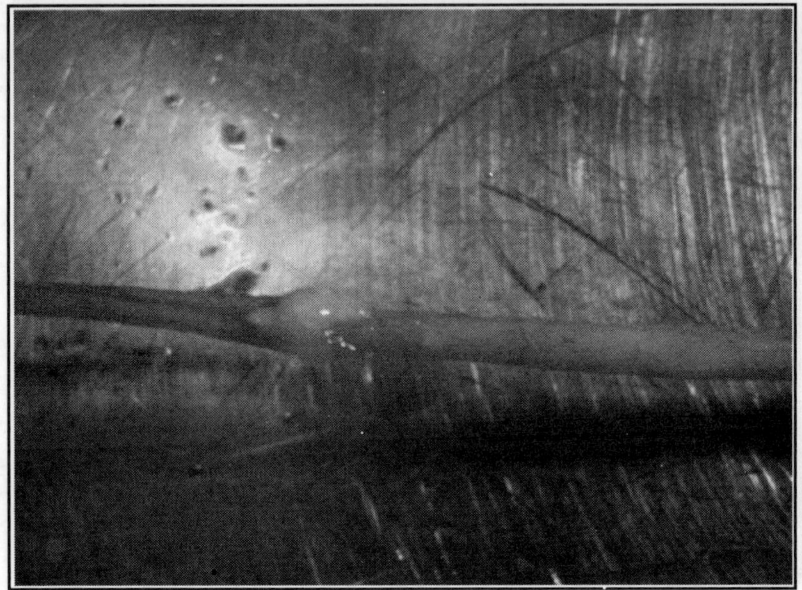

Plate 18.1 (e) Intestine of Heavily Infested Fish Occluded with Great Number of Monobothria sp.

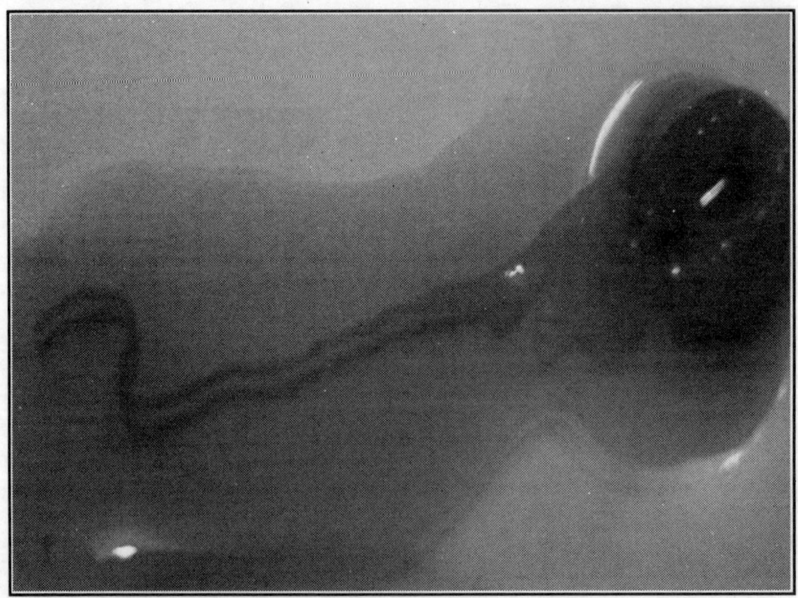

Plate 18.1 (f) Gall Bladder Containing Great Number of *Polyonchobothrium clarias*

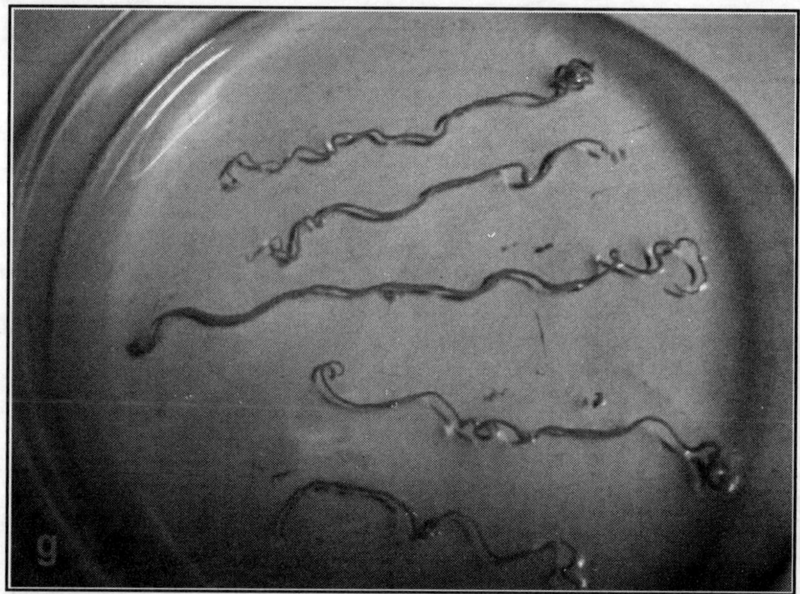

Plate 18.1 (g) Five *Polyonchobothrium clarias* Collected from One Gall Bladder of Heavily Infested Fish

Plate 18.1 (h) Scolex of *Polyonchobothrium clarias* Isolated from Gall Bladder and Stained with Carmine Stain

Plate 18.2 (a) Immature Segments of *Polyonchobothrium clarias* Isolated from Gall Bladder

Plate 18.2 (b) Scolex of *Polyonchobothrium clarias* Isolated from Glandular Stomach

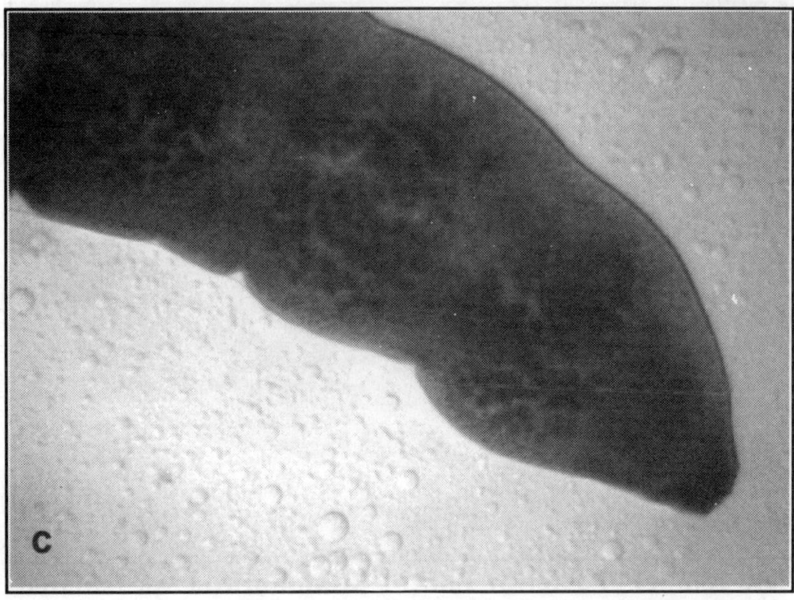

Plate 18.2 (c) Posterior Part of *Polyonchobothrium clarias* Isolated from Glandular Stomach

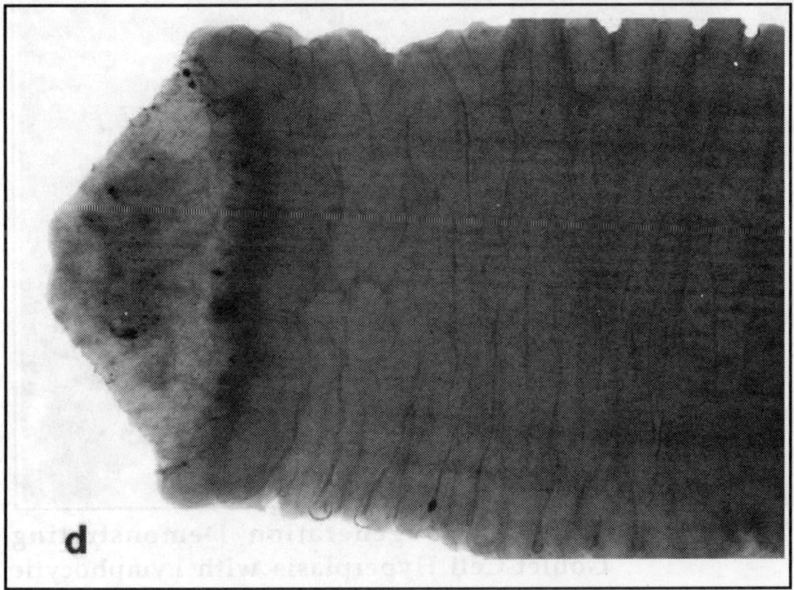

Plate 18.2 (d) Anterior End of Monobothria sp. Isolated from Intestine of Infested Fish

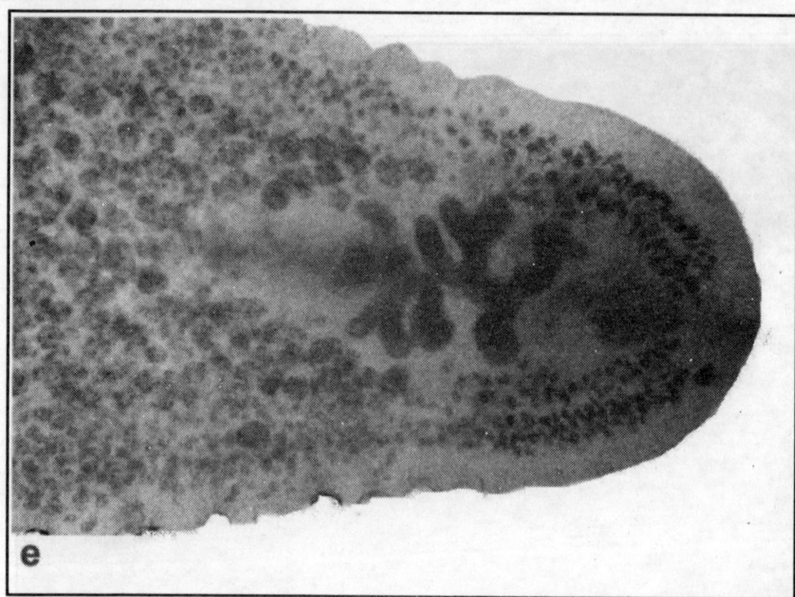

Plate 18.2 (e) Posterior End of Monobothria sp. Isolated from Intestine of Infested Fish

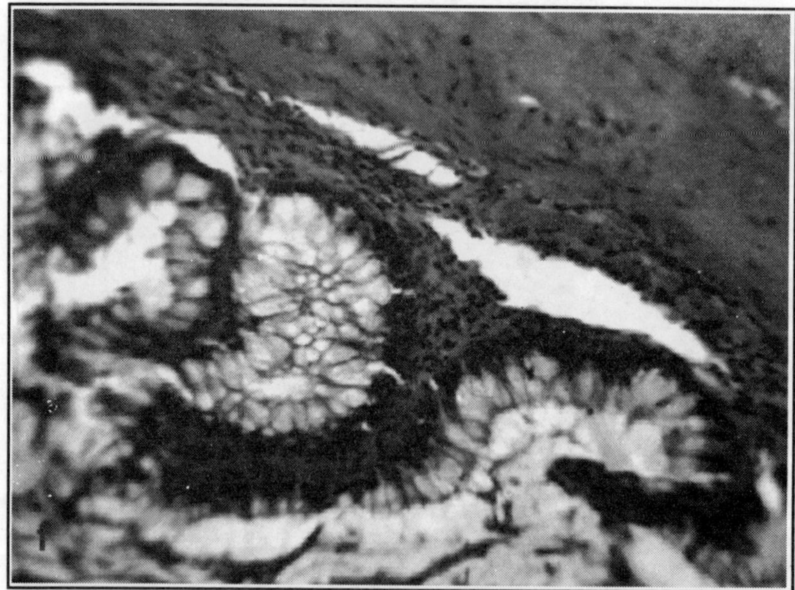

Plate 18.2 (f) Mucinous Degeneration Demonstrating Goblet Cell Hyperplasia with Lymphocytic Infiltration Observed in the Gall Bladder of Infested Fish

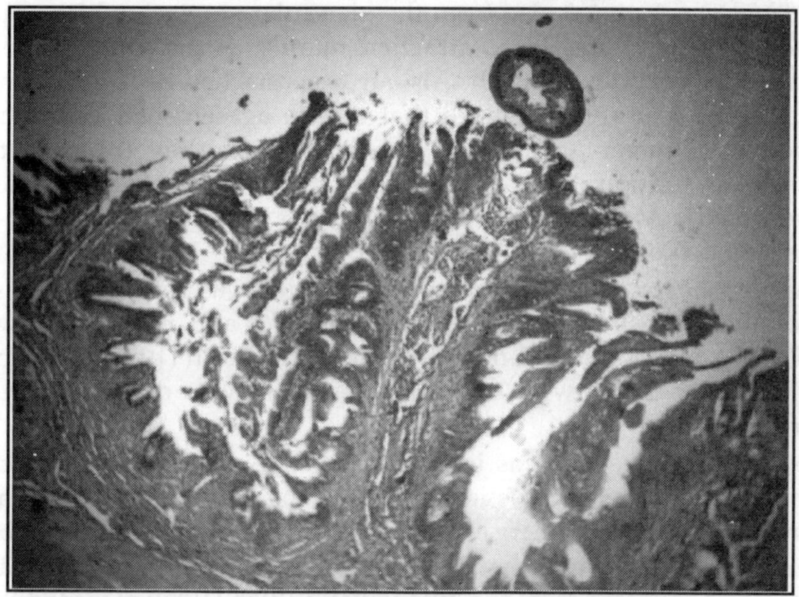

Plate 18.2 (g) **Hyperplasia and Sloughing of Gastric Mucosa of Glandular Stomach with Presence of Sub Mucosal Inflammation and Mononuclear Cell Infiltration**

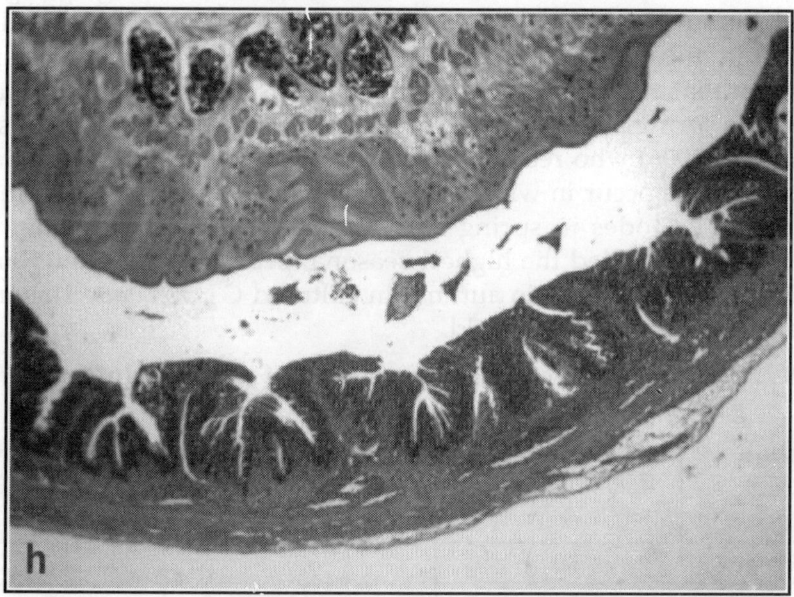

Plate 18.2 (h) **Atrophy of the Intestinal villi that became Shorten and Compressed Under the Pressure Caused Monobothria Parasite**

P clarias was isolated also from the glandular stomach which appeared congested. The parasites were attached mainly at the junction between muscular and glandular stomach. Also, it was attached near the opening of bile duct in the glandular stomach that was in agreement with the results described by Shotter and Medaiyedu (1977) as they found *P clarias* concentrated in the spiral valve in the area close to the entry of the bile duct. Moreover, Nadia Mahfouz (1991) and Moyo *et al.* (2009) isolated *P clarias* from the stomach of *Clarias gariepinus*.

The seasonal prevalence of cestode infestation was peaked during spring (96%) followed by summer (80) then winter (46) and reach the lowest in autumn (38%), also, Noor Eldin (1981) and Negm Eldin (1987) also recorded the highest prevalence with cestode infestation was during spring and summer.

Concerning, *P clarias* was isolated from the gall bladder only during spring and season while it was isolated from the glandular stomach allover the year with a total prevalence of 50.5% that was near that described by Imam (1971) who recorded, that the infestation rate with *P clarias* was 41% in *Clarias lazera* collected from the Nile while, Sahlab (1982) recorded that the infestation rate with *P clarias* was 22.22% in *Clarias lazera* from Manzala. This variation may be attributed to the difference in locality, time of collection, water temperature and size of fish.

The seasonal prevalence of *P clarias* was peaked during spring (82%) followed by summer (80%) then winter (32%) and reached the lowest infestation in autumn (8%) (Table 18.1 & 18.2). These results were nearly similar with that recorded by Abd Elaal (1996) who recorded the highest prevalence in spring and low prevalence in autumn. Also, was nearly similar to Aml Atwa (2006) who recorded the highest prevalence in spring and the lowest prevalence occur in winter and Sahlab (1982) who recorded increase prevalence of cestodes in spring and summer. On the other side, Nadia Mahfouz (1991) recorded the highest seasonal prevalence in winter and the lowest prevalence occurred in autumn in cultured *C gariepinus*. This may be explained to that our fish are wild.

Table 18.1: Showing the Seasonal Prevalence of Cestode Infestation in *C gariepinus*

Season	No. of Examined Fish	No. of Infested Fish	Infestation %
Spring	50	48	96
Summer	50	40	80
Autumn	50	19	38
Winter	50	23	46
Total	**200**	**130**	**65**

Table 18.2: Showing the Seasonal Prevalence of *Polyonchobothrium clarias* and Monobothria sp.

Cestode type		*Polyonchobothrium clarias*		Monobothria sp.	
Season	No. of Examined Fish	No. of Infested Fish	%	No. of Infested Fish	%
Spring	50	41	82	7	14
Summer	50	40	80	0	0
Autumn	50	4	8	15	30
Winter	50	16	32	7	14
Total	**200**	**101**	**50.5**	**29**	**14.5**

Monobothria sp was isolated from the intestine of C *gariepinus* with a total prevalence of (14.5%) which was higher than that described by other researchers as Negm Eldin (1987), Khattab (1990) and Nadia Mahfouz (1991) as they isolated it with an infestation rate as 6.33, 4.82 and 1.5% respectively. This may be attributed to the difference in locality and breeding. The highest seasonal prevalence of monobothria sp was recorded in autumn (30%), spring, winter (14%) and lowest prevalence occurred in summer (0 %) Table (18.2).

Table (18.3) shows that the serum total proteins, albumin and globulins were significantly decreased in heavily infested fish in comparison with non-infested fish which was similar to that described by Steinhagen *et al.* (1997) and Hamouda (2011). This decrease may be as a result of consumption of nutrient material by the parasite, also can be resulted from destruction occurred in intestinal mucosa that allow leakage of plasma protein and destruction of intestinal villi which are responsible for absorption of nutrients and protein from food materials. These findings may act as immunodepressants and open the gate to secondary infection.

Table 18.3: Showing Serum Protein Analysis of Non-infested and Infested *Clarias gariepinus* (No. 10 fish)

Parameter (g/dl)	Non-infested	Infested
Total protein	3.82 ± 0.25	3.28 ± 0.13
Albumin	1.72 ± 0.08	1.52 ± 0.13
Globulin	2.1 ± 0.27	1.76 ± 0.18

Concerning histopathological examination of the intestine of monobothria sp. infested *Clarias gariepinus* revealed presence of atrophy of the intestinal villi that became shorten and compressed under the pressure caused by the parasite that completely occupying the intestinal lumen. The glandular stomach infested with *Polyonchobothrium clarias* showing presence of hyperplasia and sloughing of gastric mucosa with presence of sub mucosal inflammation and mononuclear cell infiltration. There was observed desquamation of lining gastric mucosa with presence of transverse section in gastric lumen near the site of attachment of the parasite while, multiple longitudinal and cross sections of the parasite was observed in the gall bladder that showed degeneration and sloughing of the lining mucosa, as well as mucinous degeneration demonstrating goblet cell hyperplasia with lymphocytic infiltration. The mucosa of gall bladder showed multifocal thickening of the lining epithelium giving a feature of squamous like epithelium as a result of parasite attachment. These descriptions were nearly similar to the description given by Nadia Mahfouz (1991) and Eissa *et al.* (2010).

REFERENCES

1. Abd El-Aal, A.M.I. (1996): Some Studies on Enteric Helminthes on Nile Fishes M.V.Sc. Thesis, of Faculty of Vet. Med. Tanta Univ.
2. Aken'ova, A.A. (2000): Copepod Parasites of the Gills of *Clarias gariepinus* in Two Lakes in a River in Zaria. The Nigerian Journal of Parasitology, 20: 99-112.
3. Aml Atwa (2006): Studies on Some Prevailing Internal Parasitic Diseases in Catfish (Clarias gariepinus). M.V.Sc. Thesis Fish Dis. & Management, Fac. of Vet. Med Suez Canal Univ.
4. Austin, B. and Austin, D.A. (1987): Bacterial Fish Pathogens, Diseases in Farmed and Wild Fish. Ellis Harwood Limited England.
5. Cowx, I.G. (1992): Aquaculture Development in Africa, Training and Reference Manual for Aquaculture Extensionists. Food Production and Rural Development Division. Common Wealth Secretariat London, pp. 246-295.
6. Doumas, B.T. and Biggs, H.G. (1972): Determination of Serum Globulin. In Standard Methods of Clinical Chemistry. Vol. 7. New York, Academic Press.
7. Drury, A.A. and Wallington, T.E.A. (1980): Carletons Histological Technique. 5th Ed., Oxford Univ.
8. Eissa, A.E.; Zaki, M.M. and Abdel Aziz, A. (2010): *Flavobacterium columnare/Myxobolus tilapiae* Concurrent Infection in the Earthen Pond Reared Nile Tilapia (*Oreochromis niloticus*) during the Early Summer. Interdisciplinary Bio Central. doi: 10.4051/ibc.2010.2.2.0005.
9. Eissa, I.A.M. (2002): Parasitic Fish Diseases in Egypt. Dar El-Nahda El-Arabia Publishing, 32 Abd El-Khalek St. Cairo, Egypt.
10. Eissa, I.A.M. (2006): Parasitic Fish Diseases in Egypt. Dar El-Nahda El-Arabia Publishing, 32 Abd El-Khalek Tharwat St. Cairo, Egypt.
11. Hamouda, Awatef. H.S. (2011): Studies on Parasitic Blood Diseases in Freshwater Fish in Kafr El-Sheikh Governorate. M.V.Sc. Thesis. Fac. Vet. Med. Kafr El-Sheikh. Univ.
12. Hassen, Fatma El-Zahraa. M.: (2002): Studies on Diseases of Fish Caused by Henneguya Infestation. Ph.D. Thesis, Fac. Vet. Med., Suez, Canal University.
13. Imam, E.A.E. (1971): Morphological and Biological Studies of the Enteric Helminthes Infesting Some of the Egyptian Nile Fishes Particularly *Polyonchobothrium clarias* of the Karmot *Clarias gariepinus* and *Clarias anguillaris* Ph.D. Thesis, Faculty of Vet. Med. Cairo University.

14. Innes, W.T. (1966): Exotic Aquarium Fishes. 19 th Ed. Aquarium Incorporated. New Jersey.J. Trop. Med. Public Health J. Trop. Med. Public Health.

15. Islam, A.K.M. and Woo, P.T.K. (1991): Anorexia in Goldfish, *Carassius auratus* Infected with *Trypanosoma danilewskyi*. Diseases of Aqt Organisms,11: 45-48.

16. Khattab, M.H. (1990): Some Studies on Platyhelminthes Infecting Some Freshwater Fishes in Egypt. M.V.Sc. Thesis. Fac. Vet. Med. Alex. Univ.

17. Moyo, D.Z.; Chimbria, C. and yalala, P. (2009): Observations on the Helminth Parasites of Fish in Insukamini Dam, Zimbabwe. Research Journal of Agriculture and Biological Sciences 5(5): 782-785.

18. Mwita, C. and Nkwengulila, G. (2004): Parasites of *Clarias gariepinus* (Burchell, 1822) (Piaces: Claridae) from the Mwanza Gulf, Lake Victoria. Tanz. J. SCI. Vol. 30(1).

19. Nadia Ali (2007): Studies on Henneguya Disease Among Some Freshwater Fishes. M.V.Sc. Fish Diseases and Management Fac. Vet. Med. Kafr El-Sheikh Univ.

20. Nadia Mahfouz (1991): Studies on Round Worms and Cestodes of Some Freshwater Fish. M.V.Sc. Thesis. Fac. Vet. Med. Alex. Univ.

21. Negm El-Din, M.M. (1987): Some Morphological Studies on the Internal Parasites of Fish in Delta Nile. M.V.Sc. Thesis, Faculty of Vet. Med. Zagazig University, Benha branch (Moshtohor).

22. Noor El – Din, S.N.E. (1981): Studies on Some Parasitic Helminthes in Some Freshwater Fish. M.V.Sc. Thesis. Fac. Sci. Tanta. Univ.

23. Olofintoye, L.K. (2006): Parasitofauna in Some Freshwater Fish Species in Ekiti State, Nigeria. Pakistan Journal of Nutrition 5(4) 359-362.

24. Oniye S.J.; Adebote, D.A. and Ayanda, O.J. (2004): Studies on Helminth Parasitic Diseases in Clarias Gariepinus) (Teugels) in Zaria, Nigeria. Journal of Aquatic Sciences 19(2): 71-75.

25. Peters, T.Jr. (1970): Serum albumin, Adv. Clin. Chem. 13: 37-111.

26. Peters, T.Jr.; Biamonte, G.T. and Durnan, S. M. (1982): Protein (Total Protein) in Serum, Urine and Cerebrospinal Fluid: Albumin in Serum. In Faulkner, W.P. and Meites, S. Editors: Selected Methods of Clinical Chemistry (1982), Washington, DC, American Association for Clinical Chemistry, Inc, Vol. 9, pp. 317-325.

27. Rowely, A.F (1990): Collection, Separation and Identification of Fish Ieucocytes. In: Techniques in Fish Immunology, J.S. Stolen, T.C. Fletcher, D.P. Anderson, B.S. Robertson, W.B. Van Muiswinkel (eds.), SOS. Publications, Fair Haven, USA. Chapter 14, pp. 113-115.

28. Sabri, Dalia. M.~ El- Danasoury, M.A.~ Eissa. I.A.M. and Khouraiba, H.M. (2010): Impact of Henneguyosis Infestation on Hematological Parameters of Catfish (*Clarias garipienus*). Int. J. Agric. Biol., 11: 228-230.

29. Sahlab, A.A.M. (1982): Studies on the Enteric Helminthes Parasites of Fish from Lake Manzala. M.V.Sc. Thesis, Fac. Vet. Med. Cairo Univ. Egypt.

30. Shotter, R.A. and Medaiyedu, J.A. (1977): The Parasites of Polypterus Endlicheri Heckel (Pisces: Polypeteridae) from the River Calma at Zaria, Nigeria, with a Note on its Food. Bulletin de I´ institute fondmental d´Afrique Noire, serie A 39 (1): 177-189. Cites in Helminth. Abst. 1980, 49 (11).

31. Sineszko, S.F. (1979): Effects of Environmental Stress on Outbreak of Infectious Diseases of Fishes. Journal of Fish Biology, 6, pp. 157-208.

32. Snedecor, G.W. and Cochran, N.G. (1989): Statistical Methods, 8th (Ed.), Low State Univ., Press Ames, IOWA, U.S.A.

33. Steinhagen D.~ Oesterreich, B. and Korting. W. (1997): Carp Coccidiosis: Clinical and Hematological Observations of Carp Infected with *Goussia carpelli*. Dis Aquat Org 30: 137-143.

34. Wabuke-Bunoti, M.N.F. (1980): The Prevalence and Pathology of the Cestode *Polyonchobothrium clarias* (Woodland, 1925) in the Teleost, *Clarias mossambicus* (Peters). J. Fish Dis., 3: 223-230.

35. Woodland, J. (2006): National Wild Fish Health Survey - Laboratory Procedures Manual. 3.1 Edition. U.S. Fish and Wildlife Service, Pinetop, AZ.

36. Yamaguti, S. (1961): Systema Helminthum Vol. 111, Parts 1 and 2. The Nematodes of Vertebrates. Inter Science Publ., New York.

37. Yamaguti, S (1959): Systema Helminthum. Vol. 11. The Cestodes of Vertebrates. Inter Science Publ., New York.

38. Yamaguti, S. (1958): Systema Helminthum. Vol. 1. The Digenetic Trematodes of the Vertebrates. Parts l and 11. Inter Science Publ., New York.

19

Field Studies on Prevailing Internal Parasitic Diseases in Male and Hybrid Tilapia Relation to Monosex Tilapia at Kafr El-Sheikh Governorate Fish Farms

Eissa, I.A.M.[1]; Gado, M.S.[2]
Laila, A.M.[3]; Mona S. Zaki*[3]; Noor El-Deen, A.E[3]

ABSTRACT

The present study was carried out on 1800 specimens of *Oreochromis niloticus* (*phenotypic, hybrids and monosex* of different lengths and body weights. They were randomly collected at different seasons from Kafr El-Sheikh Governorate cultured fish farms. The clinical signs of infested fish revealed no pathognomonic abnormalities on the external body surface. Such fish were shown emaciation. The postmortem showed that the internal organs were appeared anemic with enlargement and congestion. As well as, haemorrhage and ulceration of intestine and stomach mucous membrane. Monogenetic trematode (*Enterogyrus* cichlidarum), Adult flukes including (*Orientocreadium batrochoides, Afromacroderoides sp, Astiotrema reniferum* and *Eumasenia egypticus*), Nematodes including (*Procamallanas laeviconchus* and *Paracamallanas cyathopharynx*), Cestodes including *Polyonchobothrium sp and*

1. Dept. of Fish Diseases and Management, Fac. of Vet. Med. Suez Canal University, Egypt.
2. Dept. of Fish Diseases and Management, Fac. of Vet. Med., kafr El -Sheikh University, Egypt.
3. Dept.of Hydrobiology, Vet. Division, National Research Centre, Egypt.

Acanthocephalan including *Acanthocentis tilapiae* were investigated and identified. The highest prevalence possessed in hybrids of *O. niloticus* while monosex *O.niloticus* occupied the last position.. Also some physico-chemical parameters of pond waters represented as alkalinity pH, salinity, ammonia and sulphates were examined in relation to the infestation rate with internal parasites.

Keywords: Internal parasites, *O.niloticus, Hybrids, monosex* and physico-chemical parameters.

INTRODUCTION

Internal parasitic diseases have the upper hand in fish parasitic diseases regarding the low body gain, high mortality. In addition, such diseases lead to gastrointestinal abrasions which facilitate the invasion of the opportunistic microorganisms. Where unfavourable environmental conditions contribute to stress which was weakens immunity and opens the pathway to pathogens (Kabata, 1985) and (Eissa, 2002). The clinical picture of infested fish revealed no pathognomonic abnormalities on the external body surface. Such fish were shown emaciation. The postmortem showed that the internal organs were appeared anemic with enlargement and congestion Bassiony (2000) and Ibtsam (2004).

In addation, Abd El Hady (1998) recorded presence of *Eumasenia aegyptiacus, Orientocadium batrchoides, Astiotrema reiferum* and *Afromacroids sp* from *Tilapia sp*. The highest prevalence of *Enterogyrus* was in summer by autumn then followed by spring and the lowest rate of infestation was in winter Osman (2005). Nadia Mahfouz (1991) recorded *Paracamallanus cyathopharynx* with a rate of 1.4% in *Tilapia sp* while *Procamallanus laeviconchus* 2.8% in *Tilapia sp* at Edfina and Barseek fish farms. The prevalence of nematodes were 9.25, 27.27, 2.65 and 0.0% in winter, spring, summer and autumn respectively. Omoregie *et al*. (1995) recorded that d *Polyonchobthrium sp* in *Oreochromus niloticus* from Panyam fish farm, Nigeria. Tawfik (2005) recorded that *Acanthosentis tilapiae* isolated from *Oreochromis niloticus* at Abbassa fish farms. The present investigation was planned to studying the clinical signs of the examined affected fish isolation and identification of the internal parasites infesting cultured male phenotypic, hybrids and monosex *O.niloticus* in kafr El-Sheikh fish farms, analysis of some water hydrochemistery of affected aquacultures, Studying the relationship between the seasonal prevalence of parasitic diseases and the water quality and investigation of histopathological alterations of infested male phenotypic, hybrids and monosex *O. niloticus*.

MATERIAL AND METHODS

Fish Specimens

A total number of 1800 cultured *Oreochromis niloticus (O.niloticus)* of various life stages; fry, fingerling and adult Tilapia of different Male fish types (phenotypic, hybrids and hormonally treated monosex were collected from special fish farms in Kafr El Sheikh Governorate. The length of fry, fingerlings and adult specimens were ranged from 1-1.5, 2-8 and 20-30 cm.While as their body weights were ranged from 0.9-15.0, 17-28.7 and 105-220 g respectively.

Water Samples

A clean 48 water sample flasks, one litre volume were equipped with a cork stopper. The flasks were rinsed several times with distilled water and sterilized in a hot air oven at 180 Cú for one hour.

Clinical Examination

The collected fish types were examined clinically for clinical signs and P.M. lesions according to the methods described by Noga (2010).

Parasitological Examination

The alimentary canal of each fish was separated, dissected and divided into three main parts: fore, mid and hindgut. Each part was washed with physiological saline for several times to get rid of mucus and coarse particles that may be adherent to the parasites, then each part was opened and examined in a Petri dish under binocular dissecting microscope. The parasites were collected by Pasteur pipette and dissecting needle and transferred into Petri dishes containing warm saline solution was obtaining a fully relaxed and extended parasites.

Preparation of Permanent Samples

The collected helminthes (trematodes, cestodes and acanthocephalan) were left overnight in refrigerator to allow the worm to die; then compressed gently between two glass slides and fixed in 4% formalin. The worms were washed in running water then soaked in alum carmine for 3 hrs. After staining; worms were washed in distilled water and passed through ascending grades of ethyl alcohol 50, 70, 90 and 100%, then transferred into xylol and clove oil respectively. Finally mounted with Canda balsam and covered with cover slide. Then slides were incubated at 60ºC for 24 hrs. to driving of the air bubbles (Kabata, 1985). The collected nematodes were washed in saline then relaxed in refrigerator at 4Cº and then immersed in hot alcohol-glycerin mixture until all alcohol was evaporated and the specimens remained in absolute glycerin. Worms was cleared in lactophenol and mounted in glycerin-gelatin according to Schmidely (1993).

Identification of Parasites

The helminthic parasites were morphologically and parasitologically identified according to Yamaguti (1985).

Physico-chemical Analysis of Water

pH value of water was measured at the different locations in the fish pond by means of a digital pH meter (Ph CP. Hanna instruments. Italy).

Total salinity was estimated by DR 2010 (at wave length 530, programmes 88),also ammonia (mg/l) was measured at wave length 655, programmes 342). Alkalinity was tested using (Chest own Maryland) alkalinity test kits 21620.Sulphate was measured, using HACH reagent, code 4630 in HACH apparatus, model CC. PS, (Adams 1990).

RESULTS

Clinical Examination

The infested fishes showed signs of emaciation with sunken eyes and petechial haemorrhage on the surface of abdomen and intestinal wall was congested with the presence of ulcer and protruded from anus accompanied with large amount of catarrhal mucoid secretion. Also, they revealed internal organs of naturally infested fish were pale, aneamic with enlargement and congestion of spleen, liver with distended gallbladder, enteritis, haemorrhage and ulceration of stomach as well as intestinal mucous membrane. Some fishes showed slight bulging of the stomach, congestion and haemorrhage on the mucous membrane with watery food especially in heavily infested cases. White nodules in posterior kidney (Plate, 19.1).

Parasitological Examination

Adult worms were isolated form the stomach of infested fish. Such adult worms identified as *Enterogyrus cichlidarum* and adult worms were isolated from midgut of infested fish. Identified as *Orientocreadium batrochoides and Afromacroderoides sp.* Also, adult worms were collected from foregut of infested fish identified as *Astiotrema reniferum, Eumasenia egypticus, Procamallanus laeviconchus and Paracamallanus cyathopharynx*. While, thorny-head worms were isolated from hindgut of intestine of infested Tilapia sp identified as *Acanthosentis tilapiae* (Plate 19.2).

Prevalence and Distribution of Helminthes

Internal parasitic infestations of phenotypic, hybrids and monosex *O. niloticus* with *Enterogyrus cichlidarum Orientocreadium batrochoides Afromacroderoides sp Astiotrema reniferum, Eumasenia egypticus, Procamallanus laeviconchus and Paracamallanus cyathopharynx and Acanthosentis tilapiae* were recorded in Table (19.1 and 19.2).

Water Analysis and Seasonal Prevalance

The prevalence of parasitic infestation with different water parameters were recorded in Table (19.3).

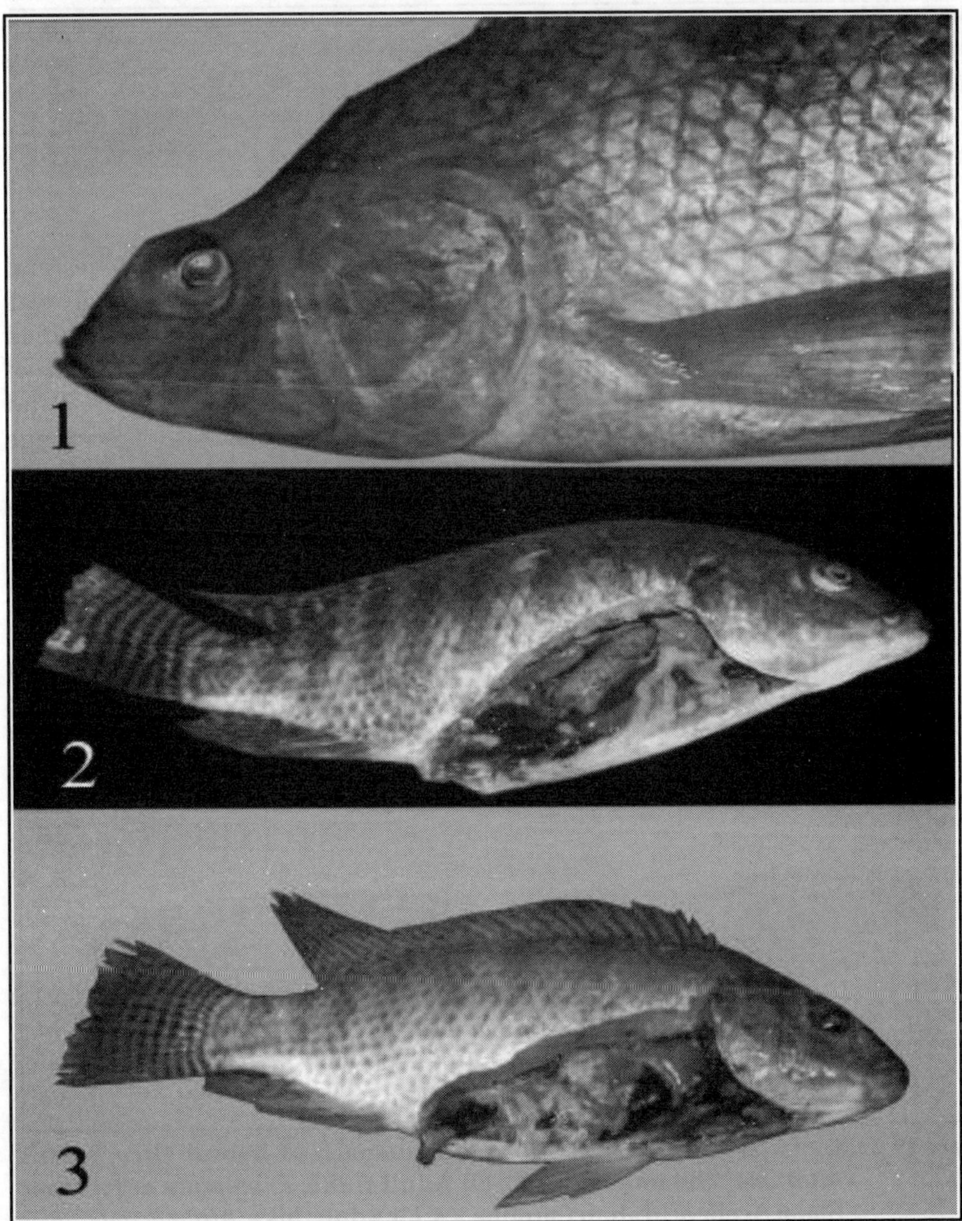

Plate 19.1: (1) Hybrid *Oreochromis niloticus* with sinking eye. (2) Hybrid *Oreochromis niloticus* with slightly turgid stomach and inflammation of the intestines. (3) Monosex *Oreochromis niloticus* showing distended of gall bladder.

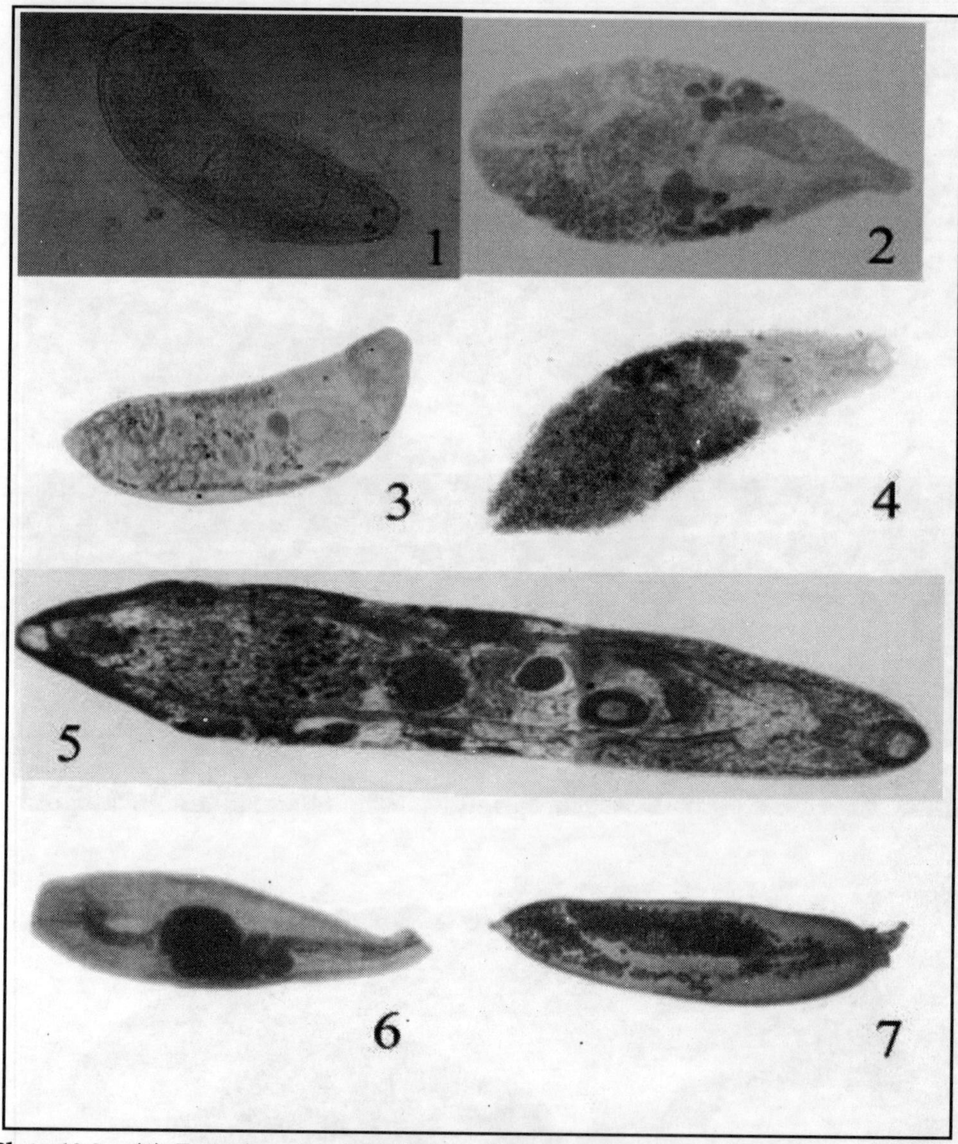

Plate 19.2: (1) *Enterogyrus cichlidarum* from stomach of hybrid *Oreochromis niloticus*. Wet mount. X 200. (2) Adult fluke, *Eumasenia aegypticus*. Stain: Acetic acid alum Carmine X 4. (3) Adult fluke, *Afromacroderoides sp*. Stain: Acetic acid alum carmine X 4. (4) Adult fluke, *Astiotrema reniferum*. Stain: Acetic acid alum Carmine X 4. (5) Adult fluke, *Orientocreadium batrochoides*. Soalted from midgut of *O. niloticus*. Stain: Acetic acid alum Carmine X 4. (6) Adult fluke, *Acanthocentis male*. Stain: Acetic acid alum Carmine X 4. (7) Adult fluke, *Acanthocentis female*. Stain: Acetic acid alum CarmineX4.

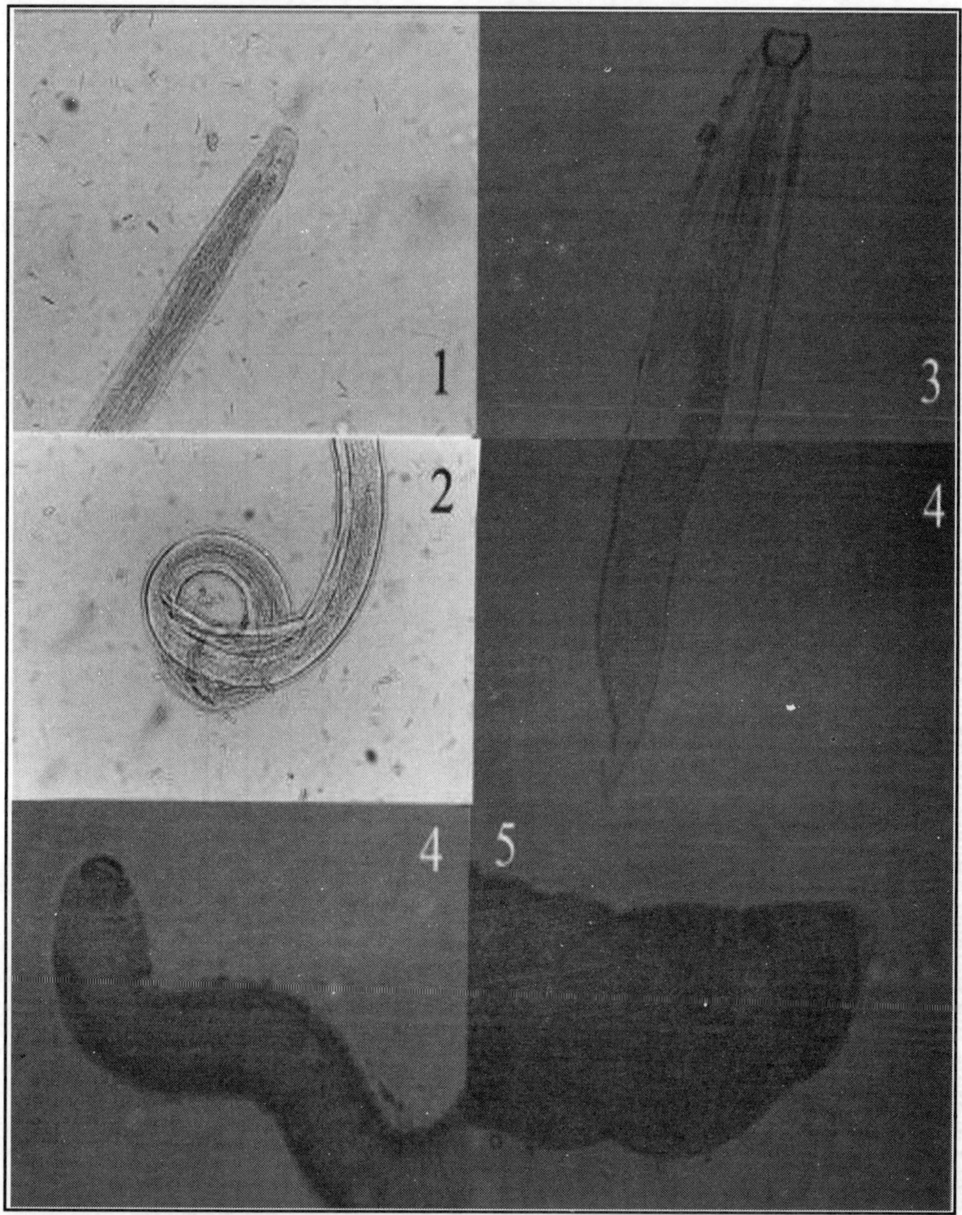

Plate 19.3: (1) *Procamallanus laeviconchus*. (Anterior end).Wet mount X10.
(2) *Procamallanus eviconchus*. (Posterior end). Wet mount X10.
(3) *Paracamallanus cyathopharynx*. (Anterior end).Wet mount X10.
(4) *Paracamallanus cyathopharynx*. (Posterior end). Wet mount X 10.
(4) *Polyonchobothrium sp*. (Anterior end).Wet mount X10.
(5) *Polyonchobothrium sp*. (Posterior end). Wet mount X 10.

Table 19.1: Prevalence of Parasitic Infestations Among Males of Phenotypic, Hybrid and Monosex *O.niloticus.*

Tilapia	No. of Exam Fish	Internal Parasites							
		Adult Trematodes		Nematodes		Cestode		Acanthocephala	
		No.	%	No.	%	No.	%	No.	%
Male phenotypic *O. niloticus.*	600	37	6.2	11	1.8	2	0.3	21	3.5
Male hybrids *O. niloticus.*	600	66	11	17	2.8	4	0.6	31	5.2
Male monosex *O. niloticus.*	600	27	4.5	5	0.9	0	0	9	1.5
Total	1800	130	21.7	33	5.5	6	1	61	10.2

Table 19.2: Distribution of Helminthes in Different Types of Tilapias

Site of Infection	Class of Parasites	Genus of Parasites	Phenotypic *O. niloticus*		Hybrids of *O. niloticus*		Monosex *O. niloticus*	
			No.	%	No.	%	No.	%
Stomach	Trematodes	*Enterogyrus cichlidarum*	2	0.3	3	0.5	1	0.2
	Nematodes.	*Procamallanus laeviconchus*	6	1	8	1.3	3	0.5
		Paracamallanus cyathopharynx	5	0.8	9	1.5	2	0.4
Intestine	Trematodes	Adult trematodes	7	1.2	13	2.2	0	0
	Cestodes	*Polyonchobothrium sp*	2	0.3	4	0.6	0	0
	Acanthocephala	*Acanthocentis tilapiae*	21	3.5	31	5.2	9	1.5

Table 19.3: The Seasonal Correlations Between the Average of Some Water Parameters in Different Fish Cultures with Endo Parasitic Infestations

Types of Tilapia Culture	No of Exam Fishes	No of Infested Fishes	Types of Parasites	Seasons										
				Spring	Summer	Autumn	Winter	Seasons	Salinity ppt	pH	Ammonia mg/L	Do	Alkalinity ppt	Sulphate ppt
Male phenotypic.	600	202	Trematodes	1.3	1.3	1.2	2.3	sp	2	7.2	0.3	8	210	90
			Cestode	0	0.3	0	0	su	1.3	6.8	0.4	6	180	50
O.nilcticu s			Nematodes	0.3	0.7	0.8	0	Aut.	1..2	6.2	0..3	8	190	53
			Acanthocephala	1	1.2	0.5	0.8	Win.	2	7.5	0.2	10	215	110
			Trematodes	1.5	1.8	3.2	4.5	sp	2	7.2	0.3	8	210	90
Male hybrids of	600	302	Cestode	0	0.3	0.3	0	su	1.3	6.8	0.4	6	180	55
O. niloticus			Nematodes	0.8	1	0.5	0.5	Aut.	1.7	6.3	0..2	8	193	52
			Acanthocephala	0.8	1	1.7	1.7	Win.	2	7.6	0.1	10	209	115
Male Monosex.	600	96	Trematodes	0.7	3	0.8	0	sp	1.0	7.5	0.1	10	160	50
O. niloticus			Nematodes	0.3	0.5	0	0	su	1.2	6.4	0.3	12	170	50
			Cestode	0	0	0	0	Aut.	1..2	6.2	0.2	8	173	41
			Acanthocephala	0.3	0.7	0.5	0	Win.	1.0	7.1	0.1	10	210	93

DISCUSSIONS

The present study deals with most of different internal parasitic diseases among naturally infested the cultured *O. niloticus* (phenotypic, hybrid and monosex) in relation to the seasonal prevalence and water parameters in Kafr El- Sheikh fish farms. The internal organs of naturally infested fish appeared pale, anemic with enlargement and congestion of spleen, liver with distended gallbladder. Signs of emaciation with petechial haemorrhage on the surface of abdomen and slight bulging of stomach was obseved. While, intestinal wall was congested with the presence of ulcer and protruded from anus accompanied with large amount of catarrhal mucoid secretion. This clinical picture nearly was similar to that recorded by Osman (2005). This picture may be explained due to the presence of Enterogyrus, nematodes, cestodes and thorny headed worms which cause harmful effect as they embedded themselves between the villi of intestine causing local damage to the intestinal mucosa and possibly peritonitis. Proteolytic enzymes may be discharged from some adult worms degrading the intestinal tissues (Woo, 1995). Regarding the internal monogenea (*Enterogyrus cichlidarum)* was morphologically and parasitologically described and was nearly similar to the descriptions given by Khidr (1996). Concerning to the cestodes (*Polyonchobothrium sp*) was isolated and identified from infested *Tilapia sp.* Such identification is nearly similar that recorded by Yamaguti (1985). Regarding to the isolated nematodes from naturally infested Tilapia fishes, isolation and identification of *Procamallanus laeviconchus* and *Paracamallanus cyathopharynx* were undertaken that nearly similar to those of original descriptions by Woo (1995). Finally, morphological and parasitological examinations of Tilapia fishes revealed isolation and identification of *Acanthosentis tilapiae* whose descriptions are nearly similar to those of original description by Yamaguti, (1985).

In the present study a total prevalence of Enterogyrosis in phenotypic, hybrid and monosex was 0.3, 0.5, and 0.2% respectively. Such results are lower than recorded by Eid and Negm, (1987) who reported that the prevalence of *Enterogyrus cichlidarum* from *O.niloticus* collected from (Bahr Mouise) was 13.3%, Ibtsam (2004) who recorded 60% of Entergyrosis. Also, disagree with that recorded by Osman (2005) who found a prevalence of Entergyrosis as 67.2%. These variations may be attributed to the water quality criteria and age of fish as such worms are stomach flukes need aged fish have well developed stomach and its wall was thicker for adaptation and fixation.

Regarding the total prevalence of adult flukes in phenotypic, hybrid and monosex were 1.2, 2.2, 0 % respectively. These results disagreed with the finding of Hassan (1992) who recorded the peak of adult trematodes in

O. niloticus were 6%. Such result was lower than recorded by Abd El- Hady (1998) who recorded that a prevalence of adult flukes was 15.58%.

Concerning the total prevalence of *Procamallanus laeviconchus* was 1.8, 2.8 and 0.9% from phenotypic, hybrid and monosex respectively. These findings nearly agree with that met by Nadia Mahfouz (1991) who recorded a prevalence of *P. laeviconchus* as 2.8% in *O.niloticus* and lower than that recorded by El- Naffer *et al.* (1983) who recorded a prevalence of *P.laeviconchus* was in *Tilapia sp* 39%. While in *Paracamallanus cyathopharynx* were 0.8, 1.5, and 0.4%. These finding nearly agree with that recorded Abd El- Wahed (1992) who recorded a prevalence of P. *cyathopharynx* was 1.4% in *O.niloticus*. These results may be attributed to different types of fish, the presence of intermediate host (Snails), the suitable temperature which consider the main survival factors for these intermediate host and aquatic birds.

The highest infestation of phenotypic, hybrid and monosex were recorded in summer 3.5%, winter 4.4% and spring 2%. These results disagreed with that recorded by Nadia Mahfouz (1991) who recorded a prevalence of nematodes infestation in winter, spring, summer and autumn were 9.25, 27.27, 2.65 and 0% respectively. This result may be attributed to different types of fish, the presence of intermediate host (*Piscivorous*), and the suitable temperature which consider the main survival factors for these intermediate host and aquatic birds.

In this study, *Polyonchobothrium sp* could be detected with a prevalence 0.3, 0.6 and 0% from phenotypic and hybrid respectively. These findings are lower than that recorded by Hassan (1992) who found up to 7.5%.

The highest infestation of phenotypic, hybrid and monosex were recorded in summer 3.5% and winter 4.4% and spring 2%. These results disagreed with that recorded by Nadia Mahfouz (1991) who recorded a prevalence of nematodes infestation in winter, spring, summer and autumn were 9.25, 27.27, 2.65 and 0% respectively. These differences may be due to variation in climatic and ecological factors which affect on intermediate host copepods (Cyclops) and aquatic birds.

Finally, the prevalence of *Acanthosentis tilapiae* in cultured (phenotypic, hybrid and monosex) was 3.5, 5.2 and 1.5% respectively. These findings nearly agree with that recorded by Eissa *et al.* (1996) and Rawia Adawy (2000) who recorded a prevalence of *A. tilapiae* in cultured *Tilapia sp* as 2.4 and 3.7% respectively and lower than that recorded by Eid (1997) who recorded a prevalence of *A. tilapiae* in *Tilapia sp* as 37.8%.

Concerning the highest infestation in phenotypic, hybrid were recorded in summer, spring, winter and autumn as 5.8, 3, 1.4 and 0% respectively. These results nearly agreed with that recorded Rawia Adway (2000) a prevalence of *Acanthocentis tilapiae* in cultured *Tilapia sp* in summer as 4.4% and disagree with Bassiony (2002) who mentioned that the highest infestation rate a prevalence of *A. tilapiae* in cultured *Tilapia sp* was in summer, autumn, spring and winter seasons were 39, 24, 21, 16.2 and 17.4% respectively. Also, Ibtsam (2004) who mentioned a prevalence of *A. tilapiae* in cultured *Tilapia sp* as in summer, autumn, spring and winter seasons were 12, 10, 17.4 and 0% respectively and in Tawfik (2005) who mentioned that the highest infestation rate a prevalence of *A. tilapiae* in cultured *Tilapia sp* in summer and winter as 14 and 7% respectively. This result may be attributed to different type of fish the presence of intermediate host (amphipod and isopod), the suitable temperature which consider the main survival factors for these intermediate host.

In the present study, all of the water parameters namely pH, salinity, ammonia, alkalinity, DO and sulphates in cultured fish farms, were within the permissible limits throughout the period of study according to APHA (1985). The epizootiological point of view to be important, are the predisposing factors for the wide spread of parasites among different Tilapia fishes in this study.

There was a positive correlation between the pH and alkalinity in water and the prevalence of each of (*Protozoa, Monogenea* and *Acanthocephala*). Negative correlation with prevalence of each of (nematodes and cestodes). These may be attributed to the fact that increasing the pH and calcium carbonate in water of fish ponds represent a stress factor on respiration process of fish, especially the gills and may be facilitate such parasites to infect fish.

The negative correlation between the DO in water and the prevalence of each of *Acanthocephala* may be attributed to the fact that low DO represent a stress factor on respiration process fish, leading to asphyxia and loss of escape reflex leading to entry of fish parasites. The present study, revealed that the levels of total ammonia and salinity in ponds containing monosex tilapias were within the normal levels. On the other side, there was increase of both parameters in ponds of hybrids and phenotypic. This may be due to receiving agricultural drainage, domestic sewage and misuse of poultry dropping (Sabla) that revealed the poor water quality in this location (ponds) which was accompanied by increase the prevalence of *Protozoa, Ergasilus sp* and trematodes infection. These results agree with that recorded by Naguib and Abu Essa (1999) who found that, the incidence of the encysted metacercariae in muscles of infected fish during the breeding season was 56.2% in fish farms received the agricultural drainage. There is a positively correlation between water sulphate levels and the prevalence of *Acanthosentis tilapiae.* It may be due to limiting factor affecting algal growth (Elewa and Mahdy., 1988).

REFERENCES

1. Abd El-Aal, A. M. I. (2002): Studies on Tissue Parasites in Fish. Ph.D. Thesis, Fac. Vet. Med., Tanta Univ. (Kafr El-Sheikh branch).
2. Abd EL- Hady. O.K (1998): Comparative Studies on Some Parasitic Infection of Fishes in Fresh and Polluted Water Sources. Ph.D. Thesis (Parasitalogy), Fac. Vet. Med., Cairo Univ.
3. Abd El-Wahed, W. M.M (1992): Epizootiological Studies on Some Gastro- Intestinal Helminthes Infestation in Fresh Water Fish in Egypt. M.V.Sc. Thesis, Fac. Vet. Med., Cairo Univ.
4. Adams, V.T (1990) Methods for the Determination of Organics. Lewis Publisher, INC. 121, South Main Street, Chelsea. Michigan, USA.
5. American Public Health Association (APHA), (1985): Standard Methods for the Examination of Water and Waste Water. 16th Ed Washington, USA.
6. Bassiony, A.E.A.A. (2002): Studies on the Prevailing Internal Parasitic Diseases Among Some Cultured Fresh Water Fishes in kafr El-Sheikh Province. M. V. Sc. Thesis, Fac. Vet. Med., kafr- El-Sheikh, Tanta University.
7. Drury, A.A. and Wallington, E.A. (1980): Carleton's Histological Technique. 5th Ed., Oxford University Press, New York, Toronto.
8. Egyptian Permissible Limits (1982): Protection of River Nile and Water Currents from Pollution. Law No. 48 at 1982, Ministry of Irrigation.
9. Eid, S.A. (1997): Studies on Parasites of Egyptian Cultured Fish.M.V.Sc. Thesis, Fac. Vet. Med, Cairo Univ.
10. Eid, N. and Negm, M.A. (1987): Some Morphological Study on a New Species of Endoparasitic Monogenetic Trematoda *Enterogyrus niloticus* in the Intestine of *Tilapia nilotica*.J. Egypt Vet.Med. Ass.,47, (1 and 2), 79-86.
11. Eissa, I.A.M. (2002): Parasitic Fish Diseases in Egypt. Dar El- Nahda El- Arabia Publishing, 23 Abd El- Khalak Tharwat St. Cairo, Egypt.
12. Eissa, I.A.M.; A.S. Diab and A.F. Badran (1996): Studies on Some Internal Parasitic Diseases Among Wild and Cultured *Oreochromis niloticus* Fish. 7th Sci. Cong., 17-19. Nov. 1996, Fac. Vet. Med., Assiut, Egypt.
13. Elewa. A.A and Mahdy. H (1988): Some Limn Logical Studies on the Nile Water at Egypt. Bull. Nat. Inst Oceanography. & Fish. ARE, 14(2): 141-152.
14. EL- Naffer, M.K.; Saoud, M.E. and Hassan, I.M. (1983): A General Survey of the Helminth Parasites of Some Fish from Lake Nasser at Aswan, Egypt. Assiut. Vet. J. 11, (21), 141-148.
15. Hassan; M.A. (1992): Studies on Some Parasitic Affection in Fresh Water Fishes in Beni Suef governorate. Ph.D. Thesis, Fac. Vet. Med., Beni- Suef. Cairo Univ.
16. Kabata, Z. (1985): Parasites and Diseases of Fish Culture in the Tropics. Printed in Great Britain by Taylor and Franks (Ltd. Basingstoke Hants). pp. 127-161.
17. Khidr, A.A. (1990): Population Dynamics of *Enterogyrus Cichlidarum* (Mongenea: Ancyrocephalinae) from the Stomach of Tilapia spp in Egypt. Int. J. Parasitol., 20 (6) 741-5.
18. Lucky, Z. (1977): Methods for the Diagnosis of Fish Diseases, Amerind. Publishing Co., Pvt. Ltd., New Delhi, Bombay, India.
19. Ibtsam, E.B.E.D. (2004): Studies on Some Prevailing Parasitic Diseases Among Cultured Tilapia Fish. Ph.D. Thesis, Fac. Vet. Med., Suez Canal University.

20. Moav, B.; Hilge, V. and Rosenthal, H. (1992): Progress in Aquaculture Research, European Aquaculture Society Special Publication No. 17, Oostende, Belgium. pp. 205-214.
21. Nadia Mahfouz, N.B.M. (1991): Studies on Round Worms and Cestodes of Some Fresh Water Fish. M.V.Sc. Thesis, Fac. Vet. Med., Alexandria University.
22. Naguib, M. and Abu Essa, J.F. K. (1999): Water Quality and its Influence on the Health Status of *Oreochromis niloticus* Fish. Beni-Suef Vet. Med. J. Vol.9, (3-A): 353-364.
23. Noga, E.J. (2010): Fish Disease Diagnosis and Treatment. Mosby-yearbook, Inc. Watsworth Publishing Co., USA. pp. 366.
24. Omoregie, E.; Ufodike,E.B.C. and Onwuliri,C.O.E.(1995): Comparative Survey of Helminthes Parasites of the Nile Tilapia. Acta Mediterranean dipato logia Infective Tropical, 12 (2): 107-110.
25. Osman, M.A.H. (2005): Studies on Monogenasis Among Fishes. Ph.D. Thesis, Fac. Vet. Med., Suez Canal Univ.
26. Rawia Adawy, S.M. (2000): Studies on the Parasitic Diseases of Some Fresh Water Fishes in Dakahlia Governorate. Ph.D. Thesis, Fac. Vet. Med., Cairo Univ.
27. Schmidely, P. (1993): Quantitative Bibliographic Review on the Use of Anabolic Hormones with Steroidogenic Action in Ruminants for Meat Production II. Principle Mode of Action " Repord. Nutr. Dev., 33 (4): 297-323.
28. Shalaby, A.A. (1982): Studies on the Enteric Helminth Parasites of Fishes from Lake Manzala. M.V.Sc. Thesis, Fac. Vet. Med., Cairo University, Egypt.
29. Tawfik, M.A.A (2005): Studies on Some Fish-borne Trematodes in Egypt. J.Vet Sci., 43: 49-58.
30. Woo, P.T.K. (1995): Fish Diseases and Disorders. CAB, Int. Wallingford, Oxon, UK.
31. Yamaguti, S. (1985): Systema Helminthes of Fish. Vol. 1.Digentic Trematodes of the Vertebrates Part 1 and 2, Interscience Publishers, Inc. New York.

20

Field Study on Cadmium Pollution in Relation to Internal Parasitic Diseases in Cultured Nile Tilapia at Kafr El-Sheikh Governorate

Eissa, I.A.M.[1]; Mona, S. Zaki*[2]; Noor El Deen[2] A I E[2]; Ibrahim, A.Z[2]; Osman, K. Abdel Hady[2]

ABSTRACT

The aim of this study is to explain the relation ship between cadmium pollution and internal parasitic infestation in tilapia fish. The present study was carried out on 400 specimens of Tilapia fish (*Oreochromis niloticus* (*O.niloticus*) ranged from 20-30 cm. While as their average body weights were ranged from 180 ± 10 g. The clinical signs revealed no pathognomonic abnormalities on the external body surface except in heavily naturally infested fish, represented as respiratory manifestation. The postmortem findings of investigated fish revealed the presence of black spots in different parts of the body in some infested fishes. While, internal organs were appeared anemic with enlargement and congestion. As well as, haemorrhage and ulceration of intestine and stomach mucous membrane, white nodules in posterior kidney. The isolated parasites from examined tilapia were 6 types namely: *Enterogyrus cichlidarum, Orientocreadium batrochoides, Heterophidae, Polyonchobothrium sp,*

1. Fish Diseases and Management Dept., Fac. of Vet. Med., Suez Canal Univ., Egypt.
2. Hydrobiology Dept., Vet Division, National Research Centre, Dokki, Egypt.

Paracamallanas cyathopharynx and *Acanthocentis tilapiae*. Helminth infestations of *O. niloticus* in Sidi Salem district fish farms in autumn season were 11, 8, 1 and 4% trematodes , nematode , cestode and *Acanthocentis tilapiae* respectively.

Also, in Alirad district fish farms were 9, 4, 1 and 2% respectively. While, in Meutobeus fish farms were 6, 3, 1 and 2% respectively. The residues of cadmium in water and *O. niloticus* tissues naturally exposed to cadmium were determined and discussed. The correlation between naturally exposed to cadmium *O. niloticus* tissues and internal parasitic diseases was studied. Also, cadmium displayed a significant decrease in PCV%, RBCs and Hb while elevation in the level of WBCs , blood glucose , serum AST, ALT, urea and creatinine at Sidi Salem district fish farms decreased in Alirad district fish farms and Metobus District fish farms throughout the periods of study.Besides, the histopathological alterations in different organs of *O. niloticus* were recorded.

Key words: cadmium, *O. niloticus*, internal parasites, histopathology, clinicopatholoy.

INTRODUCTION

Today, the contamination of freshwater with a wide range of pollutants has become a matter of great concern over the last few decades. Heavy metal levels have increased due to domestic, industrial, mining and agricultural activities (Kalay and Canli, 2000). Aquatic organisms such as fish and shellfish accumulate metals to concentrations many times higher than present in water (Olaifa *et al.*, 2004). They can take up metals concentrated at different levels in their different body organs. Cadmium concentration is higher in gills and viscera than other organs (Khaled, 2004). Studies carried out on fish have shown that cadmium heavy metal may have toxic effects, altering physiological activities in tissue and in blood of fish (Larsson *et al.*, 1985). Therefore, it is important to monitor heavy metal in aquatic environments (water and fish). Now, there is more awareness of the importance of studying fish parasites as one of the major obstacles in fish production about 80% of fish diseases are parasitic especially for warm water fish (Eissa *et al.*, 1996).

The relationship of parasitism and pollution is not simple and essence involves a double edged phenomenon which parasitism may decrease host susceptibility to toxic pollutions may result in an increase or decrease in the prevalence of certain parasites. Pollutants may affect on intermediate or alternate hosts in parasite life cycle, on free-living life cycle stages of parasite invasion (Sindermann, 1990). This study was undertaken to investigate the levels of Cadmium heavy metal in water and *O. niloticus* fish in relation to internal parasitic diseases among Kafr El Sheikh fish farms.

MATERIALS AND METHODS

Fish

A total number of 400 adult cultured *O. niloticus* were randomly collected from Kafr El- Sheikh Governorate fish farms. The collected fish were obtained in autumn season 2010 from three districts areas (Sidi-Salem, Alriad and Metobus fish farms). The length of adult specimens was 20-30 cm. While as their average body weights were ranged from 180 ± 10 g. The collected fish were transferred alive to lab of Hydrobiology Dept. in National Research Center in large plastic tanks filled with two thirds with their natural water from the same source and aerated with air battery pumps.

Water Samples

A total number of 36 water sample of 3 districts of cultured fish. They were collected from the same fish farms at the same time (midday). The collected water sample bottles were labeled with the locality, date, time and type of fish pond. The flasks, one litre volume were equipped with a cork stopper and open hand prides under water surface then equipped again. The water samples were collected as replicates from various distances along each location and the averages of their analysis were taken.

Aquaria

Fourteen fully prepared glass aquaria, 40 × 50 × 100 cm were used for holding the collected fish throughout the period of study. They were supplied with a chlorine free tap water with continuous aeration using electric air pumping compressors (Rena, France) according to Innes (1966); without water filtration or water heater.

Clinical Picture

Alive fish were clinically examined and postmortem examination according to the methods described by Noga (1996).

Parasitological Examination

Musculature, gastrointestinal tract and internal organs were examined according to Paperna (1980).

Blood Sampling

It was collected from the caudal vein of the examined fish using a plastic syringe and divided into two portions. The first portion was kept as a whole blood in heparinized tubes for hematological examination. Serum was separated from the second portion for biochemical analysis according to Dacie & Lewis (1991).

Cadmium Residues

In liver, kidneys, and musculature were estimated according to Combs *et al.* (1987).

Histopathological Examination

Autopsy specimens were taken from liver, intestine, spleen, gills and musculature of fish in different groups and fixed in 10% formalin solution for 24 hrs. Washing was done in tap water then serial dilutions of alcohol (70, 90% and absolute ethyl) were used for dehydration. Specimens were cleared in xylene and embedded in paraffin and sectioned 4 microns thickness by slidge microtome. The obtained sections were collected on glass slides, deparaffinized, stained by hematoxylin and eosin and examined microscopically (Banchroft and Stevens, 1996).

RESULTS

Clinical Picture

O.niloticus exposed to cadmium showed slimy body with pale skin, signs of restlessness, some fish suffered from emaciation. Also, abnormal movement and shape (scoliosis) were shown with loss of appetite and escape reflex. Postmortem lesions revealed inflamed, enlarged pale spleen and liver spotted with inflammatory patches, while the intestines were darker in colour (Plate.(20.1): (1 to 4).

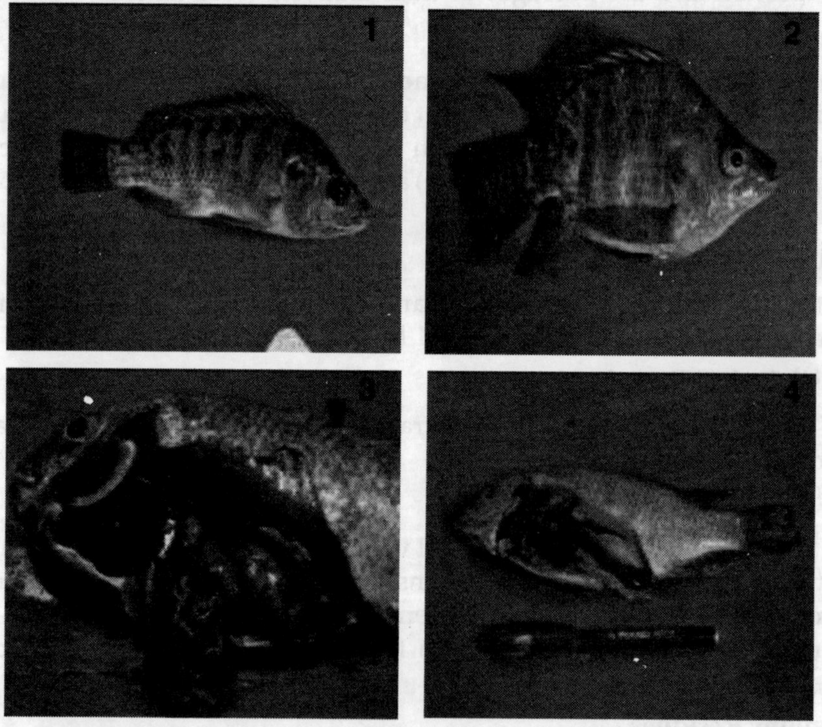

Plate 20.1: Showing *O.niloticus* naturally exposed to Cadmium suffering from emaciation (1), scoliosis (2), degeneration in overies (3) enlarged pale spleen and spotted liver with inflammatory patches (4).

Parasitological Examination

Adult worms were isolated form the stomach of infested fish. Such adult worms are trematodes belonged to class Trematoda, order Monogenea, and genus Enterogyrus and identified as *Enterogyrus cichlidarum*. They were isolated from midgut of infested fish adult worms are related to class Trematoda, order Digenea and genus Orientocreadium and identified as *Orientocreadium batrochoides*. Cysts were embedded in musculature as black colour, oval in shape with thin double wall cyst. They were related to Heterophid metacercariae. Adult worms were isolated from the intestine of infested *O. niloticus* as small whitish in colour, segmented and flat. Such adult worms belonged to subclass Eucestoda order Pseudophyllidea, family Ptychobothriidae, genus *Polyonchobothrium*. Concerning the parasitological examination it was revealed funnel shape and armed with large tridents with sclerotized posterior ends, the worm is yellowish in colour when fresh, the buccal capsule was chitinous. Such adult worms belonged to order Spiruridea, family Camallanidae, genus Paracamallanus and identified as *P. cyathopharynx*. Thorny-head worms were isolated from hindgut. Such adult worms were belonged to phylum Acanthocephala, class Eoacanthocephala, order Gyracanthocephala, family Quadrogyridae, genus Acanthosentis and identified as *Acanthosentis tilapiae* (Plate 20.2), (1-9).

Prevalence of Internal Parasitic Diseases in *O. niloticus*

From Table (20.1) it was indicated that a great variation in the infestation% in adult *O. niloticus* naturally exposed to cadmium.

Helminth infestations of *O. niloticus* in Sidi Salem district fish farms, trematodes were 11%, nematode was 8%, cestode was 1%, *Acanthocentis tilapiae* were 4% in autumn season. Also, Helminthes infestations of *O. niloticus* in Alirad district fish farms, trematodes were 9% , nematode were 4%, cestode were 1% , *Acanthocentis tilapiae* were 2%. While, Helminthes infestations of *O. niloticus* in Meutobeus fish farms, trematodes were 6%, nematode were 3%, cestode were 1%, *Acanthocentis tilapiae* were 2% in autumn season (Table 20.2).

Cadmium Residues in Water

Results are shown in tables 20.4 & 20.5 (Cadmium concentrations in water of Nile Tilapia farms).

Cadmium Residues in *Oreochromis niloticus* Tissues

Results are shown in table 20.5 (Concentration of cadmium in fresh Nile tilapia tissues). Cadmium residues were significantly increased in internal organs of *O. niloticus* tissues comparing to musculature.

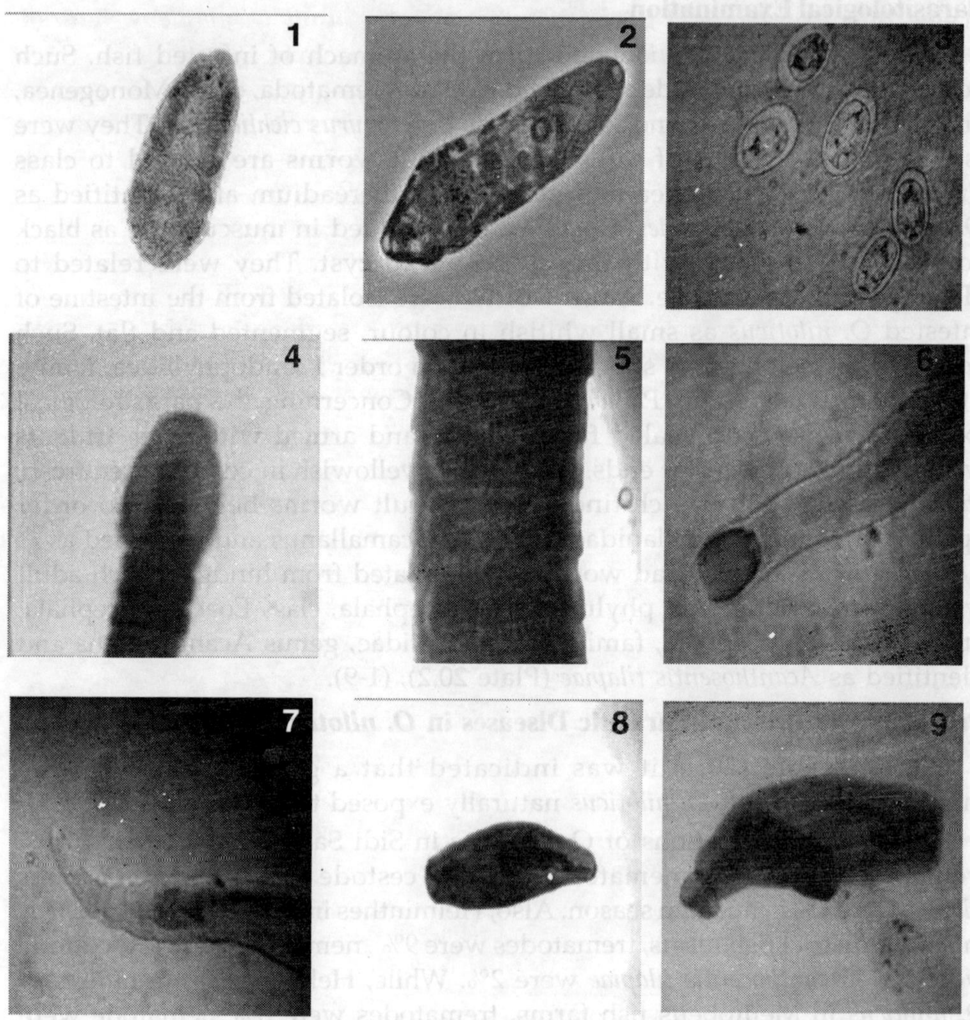

Plate 20.2: **Showing *Enterogyrus cichlidarum* wet mount (1); Adult fluke, *Orientocreadium batrochoides*. (2); heavy infestation of *Heterophidae* encysted metacercariae in musculature (3); *Polyonchobothrium sp.* (Anterior end). Wet mount (4); *Polyonchobothrium sp.* (graved segment) (5); *Paracamallanus cyathopharanuex*. (Anterior end). Wet mount (6); *Paracamallanus cyathopharanuex*. (Posterior end). Wet mount X 10. (7); *Acanthocentis tilapiae* ♀. (8); *Acanthocentis tilapiae* ♂. (9) All stained with acetic acid alum Carmine X 40 except wet mount one.**

Table 20.1: Prevalence of Parasitic Infestation in Adults *O. niloticus* Naturally Exposed to Cadmium in Relation to Different Localities

Locality	No. of Fish	Number of Infested Fish		Total
		No	%	%
Sidi Salem fish farms	200	48	24	12
Alirad fish farms	100	16	16	4
Metobeus fish farms	100	12	12	3
Total	400	76		19

Table 20.2: The Correlations Between the Average of Some Water Parameters in Different Fish Cultures with Endoparasitic Infestations

District	No. of Exam Fish	No. of Infested Fish	Type of Parasites	Infestation		Total	
				No	%	No	%
Sidi Salem fish farms	200	48	Trematodes	22	11	22	5.5
			Cestodes	2	1	2	0.5
			Nematodes	16	8	16	4
			Acanthocephala	8	4	8	2
Alirad fish farms	100	16	Trematodes	9	9	9	2.25
			Cestodes	1	1	1	0.25
			Nematodes	4	4	4	1
			Acanthocephala	2	2	2	0.5
Meutobeus fish farms	100	12	Trematodes	6	6	6	1.5
			Cestodes	1	1	1	0.25
			Nematodes	3	3	3	0.75
			Acanthocephala	2	2	2	0.5

Table 20.3: Cadmium Concentrations in Water of Nile Tilapia Farms (Three Localities)

Metal	District	In Autumn Season Water Samples (ppm)		
		Min.	Max.	Mean ± SE
	Sidi Salem fish farms	0.13	0.62	0.35 ± 0.009
Cadmium	Alirad fish farms	0.062	0.082	0.07 ± 0.002
	Meutobeus fish farms	0.01	0.07	0.04 ± 0.015

Table 20.4: Residue of Cadmium in Different *Oreochromis niloticus* Tissues

Samples / Location	Musculature			Liver			Spleen			Kidney		
	Min	Max	Mean	Min	Max	Mean	Min	Max	Mean	Min	Max	Mean
Sidi Salem fish farms	0.052	0.092	0.072 ± 0.05	0.085	0.095	0.09 ± 0.02	0.049	0.058	0.054 ± 0.02	0.035	0.049	0.036 ± 0.02
Alirad fish farms	0.026	0.046	0.036 ± 0.05	0.053	0.073	0.063 ± 0.02	0.007	0.0097	0.009 ± 0.03	0.0086	0.0098	0.009 ± 0.02
Meutobeus fish farms	0	0	0	0.008	0.01	0.009 ± 0.02	0.007	0.0095	0.009 ± 0.02	0.005	0.009	0.007 ± 0.02

Table 20.5: Residue of Cadmium in Different Fish Tissues Correlated to Internal Parasitic Infestation

Samples / Location	Musculatures	Liver	Spleen	Kidney	Infested Fish	
					%	NO
Sidi Salem fish farms	0.072 ± 0.05	0.09 ± 0.02	0.054 ± 0.02	0.036 ± 0.02	48	24
Alirad fish farms	0.036 ± 0.05	0.063 ± 0.02	0.009 ± 0.03	0.009 ± 0.02	16	16
Meutobeus fish farms	0	0.009 ± 0.02	0.009 ± 0.02	0.007 ± 0.02	12	12

Hematological Studies

The present study demonstrated that *O. niloticus* naturally exposed to cadmium displayed a significant decrease in P.C.V, RBCs and Hb while elevation in the level of WBCs at Sidi Salem district fish farms theese parameters were decreased in Alirad and Meutobeus Districted fish farms throughout the periods of study (Tables 20.6 and 20.7).

Table 20.6: Erythrogram (RBCs (10^6), Hb and P.C.V.) in Naturally Exposed *O. niloticus* to Cadmium Pollution in Three Different Locations in Kafr El Sheikh Governorate Fish Farms (10 Samples from Each Location)

Districts	Parameters	Control Fish		Naturally Exposed Fish	
		Range	Mean	Range	Mean
Sidi Salem fish farms	R.B.Cs (10^6)	1.7 -1.9	1.8 ± 0.08Aa	1.6 -1.7	1.65 ± 0.07Cb
	Hb (g%)	8.3-8.6	8.45 ± 1.45Ba	6.6-7.4	7 ± 2.75Aa
	P.C.V%	19.5-22.5	21 ± 2.22Ab	16-18.5	17.25 ± 2.75Ab
Alirad fish farms	R.B.Cs (10^6)	1.7-1.8	1.75 ± 0.07Bb	1.8 -1.9	1.85 ± 0.08Aa
	Hb (g%)	8.1-8.4	8.22 ± 1.22Ca	7.1-8.2	7.65 ± 1.65Cb
	P.C.V%	19-21	20 ± 2.10Bb	20.5-23	21.75 ± 2.15Ca
Meutobeus fish farms	R.B.Cs (10^6)	1.75-1.85	1.8 ± 0.08Aa	1.7-1.75	1.725 ± 0.05Bb
	Hb (g%)	8.3-8.8	8.55 ± 1.55Aa	7.9-8.7	8.3 ± 1.13Bb
	P.C.V%	20-22.5	21.5 ± 2.15Ab	21-23.5	22.25 ± 2.12Ba

For the same parameter of different locality under study:
Capital letters: Means within the same column of different letters are significantly different at ($P < 0.05$).
Small letters: Means within the same row of different letters are significantly different at ($P < 0.05$).

Table 20.7: Leukogram Parameter (Total WBCs and Differential Count) in Naturally Exposed *O. niloticus* to Cadmium Pollution in Three Different Locations in Kafr El Sheikh Governorate Fish Farms (10 Samples from Each Location)

Districts	Parameters	Control Fish		Naturally Exposed Fish	
		Range	Mean	Range	Mean
Sidi Salem fish farms	W.B.Cs (10 3)	40-44	42 ± 2.40Ab	108-116	112 ± 12.11Aa
	Heterophiles%	3.35-4	3.75 ± 3.15Bb	25.1-27.3	26.5 ± 2.65Aa
	Agranulocytes%	95-98	96.25 ± 2.65Ba	70.3-75-1	73.5 ± 7.33Cb
Alirad fish farms	W.B.Cs (10 3)	38-40	39 ± 2.39Cb	48-54	51 ± 5.11Ca
	Heterophiles%	4.25-4.65	4.5 ± 0.45Ab	8-8.40	8.25 ± 5.22Ba
	Agranulocytes%	90-98	95.5 ± 5.62Ca	90-92.15	91.25 ± 9.25Bb
Meutobeus fish farms	W.B.Cs (10 3)	40-42	41 ± 4.11Bb	52.5-57.5	54±4.53Ba
	Heterophiles%	2.75-3.25	3 ± 3.14Cb	5.1-5.85	5.75 ± 1.75Ca
	Agranulocytes%	95-99	97 ± 7.98Aa	92.3-96.35	94.25 ± 4.25Ab

For the same parameter of different locality under study:
Capital letters: Means within the same column of different letters are significantly different at ($P < 0.05$).
Small letters: Means within the same row of different letters are significantly different at ($P < 0.05$).

Biochemical Studies

The present study demonstrated that *O. niloticus* naturally exposed to cadmium displayed a significant elevation in the level of blood glucose, serum AST, ALT, UREA, Creatinine. at Sidi Salem district fish farms these parameters were decreased in Alirad and Meutobeus Districted fish farms throughout the periods of study (Table 20.8).

Table 20.8: Biochemical Parameters in Naturally Exposed *O. niloticus* to Cadmium Pollution in Three Different Locations in Kafr El Sheikh Governorate Fish Farms (10 Samples from Each Location)

District	Parameters	Control Fish		Naturally Exposed Fish	
		Range	Mean	Range	Mean
Sidi Salem fish farms	AST(u/l)	88-94	91 ± 9.11Bb	126-146	136 ± 11.36Aa
	ALT (u/l)	18-27	22.5 ± 2.25Bb	37-43	40 ± 4.11Aa
	Urea(mg/dl)	2.9-3.45	3.175 ± 0.03Ab	3.8-4.5	4.15 ± 0.04Aa
	Creatinine(mg/dl)	0.68-0.97	0.74 ± 0.07Ab	0.8-1.3	1.05 ± 0.05Aa
	Glucose(mg/dl)	58-63	60.5 ± 6.50Bb	71-93	82 ± 8.12Aa
Alirad fish farms	AST(u/l)	90-96	93 ± 9.3Ab	120-136	128 ± 12.18Ba
	ALT (u/l)	18-23	20.5 ± 2.05Cb	33-42	37.5 ± 3.75Ba
	Urea(mg/dl)	2.7-3.33	3.015 ± 0.03Aa	2.8-3.7	3.25 ± 0.03Ba
	Creatinine(mg/dl)	0.63-0.68	0.65 ± 0.06Bb	0.63-1.1	0.85 ± 0.08Ba
	Glucose(mg/dl	60-62	61 ± 6.11Ab	67-73	73 ± 7.3Ba
Meutobeus fish farms	AST(u/l)	84-93	88.5 ± 8.55Bb	96-107	103.5 ± 10.37Ca
	ALT (u/l)	20-28	24 ± 4.22Ab	19-33	26 ± 2.66Ca
	Urea(mg/dl)	2.15-2.85	2.5 ± 0.02Ba	2.3-3.1	2.7 ± 0.02Ca
	Creatinine(mg/dl)	0.71-0.78	0.74 ± 0.07Ab	0.54-1.1	0.82 ± 0.08Ba
	Glucose(mg/dl)	57-64	60.5 ± 6.05Bb	63-69	66 ± 6.16Ca

For the same parameter of different locality under study:
Capital letters: Means within the same column of different letters are significantly different at ($P < 0.05$).
Small letters: Means within the same row of different letters are significantly different at ($P < 0.05$).

Histopathological Examination

The histopathological alterations in the affected liver was manifested as melanin pigmented cells with leucocyte inflammatory cells infiltration were observed in the portal vein associated with congestion in the central vein.while in the affected kidney was manifested as focal haemorrhage in between the degenerated and necrosed tubules associated with dilatation and congestion in the blood vessels with perivascular deposition of melanin pigmented cells also, in the affected musculature was manifested as hyalinization in some muscular bundles. Oedematus musculature and infested with encysted metacercariae were appear surrounded with serous fluid which contain a network of fibrin and in the affected intestine was manifested as hypertrophy, hyperplastic, proliferation and necrobiosis in the lining epithelium associated with inflammatory cells infiltration in the lamina propria. There was Variations were observed in the thickness of the villi , while the goblet cells were observed in diffuse manner allover the mucosal epithelium. The histopathological alteration in the affected spleen was manifested as hemosiderin was detected in the congested red pulps, focal melanin pigment cells deposition was observed in the white pulps and in the perivascular tissue of the dilated and congested blood vessels (Plate 20.3) (1-5).

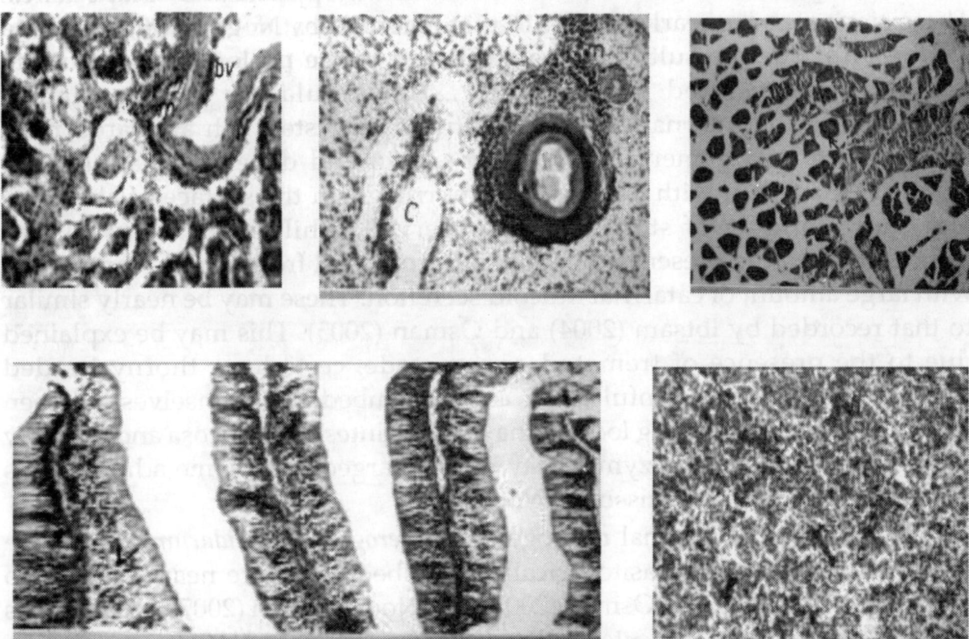

Plate 20.3: Showing Liver of *O.niloticus* naturally exposed to Cadmium suffered from melanin pigmented cells and leucocyte inflammatory cells infiltration (m) were observed in the portal area associated with congested central vein © (1), kidney suffered from degeneration in the tubules with dilatation in the blood vessels (bv) (2), hyalinization in some muscular bundles (3), necrobiosis in the mucosal epithelium with inflammatory cells infiltration (v) of villi. (4) and hemosiderin (h) and congested red pulps © (5). All stained by (H& E) X 40.

DISCUSSION

In Egypt, some areas especially those of Kafr El-Sheikh Governorate, fish farms are depending on agriculture drainage water mixed with industrial and the phosphate fertilizer which is considered the main source of Cd in the environment (Osman, 2009). Both types are considered an important source of cadmium pollution affecting the prevalence of internal parasitic diseases in cultured fishes similar to recorded by Dimari *et al.* (2008). The present study deals with most of different internal parasitic diseases among naturally infested cultured *O. niloticus* in relation to the cadmium concentration in water in Kafer El- Sheikh fish farms. In this work, the main clinical picture in naturally infested *O. niloticus* revealed that some aggregated on the water surface, accumulated at the water inlet of the pond. Also, some fish showed abnormal movement and shape (scoliosis). The results in this investigation showed that cadmium can primarily cause the backbone deformities in fish due to musculature spasms. This result is in agreement with that reported by Olsson (1998). Also, loss of appetite and escape reflex. These signs may be nearly similar to that recorded by Noga (1996) and Eissa *et al.* (2010). These results may be attributed to the prolonged exposure to heavy metals resulted in respiratory, osmoregulatory and circulatory impairment. The internal organs of naturally infested fish appeared pale, anemic with enlargement of liver and spleen and distended gallbladder. Signs of emaciation with petechial haemorrhage on the surface of abdomen and slight bulging of stomach was observed, while intestinal wall was congested with the presence of ulcer and protruded from anus accompanied with large amount of catarrhal mucoid secretion. These may be nearly similar to that recorded by Ibtsam (2004) and Osman (2005). This may be explained due to the presence of trematodes, nematode, cestode or thorny headed worms which cause harmful effect as they embedded themselves between the villi of intestine causing local damage to the intestinal mucosa and possibly peritonitis. Proteolytic enzymes may be discharged from some adult worms degrading the intestinal tissues (Woo, 1995).

Regarding the internal monogenea (*Enterogyrus cichlidarum*) they were morphologically and parasitologically described and were nearly similar to the descriptions given by Osman (2005) and Noor El Deen (2007).Adult flukes isolated from midgut (*Orientocreadium batrochoides*) was identified depending on the morphological and parasitological characters and the encysted metacercariae, were identified as (Heterophidae). These findings are nearly similar that recorded by Yamaguti (1985). Concerning to the cestodes it was identified as (*Polyonchobothrium sp*). Such identification is nearly similar that recorded by Ibtsam (2004).

Regarding to the isolated nematodes from naturally *O.niloticus*, isolation and identification of *Paracamallanus cyathopharynx* were undertaken that nearly similar to those of original descriptions by Woo (1995). Finally, the morphological and parasitological examinations of Tilapia fish revealed isolation and identification of *Acanthosentis tilapiae* whose descriptions are nearly similar to those of original description by Yamaguti, (1985) and Ibtsam, (2004).

In the present study a total prevalence of helminth infestations of *O. niloticus* in Sidi Salem district fish farms represented trematodes as 11%, nematode 8%, cestode 1% and *Acanthocentis tilapiae* 4% in autumn season.

Such results are lower than recorded by Osman (2005) who found a prevalence of Entergyrosis as 67.2%. These variations may be attributed to the water quality criteria and age of fish as such worms are stomach flukes need aged fish have well developed stomach and its wall was thicker for adaptation and fixation for such parasite. These results higher than that recorded with Hassan (1992) who found prevalence as 6% in *O.niloticus.* Such result disagree with that recorded by Tawfik (2005) who recorded a prevalence of digenia in autumn 22.7%. These results may be attributed to different types of fish, the presence of intermediate host (snails), the suitable temperature which consider the main survival factors for these intermediate hosts and aquatic birds (piscivorous birds) according to Noor El Deen (2007). Concerning a total prevalence of *P. cyathopharynx* was 8% from *O.niloticus.* These findings disagree with that met by Abd El- Wahed (1992) who recorded a prevalence of P. *cyathopharynx* was 1.4% in *O.niloticus.* These results may be attributed to different types of fish, the presence of intermediate host copepods and the suitable temperature. In this study, *Polyonchobothrium sp* could be detected with an prevalence 1% from O.niloticus. These findings are lower than that recorded by Hassan (1992) who found 7.5%. These results disagreed with that recorded by Nadia Mahfouz (1991) who recorded a prevalence of nematodes infestation in autumn were 0%. These differences may be due to variation in climatic and ecological factors which affect on intermediate host copepods (Cyclops) and aquatic birds.

Finally, the prevalence of *Acanthosentis tilapiae* in cultured *O. niloticus* was 4%. These findings nearly higher than with that recorded by Rawia Adawy (2000) who recorded a prevalence of *A. tilapiae* in cultured two Tilapia sp as 2.4 and 3.7% and lower than that recorded by Eid (1997) who recorded 37.8% in tilapia sp. Also, disagree with Bassiony (2002) who mentioned that the highest infestation rate a prevalence of A. *tilapiae* in cultured Tilapia sp was in autumn 16.2%. Also, Ibtsam (2004) in cultured tilapia sp in autumn season as 10%. This result may be attributed to different types of fish the presence of intermediate host (amphipod and isopod), the suitable temperature which consider the main survival factors for these intermediate host.

Cadmium concentration in water of Sidi Salem farms was 0.35 ± 0.009 ppm which higher than the maximum permissible limits recommended by WHO (1984) 0.005 ppm, FAO/WHO (1992) [0.05 ppm] and Egyptian Organisation for Standardization and Quality Control "E.O.S.Q.C". [0.1 mg kg1]. This result may be attributed to presence of industrial activity and agriculture drench branches were supply Sidi Salem fish farms. While in Alrad and Metobus areas were 0.07 ± 0.002 and 0.04 ± 0.015 ppm respectively within the permissible limits. This result may be attributed to absence of industrial activity.

It was observed that cadmium concentration in liver, kidney, intestine and spleen was significantly higher in fish exposed to cadmium. While cadmium concentration was in the permissible limits in musculature. The high contents of heavy metal found in viscera may be due to the fact that most of the heavy metal are accumulated in the liver, spleen, intestine and kidney after ingestion. Khaled, (2004) reported that Cadmium is stored in the body in various tissues but the main site of accumulation in aquatic organisms is in the kidney and liver. Fish musculature is important part to be used for human consumption. This result recorded with Yielmaz (2003) who found that concentrations of heavy metals were higher in all internal organ samples than in muscles.

The results recorded elevation of internal parasites with increase of Cd pollution comparing with that observed in control one. The relationship of parasitism and pollution is not simple and essence involves a double edged phenomenon which parasitism may decrease host susceptibility to toxic pollutions may result in an increase or decrease in the prevalence of certain parasites. Pollutants may affect on intermediate or alternate hosts in parasite life cycle, on free-living life cycle stages of parasite invasion (Sindermann, 1990).

Regarding hematological and biochemical parameters, a decrease in the concentration of haemoglobin in blood, which is usually caused by the effect of toxic metals on gills, as well as a de-crease in oxygen also indicates anaemia that confirms negative changes occurring in fish. Glucose is one of the most sensitive indices of the stress state of an or-ganism: its high concentrations in blood indicate that the fish is in stress and it is intensively using its energy reserves i.e. glycogen in liver and muscles. Meanwhile, a decreased concentration of glucose indicates the exhaustion of energy (glycogen) resources and, sub-sequently, the worsening of an organism status. Namely, a decrease in glucose in the blood of fish is observed during long-term exposure to heavy metals.

The present study demonstrated that *O. niloticus* naturally exposed to cadmium revealed a decrease in RBCs count (erythropenia) ($1.65 \pm 0.07 \times 10^6$) while Hb ($7 \pm 2.75$ g%) and P.C.V% (17.25 ± 2.75) in Sidi salim district area at Cd level (0.35 ppm). While RBCs count ($1.85 \pm 0.08 \times 10^6$), Hb ($7.65 \pm 1.65$ g%) and P.C.V% (21.75 ± 2.15) in Alriad districted area at Cd level (0.07 ppm). In Metabus distract area, RBCs count ($1.725 \pm 0.05 \times 10^6$), Hb ($8.3 \pm 1.13$ g%) and P.C.V% (22.25 ± 2.12) at Cd level (0.04 ppm). The later 2 areas displayed nearly similar level with the finding net with control levels. This may be attributed to their water supply coming directly from Rasheed branch. Regarding Sidi salim district area its water supply coming directly from agriculture and industrials discharges. These results are similar with observations reported by Osman (2009) and Mona Zaki *et al* (2010).

However, an increase in WBCs count (leukocytosis) (112 ± 12.11 x 10^3) and heterophlis (26.5 ± 2.65%) ,while a decrease in agranulocytes (73.5 ± 7.33 %) in comparing to control in Sidi salim district area at Cd level (0.35 ppm). The results showen in Alriad district area at Cd level (0.07 ppm) concerning WBCs count (51 ± 5.11 x 10^3), heterophlis (8.25 ± 5.22) and agranulocytes (91.25 ± 9.25%). In Metabus district area, concerning WBCs count (54 ± 4.53 x 10^3), heterophlis (5.75 ± 1.75%) and agranulocytes (94.25 ± 4.25%). This result is nearly similar to control. It may be attributed to the increase of cadmium level in Sidi Salim than Alriad and Metabus districts. These results are nearly similar to what recorded by Gill and Pant (1986) and Ahmed (1996) who recorded that the lymphocytosis condition may be occur due to the stimulatory effect of cadmium on haematopiotic tissues.

The present study showed that the exposure of cadmium was observed an elevation in the blood glucose (82 ± 8.12 mg/dl), serum AST and ALT (136 ± 11.36 and 40 ± 4.11 u/l) in Sidi salim district area respectively. While the glucose , AST and ALT (73 ± 7.3 mg/dl, 128 ± 12.18 and 37.5 ± 3.75 u/l) in Alriad district area respectively and in Metabus district area, the glucose , AST and ALT (66 ± 6.16 mg/dl, 103.5 ± 10.37 and 26 ± 2.66 u/l) respectively. These results in agreement with Mona Zaki *et al.*, (2010) who reported that experimintal exposure of *Tilapia zillii* to cadmium sulphate at 0.25 ppm. Several investigations showed that these blood enzymes were highly increased in the fish treated with cadmium. In addition, Shakoori *et al.* (1990) who reported that the increase of blood enzymatic activity is either due to leakage of these enzymes from hepatic cells and thus raising levels in blood, increased synthesis and enzyme induction of these enzymes. Also, Campbell *et al.* (1984) who reported that these enzymes liberate to the blood stream when the hepatic parenchyma cells are damaged Thophon *et al.* (2003) who found structural and ultrastructural damage in the liver of rainbow trout and white Sea bass following cadmium exposure. These results are nearly similar to what recorded by Attef, (2005) who reported that the fish *O. niloticus* exposed to sublethal concentration of cadmium displayed a significant elevation in the level of blood glucose after one day till the end of the experimental period.

Regarding the naturally exposed fish to cadmium revealed an increase of glucose level may be attributed to stress. Also, De Smet and Bulst, (2002) who observed an increase in. the activities of AST and ALT and they suggested that the observed proteolysis is intended to increase the role of protein in the energy production during cadmium stress. The results indicated that cadmium produces severe toxic effects in fish blood.

In the present study, in naturally exposed fish to cadmium was observed an elevation in the serum urea (4.15 ± 0.04 mg/dl) and Creatinine (1.05 ± 0.05 mg/dl) in Sidi Salim district area at Cd level (0.35 ppm) while the serum urea (3.25 ± 0.03 mg/dl) and Creatinine (0.85 ± 0.08 mg/dl) in Alriad district area at Cd level (0.07 ppm) and Metabus district area, the serum urea (2.7 ± 0.02

mg/dl) and Creatinine (0.82 ± 0.08 mg/dl) at Cd level (0.04 ppm). These results in agreement with Mona Zaki et al. (2010) who reported that expermintal exposure of *Tilapia zillii* to cadmium sulphate at 0.25 ppm induced deleterious effects in fish such as damage of Kidney, liver, spleen and gills, which were reflected on the biochemical and hematological parameters. Also, this result agree with Abbas *et al.*, (2002) and Mona Zaki *et al.*,(2010) who recorded that a significant increase of urea and Creatinine of *Tilapia zillii* exposure to cadmium sulphate at 0.25 ppm.

Histopathologically, the liver showed degeneration of the hepatocytes, congestion of central vein and nuclear pyknosis in the majority of hepatic cells. These findings were apparent as the liver considered the organ of detoxification. Similar results were observed by Van Dyk (2007) who found that liver of fish is sensitive to environmental contaminants because many contaminants tend to accumulate in the liver and exposing it to a much higher levels than in the environment. In this study, the intestine of *O. niloticus* showed, hypertrophy and hyperplastic proliferation of intestinal villi, severe dilatation of blood vessels of the sub mucosa and desquamation of the epithelial lining of the interstitial villi attributed to mechanical injury of the infested parasites and the effect of toxic product. These findings are nearly similar to that recorded with Ibtsam (2004). Concerning histopathological alteration in the affected kidney was manifested as focal haemorrhage in between the degenerated and necrosed tubules associated with dilatation and congestion in the blood vessels with perivascular deposition of melanin pigmented cells.The results of this investigation related to the kidneys of fish that were purposely poisoned. These results may be similar to that recorded with Tanimoto *et al.* (1999) who recorded that cadmium causing pathological changes of kidney tubules. Similar alterations in musculatures and kidney of Tilapia were observed in several species of fish exposed to heavy metals and these alterations were described by Gupta and Srivastava (2006). Regarding histopathological alteration in the affected musculature was manifested as hyalinization in some muscular bundles. Oedematus musculature and infested with encysted metacercariae were appear surrounded with serous fluid which contain a network of fibrin. These results may be attributed to cadmium pollution. This may be similar to that recorded with Kaoud and El-Dahshan (2010) who recorded that that several histopathological alterations were seen in the muscles of Tilapia which included degeneration in muscle bundles with aggregations of inflammatory cells between them and focal areas of necrosis. Also, atrophy and edema of muscle bundles as well as splitting of muscle fibers. The pathological findings in the intestine included atrophy in the muscular is, degenerative and necrotic changes in the intestinal mucosa and submucosa with necrotized cells aggregated in the intestinal lumen, edema and atrophy in the submucosa.

Finally, regarding histopathological alteration in the affected spleen was manifested as hemosiderin was detected in the congested red pulps and focal melanin pigment cells deposition was observed in the white pulps and in the per vascular tissue of the dilated and congested blood vessels. These observations in agreement with that recorded by Pirarat *et al*. (2008) Who observed histopatholigical change in the spleen of *Oreochromis niloticus* fish exposed to different concentration of cadmium. Histopatholigical change including ellipsoidal tissue enlargement , melanomacrophage cell aggregation, vacuolar degeneration and edematous capillary and also with Suresh (2009) who observed a significant difference in the frequency and size of melano macrophage centres (MMC) and free macrophage found in, spleen of *Tilapia mossambica* exposed to 20.93 mg l-1 of cadmium chloride and observed also two pigments hemosiderin and melaninare.

From the present study, it was concluded that, scoliosis in *O. niloticus* may be an indicator to cadmium pollution and there was a positive correlation between cadmium pollution in water and the prevalence of internal parasitic infestation in *Oreochromis niloticus*. Finally, cadmium residues in musculature was found in the permissible limits, while in internal organs were relatively high.

REFERENCES

1. Abbas, H.H; Zaghloul, K.H. and Mousa, M.A (2002): Effect ot Some Heavy Metals Pollutants on Some Biological and Histopatholigical Changes in the Blue Tilapia, Oreochromis Aureus. Egypt. J.Agric. Res.80 (3); 1395-1411.
2. Abd El-Wahed, W.M.M (1992): Epizootiological Studies on Some Gastro-intestinal Helminthes Infestation in Fresh Water Fish in Egypt. M.V.Sc. Thesis, Fac. Vet. Med., Cairo Univ.
3. Attef M.EL-Attar (2005): Biochemical Effect of Short Term Cadmium Exposure of Fresh Water Fish (Oreochromis Niloticus). Journal of Biological Sciences 5(3): 260-265.
4. Bancroft, J.D. and Stevens, A. (1996): Theory and Practice of Histological Techniques. Fourth Edition, Churchill Living Stone, Edinburgh London, Melbourne. pp. 304-307.
5. Bassiony, A.E.A.A. (2002): Studies on the Prevailing Internal Parasitic Diseases Among Some Cultured Fresh Water Fishes in Kafr El-Sheikh Province. M.V.Sc. Thesis, Fac. Vet. Med., kafr- El-Sheikh, Tanta University.
6. Campbell, E.J., C.J. Dickinson, J.D. Spater, C.W., Edwards and K. Sikora, (1984): Clinical Physiology. Bulter and Tanner Ltd. London.
7. Combs, G.F., O.A Levander, J.E. Spallholz and J.E. Oldfield, (1987): Textbook of Selenium in Biology and Medicine, Part B, Van Hostrand Company, New York, pp. 752.
8. Dacie, S. and Lewis,S. (1991): Practical Hematology. 7th Ed., Churchill Living Stone.
9. Dimari GA, Abdulrahman JC and Garba ST. (2008): Metals Concentrations in Tissues of Tilapia Galli, Clarias Lazera and Osteoglossidae Caught from Alau Dam, Maiduguri, Borno State, Nigeria. American Journal of Environmental Sciences 4: 373-379.

10. Egyptian Organisation of Standardization and Quality Control (EOSQC) (1993): Maximum Residue Limits for Heavy Metals in Food. Ministry of Industry. 2360.
11. Eid, S.A. (1997): Studies on Parasites of Egyptian Cultured Fish. M.V.Sc. Thesis, Fac. Vet. Med. Cairo Univ.
12. Eissa, I.A.M.; A.S. Diab and A.F. Badran (1996): Studies on Some Internal Parasitic Diseases Among Wild and Cultured *Oreochromis niloticus* Fish. 7th Sci. Cong., 17-19. Nov. 1996, Fac. Vet. Med., Assiut, Egypt.
13. Eissa, I.A.M.; Gado, M.S; Lila, A.M. and Noor El Deen, A I.E. (2010): The External Parasitic Diseases Prevailing in Male and Monosex Tilapias in Kafr El-Sheikh Governorate Fish Farms. The 5th Inter. Conf. Vet. Res. Div., NRC, Cairo, Egypt, 22-24 febary, 2010.
14. FAO/WHO (1992): Food Monitoring and Assessment Programme, WHO, Geneva 5, UNEP, Nairobi. 52. Report of the Third Meeting of the GEMS/Food.
15. Gupta P and Srivastava N. (2006): Effects of Sublethal Concentrations of Zinc on Histological Changes and Bioaccumulation of Zinc by Kidney of Fish Channa Punctatus (Bloch). Journal of Environmental Biology 27: 211-215.
16. Hassan, M.A. (1992): Studies on Some Parasitic Affections in Fresh Water Fishes in Beni Suef Governorate. Ph.D. Thesis, Fac. Vet. Med., Beni-Suef. Cairo Univ.
17. Ibtsam, E.B.E.D. (2004): Studies on Some Prevailing Parasitic Diseases Among Cultured Tilapia Fish. Ph.D. Thesis, Fac. Vet. Med., Suez Canal University.
18. Innes, W.T. (1966): Exotic Aquarium Fishes 19th Ed., Aquarium Inc., New Jersy. pp. 530-531.
19. Kalay M and Canli M. (2000): Elimination of Essential (Cu and Zn) and Non Essential (Cd and Pb) Metals from Tissues of a Fresh Water Fish, Tilapia Zillii. Tropical Journal of Zoology 24: 429-436.
20. Kaoud H.A. and A.R. El-Dahshan (2010): Bioaccumulation and Histopathological Alterations of the Heavy Metals in Oreochromis Niloticus Fish., Nature and Science. 2010; 8(4): 147-156.
21. Khaled A. (2004): Heavy Metal Concentrations in Certain Tissues of Five Commercially Important Fishes from El-Mex Bay, Al-Exandria , Egypt. pp. 1-11.
22. Mona S. Zaki, Olfat M. Fawzi Suzan O. Mostafa, Isis Awad, Mostafa fawzy (2010): Biochemical Studies on Tilipia Nilotica Exposed to Climate Change and Cadmium Sulphate (0.50 p.p.m.) New York Science Journal. 3(4): 90-95.
23. Nadia Mahfouz, N.B.M. (1991): Studies on Round Worms and Cestodes of Some Fresh Water Fish. M.V.Sc. Thesis, Fac. Vet. Med., Alexandria University.
24. Noga, E.J. (1996): Fish Disease Diagnosis and Treatment. Mosby-yearbook, Inc. Watsworth Publishing Co., USA. pp. 366.
25. Noor El Deen, A.E. (2007): Comparative Studies on the Prevailing Parasitic Diseases in Monosex Tilapia and Natural Male Tilapias in Kafr El-Sheikh Governorate Fish Farms. Ph.D. Thesis, Fac. Vet. Med., Kafr El-Sheikh University.
26. Olaifa F.E, Olaifa AK, Adelaja AA, and Owolabi AG. (2004): Heavy Metal Contamination of Clarias Garpinus from a Lake and Fish Farm in Ibadan, Nigeria. Afric. J. of Biomed. Res. 7: 145-148.
27. Olsson, P.E. (1998): Disorders Associated with Heavy Metal Pollution. In: J.F. Leatherland and P.T.K. Woo (eds), Fish Diseases and Disorders, Non-infectious Disordes. CABI Publishing, Wallingford: 105-131.

28. Osman, M.A.H. (2005): Studies on Monogenasis Among Fishes. Thesis Ph.D. Thesis, Fac. Vet. Med., Suez Canal Univ.
29. Osman, H.A.M., T.B. Ibrahim, A.T. Ali and H.I.M. Derwa, (2009): Field Application of Humic Acid Against the Effect of Cadmium Pollution on Cultured Tilapia Oreochromis Niloticus. World Applied Sci. J., 6: 1569-1575.
30. Paperna, I. (1980): Parasitic Infestation and Diseases of Fish in Africa. FAO, CIFA Technical Paper, 51-62.
31. Pirarat n., P. Chotipong, P.S. Inghasenee (2008): Toxicity of Cadmium on Tilapia (Oreochromius Niloticus) Spleen, Proceeding the 15 th Congress of FAVA 27-30 October, Bangkok, Thailand.
32. Rawia Adawy, S.M. (2000): Studies on the Parasitic Diseases of Some Fresh Water Fishes in Dakahlia Governorate. Ph.D. Thesis, Fac. Vet. Med., Cairo Univ.
33. Shakoori, A.R., J. Alam, F. Aziz and S.S. Ali,(1990): Biochemical Effects of Bifenthrin (talstar) Administered Orally for One Month on the Blood and Liver of Rabbit. Proc. Pak. Congr. Zool., 10: 61-81.
34. Sindermann,C.J.(1990): Principal of Marine Fish and Saltwater Diseases Fish. Academic Press, Inc. Oxford, Maryland, pp. 432-438.
35. Tanimoto, A., Hamada, T., Higashi, K., and Sasaguri, Y. (1999): Distribution of Cadmium and Metallothionein in CdCl2 – Exposed Rat Kidney: Relationship with Apoptosis and Regeneration. Pathology International, 49: 125-132.
36. Suresh, N (2009): Effect of Cadmium Chloride on Liver, Spleen and Kidney Melano Macrophage Centres in Tilapia Mossambica. Journal of Environmental Biology Triveni Enterprises, Lucknow (India) July 2009, 30(4) 505-508 (2009).
37. Tawfik, M.A.A (2005): Studies on Some Fish–borne Trematodes in Egypt. J.Vet Sci. Vol. 43, pp. 49-58.
38. Thophon, S., M. Kruatrach uc, E. Upathau,(2003): Histopatholigical Alteration of White Sea Bass, (Lates calcartfer) in Acute and Subchoronic Cadmium Exposure. Environ. Pollut. 121: 307-320.
39. Van dyk, J.C.; Pieterse, G.M. and Van Vuren, J.H.J. (2007): Histological Changes in the Liver of Oreochomius Mossambicus (Cichlidae) after Exposure to Cadmium and Zinc. Ecotoxocology and Enviromental safty, 66: 432-440.
40. WHO World Health Organisation, (1984): Guidelines for Drinking Water Quality WHO, Vol. 1, Recommendation, Geneva.
41. Witeska M (1999): Changes in Selected Blood Indices of Common Acute Exposure to Cadmium. Acta vet. Brno. 67: 289-293.
42. Woo, P.T.K. (1995): Fish Diseases and Disorders. CAB, Int. Wallingford, Oxon, UK.
43. Yamaguti, S. (1985): Systema Helminthes of Fish.Vol. 1. Digentic Trematodes of the Vertebrates Part 1 and 2, Interscience Publishers, Inc. New York.
44. Yilmaz AB. (2003): Levels of Heavy Metals (Fe, Cu, Ni, Cr, Pb and Zn) in Tissue of Mugil Cephalus and Trachurus Mediteraneus from Iskenderun Bay, Turkey. Environ. Res., 92: 277-281.

Index